INDIRECT TRANSLATION EXPLAINED

Indirect Translation Explained is the first comprehensive, user-friendly book on the practice of translating indirectly in today's world. Unlike previous scholarly approaches, which have traditionally focused on translating from the original, this textbook offers practical advice on how to efficiently translate from an already translated text and for the specific purpose of further translation.

Written by key specialists in this area of research and drawing on many years of translation teaching and practice, this process-focused textbook covers a range of languages, geographical settings and types of translation, including audiovisual, literary, news, and scientific-technical translation, as well as localization and interpreting. Since this topic addresses the concerns and practices of both more peripheral and more dominant languages, this textbook is usable by all, regardless of the language combinations they work with.

Featuring theoretical considerations, tasks for hands-on practice, suggestions for further discussion and diverse, real-world examples, this is the essential textbook for all students and autodidacts learning how to translate via a third language.

Hanna Pięta is an assistant professor at Universidade NOVA de Lisboa (FCSH), Portugal, and a researcher at CETAPS (Translationality Research Group). She is co-coordinator of the international research network IndirecTrans and associate editor of the *Translation Matters* journal. She has recently co-edited a special issue of *Target* on what indirect translation can do for translation studies (2022) and is now co-editing a special issue of *Perspectives* on pivot audiovisual translation (2023).

Rita Bueno Maia is Assistant Professor of Spanish and Translation in the School of Human Sciences at the Catholic University of Portugal and a member of the Research Centre for Communication and Culture. She has recently co-edited *Indirect Translation: Theoretical, Terminological and Methodological Issues* (Routledge, 2019).

She is co-coordinator of the international research network IndirecTrans and has worked as a literary translator for the theatre.

Ester Torres-Simón is an assistant professor at Universitat Autònoma de Barcelona (UAB), Spain. She is a researcher at GREGAL Research Group (at UAB), an external collaborator of the Research Group on Reception and Translation Studies (at the University of Lisbon, Portugal) and a member of the European Society for Translation Studies Wikipedia Committee. She has a keen interest in innovative teaching practices and has published about the topic in *The Interpreter and Translator Trainer*, the *Journal of Higher Education Outreach and Engagement* and *Perspectives*, among others.

"I am delighted by the innovative take of this textbook. With a rigorous focus on indirect translation, it caters for many different specialisations and course contexts. The approach is pragmatic, and chapters come with a plethora of ready-made assignments, but I trust the broad focus will also open up new avenues of thought in research."

Kaisa Koskinen, *Tampere University, Finland*

"A necessary and most timely textbook on how to translate through another language. The chapter on pivot audiovisual translation is a must-read for template makers."

Stavroula Sokoli, *Computer Technology Institute & Press, Diophantus, Greece*

"*Indirect Translation Explained* is a richly described, theoretically motivated introductory coursebook dedicated to indirect translation in its many forms. Full of scaffolded activities and discussion points, this volume is certain to open new opportunities for instructors and students alike to delve into the increasingly complex nature of multilingual communication."

Christopher D. Mellinger, *UNC Charlotte, USA*

"This book provides excellent practical grounding and training for a vital yet often overlooked—and even stigmatised—area of the language services industry. Through the authors' methodical approach and thorough coverage, readers will understand much better how and where to use indirect translation with success, and avoid many common pitfalls."

Richard Mansell, *University of Exeter, UK*

TRANSLATION PRACTICES EXPLAINED
Series Editor: Kelly Washbourne

Translation Practices Explained is a series of coursebooks designed to help self-learners and students on translation and interpreting courses. Each volume focuses on a specific aspect of professional translation and interpreting practice, usually corresponding to courses available in translator- and interpreter-training institutions. The authors are practicing translators, interpreters, and/or translator or interpreter trainers. Although specialists, they explain their professional insights in a manner accessible to the wider learning public.

Each volume includes activities and exercises designed to help learners consolidate their knowledge, while updated reading lists and website addresses will also help individual learners gain further insight into the realities of professional practice.

Most recent titles in the series:

Subtitling
Concepts and Practices
Jorge Díaz Cintas and Aline Remael

Diplomatic and Political Interpreting Explained
Mira Kadrić, Sylvi Rennert and Christina Schäffner

Indirect Translation Explained
Hanna Pięta, Rita Bueno Maia and Ester Torres-Simón

For more information on any of these and other titles, or to order, please go to www.routledge.com/Translation-Practices-Explained/book-series/TPE

Additional resources for Translation and Interpreting Studies are available on the Routledge Translation Studies Portal: http://routledgetranslationstudiesportal.com/

INDIRECT TRANSLATION EXPLAINED

Hanna Pięta, Rita Bueno Maia and Ester Torres-Simón

LONDON AND NEW YORK

Cover image: Getty Images

First published 2023
by Routledge
4 Park Square, Milton Park, Abingdon, Oxon OX14 4RN

and by Routledge
605 Third Avenue, New York, NY 10158

Routledge is an imprint of the Taylor & Francis Group, an informa business

© 2023 Hanna Pięta, Rita Bueno Maia and Ester Torres-Simón

The right of Hanna Pięta, Rita Bueno Maia and Ester Torres-Simón to be identified as authors of this work has been asserted in accordance with sections 77 and 78 of the Copyright, Designs and Patents Act 1988.

All rights reserved. No part of this book may be reprinted or reproduced or utilised in any form or by any electronic, mechanical, or other means, now known or hereafter invented, including photocopying and recording, or in any information storage or retrieval system, without permission in writing from the publishers.

Trademark notice: Product or corporate names may be trademarks or registered trademarks, and are used only for identification and explanation without intent to infringe.

British Library Cataloguing-in-Publication Data
A catalogue record for this book is available from the British Library

Library of Congress Cataloging-in-Publication Data
A catalog record has been requested for this book

ISBN: 978-0-367-47381-5 (hbk)
ISBN: 978-0-367-47365-5 (pbk)
ISBN: 978-1-003-03522-0 (ebk)

DOI: 10.4324/9781003035220

Typeset in Bembo
by Newgen Publishing UK

We dedicate this book to all the working mothers in academia: nobody knows how we do it, and yet here we are!

CONTENTS

List of figures — xii
List of tables — xiv
About this book — xv
Acknowledgements — xix

1 Introduction — 1
   Introduction 1
   Learning outcomes 1
   What is indirect translation? 2
   When does indirect translation happen? 3
   Where do you translate indirectly? 4
   How do you translate indirectly? 6
   Who are the main stakeholders in indirect translation? 7
   Why translate indirectly? 9
   What are the consequences of translating indirectly? 10
   Indirect translation in the foreseeable future 11
   Activities 16

2 Interpreting — 22
   Introduction 22
   Learning outcomes 22
   Relay in the history of interpreting 23
   Relay interpreting today 23
   Tips on how to deal with pivot interpreting situations 31
   Activities 43

3 Scientific-Technical Translation 51

Introduction 51
Learning outcomes 51
Indirect translation in scientific-technical translation 52
Quality control and quality assurance and how they relate to indirect translation 53
Indirect translation in international patenting activity 54
Indirect translation as part of instructional text production 57
Indirect translation in international scientific publishing 64
Indirect translation in popularizing science 66
Activities 70

4 Localization 78

Introduction 78
Learning outcomes 78
Indirect translation and localization 79
Indirect translation in the history of localization and today 80
Localization processes 81
Challenges brought about by localization processes and ways to go about them 95
Silver linings 102
Activities 103

5 Literary translation 109

Introduction 109
Learning outcomes 109
Indirect translation and cultural awareness issues 110
Ethical challenges 114
Legal challenges 117
Activities 123

6 Audiovisual translation 133

Introduction 133
Learning outcomes 133
Indirect translation in the history of audiovisual translation 134
Indirect translation in AVT today 135
Pivot language templates in professional subtitling 136
Main challenges brought about by pivot templates 139
Silver linings 146
Tips on how to create a fit-for-purpose pivot template 146
Tips on how to translate from a pivot template 151
Activities 154

7　News translation　　　　　　　　　　　　　　　　　　　　　　159
　　Introduction 159
　　Learning outcomes 159
　　Indirect translation in the history of news translation 160
　　Indirect translation in news translation today 162
　　Indirect translation and fact-checking 166
　　Challenges in news translation (and some ways to go about them) 169
　　Activities 178

8　Project management　　　　　　　　　　　　　　　　　　　　185
　　Introduction 185
　　Learning outcomes 185
　　What does a PM do? 186
　　Project management in interpreting 191
　　Project management in scientific-technical translation 193
　　Project management in localization 193
　　Project management in literary translation 195
　　Project management in AVT 195
　　Project management in news translation 196
　　Activities 198

9　Conclusions　　　　　　　　　　　　　　　　　　　　　　　　203
　　Introduction 203
　　Bringing it all together 203
　　Activities 207

Glossary　　　　　　　　　　　　　　　　　　　　　　　　　　210
Index　　　　　　　　　　　　　　　　　　　　　　　　　　　215

FIGURES

1.1	Simulation of raw output generated by an MT engine in July 2021	2
1.2	Variables in indirect translation	6
1.3	Key stakeholders in indirect translation	8
2.1	Interpreter booths	23
2.2	Settings where relay interpreting is most common	24
2.3	Positioning in relay consecutive interpreting	41
2.4	Proposal for relay interpreting process (Activity 1.3)	45
3.1	Language options for the Wikipedia article "Translation"	52
4.1	The landing page of www.indirectrans.com	79
4.2	Localization process (from Valdez 2019)	94
4.3	Language length problems for button display	96
4.4	Different ways of indicating the number three in Polish, Japanese and Portuguese	97
4.5	Incorrect localization into Hebrew	99
4.6	Dialogue window in Polish	103
5.1	*Zaproszenie do Moskwy* [Invitation to Moscow] by Zbigniew Stypułkowski in Polish (1951/1977), English (1951) and Portuguese (1952)	110
6.1	Screenshot of an English language template in OOONA	134
6.2	Screenshot of an English language template in OOONA (with annotations)	137
6.3	Production of pivot template and final subtitles into multiple languages: a sample workflow	139
7.1	(Mock) international newspaper with several locales	160
7.2	Circular indirect translation / back translation	167

8.1	Multilingual exchanges during the production of a news translation for a local radio station in South Africa (adapted from van Rooyen 2019)	186
8.2	Screenshot of spreadsheet-based content manager Gridly (sample multi-step localization project)	189
8.3	Hub-style communication flow	191
9.1	The logo of IndirecTrans Network	204

TABLES

4.1	Name conventions according to different locales	98
4.2	Examples of different postcodes	100
4.3	Character names for the video game *The Witcher*	105
7.1	Translating for and from and crediting translation in news agencies and newspapers	164
7.2	Reuters' guidelines for producing translator-friendly news stories	171
8.1	Authors' divisions of PM tasks	187

ABOUT THIS BOOK

Indirect translation creates particular challenges, be they ethical, technological, textual, etc. These challenges require specific competences. For example, to be efficient in translating indirectly, you need to be able to critically approach the use of mediating languages. You also need to know how to review your own work to ensure that previous translation mistakes do not reach the target text or identify potential translation difficulties that are likely to hinder the work of further translators (such as the presence of domesticated cultural items or displaced indexicality).

Some time ago, several researchers and trainers stressed the importance of specific training in indirect translating. However, our recent survey of translation courses, trainers and coursebooks suggests that indirect translation is not as widely taught as it should be. Therefore, there is a shortage of training aids and guidelines for translators who need to translate from translation or with a further translation in mind. One reason behind this is that there is still a misconception among some that indirect translation is no longer practiced or is a deformation that can never be as good as a direct translation.

With this textbook, we want to help break these misconceptions and address the urgent gap in translator education. This is why our focus is not on describing and analysing how people in the past translated indirectly. Rather, our focus is on encouraging reflection on how indirect translation is done today, on how it could be done, and on fostering discussion about potential challenges and solutions. With this, we hope to promote new and better ways of doing indirect translation today and in the foreseeable future.

To this end, the textbook covers the ins and outs of the various settings where indirect translation is most likely to be commissioned, while discussing the most common pitfalls and guiding the trainee translators in their decision-making processes. *Indirect Translation Explained* is designed to introduce you to the knowledge and skills necessary to perform as an indirect translator. At the same time, the book offers tips and tools to build your own knowledge of indirect translation processes, providing the time and space for reflective learning. Against this backdrop, the textbook also provides insight for research into indirect translation.

The information and suggestions you will find in this book are based on our first-hand experience teaching, researching and practicing indirect translation in Poland, Portugal and Spain. The book includes translation examples in Catalan, Chinese, English, French, Hebrew, Italian, Japanese, Korean, Portuguese, Polish, Spanish and Turkish. These are properly contextualized to illustrate situations that occur in various linguistic and geographic settings, so a knowledge of these languages is not required. Since this topic addresses the concerns and practices of both more peripheral languages (often in the position of translating for) and more dominant languages (often the pivot languages translated from), this textbook is intended for all, regardless of the language combinations they work with.

This textbook wants to enlarge and enrich your translator toolbox and your knowledge of settings in which you are likely to work after graduation. It therefore presupposes that you have already been introduced to basic concepts and skills that are necessary to translate in various domains.

This book focuses on indirect translation as a field of specialization and inquiry in its own right. We understand that indirect translation will be a common practice for still many years to come, and therefore it must be carried out in the best possible way. As a disclaimer, we want to stress that such a conviction permeates this book. However, empirically supported claims, facts and opinions are clearly distinguishable in the hope that you can extract what is useful for you in each of these.

The starting point for this book was a list of competences specific to indirect translation, which we drafted drawing loosely on the 2017 edition of the EMT competence framework (the list is available online on the Translation Studies Portal). For the purpose of this book, we linked these competences to different fields. This enabled us to present each chapter with specific learning outcomes. Please note that just because a specific competence is linked to a specific domain, it does not mean that is the only domain where that competence will be relevant. It only means that, from the pedagogical perspective we apply in this book, it makes more sense to match a given competence with a given domain.

Using the textbook

This textbook is primarily aimed at advanced undergraduate and postgraduate students of translation (including interpreting), as well as self-learners, regardless of their language combination. However, it can also be useful to a variety of other readers who, for different reasons, may wish to explore the intricacies of indirect translation:

- Translator trainers looking for innovative ways of teaching translation or interpreting (for example, in multilingual classrooms).

- Professional translators who are already in the market and want to refresh their skills (e.g., video game localisers, subtitlers, translators and interpreters working in international organizations).
- Non-professional translators, i.e., bilinguals who volunteer or are asked to translate without financial compensation.
- Journalists, post-editors, template makers, technical writers, and multilingual technical writers.
- Researchers interested in indirect translation.
- Scholars in the general field of translation studies who want to learn more about the role translation can play in multilingual environments, in mitigating inequalities, and in enhancing inclusivity and accessibility.

Not counting the introduction and conclusion, the textbook is organized into seven core chapters. Added to these are a glossary and an index. Further resources and tips for some activities can be found at the Routledge Translation Studies Portal.

Each core chapter follows a similar formula and is devoted to one particular translation domain that acts as a possible background. Each chapter starts with an outline of the main problems to be tackled, a checklist of expected learning outcomes, and snapshots of real-life situations where indirect translation happens. These snapshots are meant to serve as a springboard for preliminary discussions. Then, the chapters go on to provide theoretical considerations, which allow us to identify the typical challenges involved in translating for further translation and from translation in a specific translation domain. These considerations are followed by points for further discussion so that you can further explore and reflect on the topics at hand. Please bear in mind that, throughout this book, indirect translation is mainly taken in narrow terms (a translation via a third language). However, the section on further discussion amplifies this view and goes beyond this narrow definition to explore interactions with other theoretical considerations in translation studies. After the "Further discussion" section you will find activities so that you can practice what you have learned. The activities vary in terms of type and workload: some are more theoretical and demand extra reading, while others are very practical but at the same time might require more leg work. At the end of each chapter, you will find brief information about the accompanying material that can be found on the Translation Studies Portal and the references used in the chapter.

Throughout the book, words that are used meta-linguistically, as well as the titles of publications, are italicized. Terms that are explained in the glossary are marked in bold.

Each core chapter adds a new set of competences and deals with a different area of the translation industry in which translating for/from a translation is likely to occur. As each chapter builds on the previous one, the book lends itself well to sequential reading. However, it is also possible for each chapter to be approached autonomously.

Using the Routledge Translation Studies Portal

Additional resources for students and teachers are available at the Translation Studies Portal (http://routledgetranslationstudiesportal.com/). Once in the portal, the material is structured following the order of chapters in the book. Below each chapter you can find "Resources" and "Tasks." In "Resources" you will find links to readings, recommendations and useful material. All these resources aim to help you learn more about a given topic or carry out the activities described in the book. "Tasks" includes extra activities and tips on how to adapt activities from specific chapters to different settings (e.g., classes focused on other translation domains or a particular language combination or directionality, and different educational environments). The section also includes solutions for some tasks.

ACKNOWLEDGEMENTS

This book has three authors, but it took a village to complete. We would like to thank many people who have kindly helped us to prepare and finalize this book project. For their insightful advice, useful material and invaluable help with activities and theoretical considerations, special thanks go to:

Alexandra Assis Rosa	Lynne Bowker
Anthony Pym	Magdalena Oziemblewska
Catherine Fuller	Marco Neves
Cláudia Martins	Marlie van Rooyen
Chris Mellinger	Minako O'Hagan
David Orrego-Carmona	Mireia Vargas-Urpi
Elena Aguirre Fernández-Bravo	Nuno Vieira
Elena Zavar Galvão	Pieter Boulogne
Franz Pöchhacker	Renata Milczak
Haidee Kotze	Rita Menezes
James Hadley	Richard Mansell
Joss Moorkens	Roberto Valdéon
Kaisa Koskinen	Stavroula Sokoli
Karen Bennett	Susana Valdez
Kate Pool	Verónica Calafell
Laura Ivaska	Wine Tesseur
Lucile Davier	Yves Gambier

Our gratitude also goes to many colleagues in academia and the industry worldwide, who participated in online surveys we conducted for the purpose of this study. Warm thanks to our students, on whom we tested some of the activities published in this book; to participants of our pre-conference workshop at the IATIS

2021 congress, who helped us fine-tune these activities; and to our colleagues at Universidade NOVA de Lisboa, Universidade de Lisboa, Universidade Católica Portuguesa, Universitat Rovira i Virgili, Universitat Autònoma de Barcelona and the IndirecTrans network, who acted as very productive resonance groups. This work was supported by Fundação para a Ciência e a Tecnologia (SFRH/BPD/100800/2014, UIDB/00114/2020, UIDP/00114/2020, UIDB/04097/2020, UIDP/04097/2020, UIDB/00126/2020, UIDP/00126/2020).

We would like to gratefully acknowledge the tireless support we received from Eleni Steck, Louisa Semlyen and the rest of the team at Routledge. They are responsible for the book's title. We are also indebted to Kelly Washbourne for his thorough reading and enriching feedback.

Finally, we would like to thank our family and friends for their patience and constant support in challenging times, and for all the various reasons that they know best. In a way, this book is also for them (and especially for Marysia, Adam, Manuel, Lurdes, Pol and Leo).

Permissions

Every effort has been made to secure permission to reproduce copyrighted material. Any omission brought to our attention will be amended in future editions.

We would like to thank the following copyright holders for granting permission for the use of their material:

António Valente	Marlie van Rooyen
Daria Maslona	Nuno Vales
Kuba Mikurda	OOONA
Festival de Cinema Avanca	Stanisław Zaborowski
Gridly	Susana Valdez
M.F. Costa e Silva	

1
INTRODUCTION

Introduction

In this chapter we will familiarize ourselves with the concept of indirect translation by looking at the key main trends in past and present-day indirect translation situations. We will also discuss the future prospects of this practice and outline how indirect translation is handled in research and training.

Learning outcomes

This chapter prepares the ground for what will be discussed in the eight core chapters to follow. Upon successful completion of this chapter, you will be able to:

- Problematize the concept of indirect translation using appropriate terminology.
- Discuss common misconceptions associated with this practice.

> **Warm-up activity**
>
> Look at the raw output generated by a machine translation engine in Figure 1.1. Can you spot the English pivot hack? What does this image say about the relevance of indirect translation today?

FIGURE 1.1 Simulation of raw output generated by an MT engine in July 2021

What is indirect translation?

Indirect translations are translations of translations. In the English language, the terminology that translators use to label this practice varies immensely and is in constant flux. Possible alternatives include compilative, double, eclectic, intermediate, mediated, pivot, relay, retranslation, second-hand and secondary translation. Sometimes the choice depends on the translation domain in which a translator works. For instance, interpreters typically talk about relay interpreting, whereas subtitlers and people specializing in machine translation tend to opt for pivot (translation). The choice may also be informed by the linguistic tradition you come from: translators working with Romance languages often prefer to call this practice "indirect translation", while those working with the Chinese language tend to prefer "relay" when describing this practice in English (Assis Rosa, Pięta and Maia 2017, 117).

Some people understand indirect translation in a narrow sense: as a translation via a third language (e.g., St. André 2019; Landers 2001, 130). In these narrow terms, a translation is achieved in two steps: a first translation from language A into language B, then a second translation by a different translator from language B into language C.

However, others take indirect translation more broadly (e.g., Gambier 1994; Toury 2012, 82). They recognize that the definition is broad enough to include, or at least overlap with, a great diversity of **intralingual, interlingual, intramodal** and **intermodal translation** processes. Possible examples include:

- **Retranslation**: adapting the text to a new audience or to new times.
- **Back translation**: translating back to the source language to, for example, look for discrepancies.

- **Support translation**: using target texts in other languages when you are looking for alternative solutions in your target language (Dollerup 2000).
- **Novelization** of a film or video game which is itself based on a book. For example, Christopher Wood wrote a novelization of the James Bond film *The Spy Who Loved Me*. The film itself is a cinematographic adaptation of an Ian Fleming novel.
- **Speech-to-text interpreting** (also referred to as live subtitling): interpreting into another language which is then rendered as written text with keyboards (e.g., stenotype, velotype) or speech recognition software.
- **Compilative translation**: when you translate not from one but several source texts, thus compiling different sources in one plural target text. Literary classics such as Boccacio's *Decameron* may be read as this type of compilative patchwork of short stories, coming from different languages, genres and oral traditions (Maia 2021).

In this book we pay particular attention to indirect translation understood in the narrow sense (as a translation via a third language). However, when relevant, we also refer to other practices that can be subsumed under the broad term of indirect translation, such as the ones listed above.

Whether understood in a narrow or broad sense, indirect translation includes at least one of the two processes that form two sides of the same coin, requiring overlapping competences: translating from a translation and translating with a further translation in mind.

When does indirect translation happen?

Indirect translation has an age-old history. Take, for example, the Bible. The Old Testament, originally written in Hebrew, Aramaic and Greek, was translated into Latin and from there into many different **vernacular languages.** Jesus is claimed to have spoken Aramaic. However, no written version in Aramaic has been preserved. This is why, when St. Jerome translated the Bible into Latin (in the early fourth century), he used other Latin and Greek sources. Over time, St. Jerome's version (commonly known as the Vulgate) overtook the original version. When, in the sixteenth century, after centuries of bans and persecutions, the Catholic Church finally began to sponsor vernacular translations of the Bible, the only acceptable source text was not the Hebrew/Aramaic/Greek original but St. Jerome's Latin translation. This indirect route was standard procedure for many Bible translations until the early twentieth century.

Other historical examples can be found in the literary domain, as many world literature classics have been subject to indirect translation. The pivotal role of French and German in further European translations of Dostoyevsky (Boulogne 2015) or the developments around the *Arabian Nights* (Borges 1997) are examples of how translations would serve as source texts for further translation. In some cases, these source texts are preserved (published or archived). In other cases, these source texts are lost to history (e.g., cribs or oral translations by an informant).

There are also many historical examples of indirectness related to the translation of philosophical, scientific and technical texts. One telling example is Chinese law, which was transplanted at the beginning of the twentieth century from Europe via Japan. From the standpoint of translation, this means that some laws of civil law countries such as Germany or France were first translated into Japanese, and from there into Chinese (Ng 2014). Another case in point is the activity of the so-called Toledo School, which, in the twelfth and thirteenth centuries, made the scientific and philosophical heritage of the Islamic world available to medieval Europe. Many of these Arabic texts were themselves translations of Greek and Roman works, which adds an extra element to this indirect trajectory. This long-standing indirect transmission of astronomical, medical and philosophical knowledge, from Europe to the Middle East and then back to Europe, paved the way for the Renaissance. Without all these indirect translations, the world as we know it would not be the same.

At the same time, in certain periods and geopolitical regions, some languages became more powerful than others. They often served as regional pivots for linguistic contacts in these regions. Pivot languages facilitate translation between two (or more) other languages. For example, between the fourteenth and eighteenth centuries, when Latin was still the main **pivot language** across Europe, Middle Low German acted as a regional hub language for contacts within the Hanseatic League—a network of merchant communities in northwestern and central Europe. Another telling example is Russian, which roughly between the 1950s and 1990s—at a time when English was already assuming its position as the main pivot language worldwide—worked as a regional pivot in the transfer of texts between the former Soviet republics, and between these republics and Western countries (Witt 2013; Witt 2017). It thus became the language of censorship, controlling what got in and got out (Gambier 2003). In turn, Portuguese, as the language of the metropole of the Portuguese Empire, has for centuries worked as an important pivot for contacts between local languages of Lusophone Africa, and between these languages and the rest of the world (Halme-Berneking 2019).

Where do you translate indirectly?

From the discussion so far, it should be clear that indirect translation is not restricted to a specific geographic or linguistic area but is performed the world over. Typically, indirect translation is done from one **peripheral language** into another via a more **central language**. This means that indirect translation is a matter relevant to both more peripheral languages and more central languages.

It should also have become clear that, although it tends to be associated almost exclusively with printed books and conference interpreting, indirect translation can be easily found in myriad multimodal, multimedia and interactive textual forms currently available, as well as various language learning situations and settings (the marketplace, international trains, museums, learning environments, live festivals, etc.). Some examples of other domains where indirect translation is most likely to be commissioned include:

Interpreting. Relay arrangements play an important role both in conference and community settings (courts, police, social services, etc.) and they are incorporated into different working modes (e.g., consecutive, simultaneous, whispered). The role of technology has facilitated this modality in simultaneous interpreting (via the use of, for example, pivot booths). For example, in Canada's Northwest Territories, relay in consecutive mode is part of public service interpreting practices, serving various aboriginal languages in combination with English and French (Biscaye 1993).

Institutional translation. With the increase in the number of language combinations in many intergovernmental (e.g., the European Union and the United Nations) and non-governmental institutions (e.g., Amnesty International), a system of relay languages is used. Documents are first translated into a major language, for example English, French or German, then from that language into many others (Tesseur 2015).

Localization. In **localization**, translation needs to be planned for from the very outset and at every stage of product development (whether it is software, a video game, a website, etc.). This is particularly clear in the process known as **internationalization** (which takes place at the stage of programme design and document development), when a product is generalized so that it can be adapted to various languages and regions without requiring engineering changes. Internationalization can therefore be seen as an extended version of translating for translation. Indirect translation has also been commonly used in video game localization. Games developed in languages other than English are first localized into English for the North American region, which constitutes a major market for these products. Other localized versions are based on these English pivots and subsequently released in further markets.

Audiovisual translation. More and more content is being translated between two non-English languages. In such situations, the second translator often works from an English **template**, without knowing the foreign language in the audio. At the same time, in order to sell their audiovisual products abroad, many broadcasting companies from non-English language contexts present their marketing material (programme synopses, scripts or dialogue lists) into English. This means that indirect translation is not only visible on screen: a large share of the behind-the-scenes negotiations involves resorting to English language mediation as well.

News translation. In journalistic translation, direct translations are very rare. Indirect translations take place in oral and verbal form, either through a published mediating text or a verbal mediation. Just consider the compilations of translated quotes from different ultimate source language texts, including interviews and PR material, as well as situations in which a media outlet rewrites a wire dispatch that already includes translations (Davier and Van Doorslaer 2018).

6 Introduction

Machine translation. Indirect translation is exactly how many machine translation engines (such as Google Translate) do their magic when translating between "unusual" language pairs. These engines rely on machine learning and hence the availability of large parallel data for training. In other words, to know how to translate well, typically these engines first need access to a high number of bilingual sentence pairs. Since such data are not available for most language pairs, present-day technologies often fall short in their ability to translate between unusual language combinations. They thus often need to use pivoting (aka bridging) methods as a workaround. For example, if we wanted to build a machine translation system translating from Nepali into Swahili, then, instead of building one direct system to do that, we would build two parallel systems, first translating from Nepali into English, then from English into Swahili (Liu et al. 2019). This is because both Nepali and Swahili are **low-resource languages**, so we have much more parallel data in the two language pairs of Nepali–English and English–Swahili than the direct Nepali–Swahili corpus.

How do you translate indirectly?

Indirect translations can be performed in all sorts of ways and an all-encompassing classification is impossible here. Below is only a glimpse into some aspects of *how* indirect translations tend to be made (summarized in Figure 1.2). These aspects are further explored throughout the book.

- *Knowledge about indirectness.* The first and second translator may be perfectly aware that they are not working from the original or they may be completely in the dark about this (thus unknowingly risking a breach of copyright, etc.).

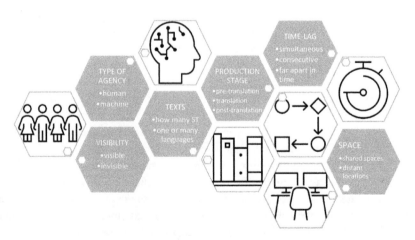

FIGURE 1.2 Variables in indirect translation

- *Access to the source text and/or language.* The second translator may or may not have access to the source text but only to a mediating text. In cases where the relay-taker does not know the language but has access to the original content, they can try to incorporate some of its elements into the final product. For example, in all-on-site, bilateral consecutive interpreting operated in relay mode, the relay-taker may not understand the verbal component of the original utterance, but they may understand and make use of the non-verbal elements to which they have access, such as facial expression, posture, gestures.
- *Number of languages and text.* The second translator can make use of only one or many versions of the original, in the same or various languages. These versions can be used simultaneously or alternately, as starting points or merely as a control.
- *Space and time sharing.* The first and the second translator may share the same space (as in relay interpreting, where the utterances are rendered with a relatively small delay and the interpreters can be located in the same building, booth or online environment) or they can work in distant locations (as in many other subtitling workflows, e.g., in video game localization). Their work may be separated by a very small time lag (e.g., a subtitler working from a template) or it may be separated by decades (literary translation).
- *Type of agency.* The mediating or target text can be produced by a human (as is often the case in, for example, consecutive interpreting in community settings). Alternatively, it can be generated by a non-human agent (for instance, when speech is first turned into text by an automatic speech recognition system and then processed through machine translation) (Pöchhacker 2022).
- *Stage of translation production.* A translation process can go indirect during the pre-translation, translation or post-translation stage. For example, in the case of literary translation, the choice to translate can be triggered by the success of a different language version of the original; a translator can work from a non-original; or a reviser can add changes based on a parallel language version.

For more developed classifications, see Assis Rosa, Pięta and Maia (2017), Davier (2022), Dollerup (2014) and Washbourne (2013).

Who are the main stakeholders in indirect translation?

There are a number of agents who make translation more or less indirect, and their impact may happen during the pre-translation, translation or post-translation stage (see Figure 1.3). We have identified the following stakeholders in a process of indirect translation:

- The *first translator*, or **relayer**, who creates a pivot version. They can be more or less aware of their pivoting role. This is likely the case for a subtitler (**template**

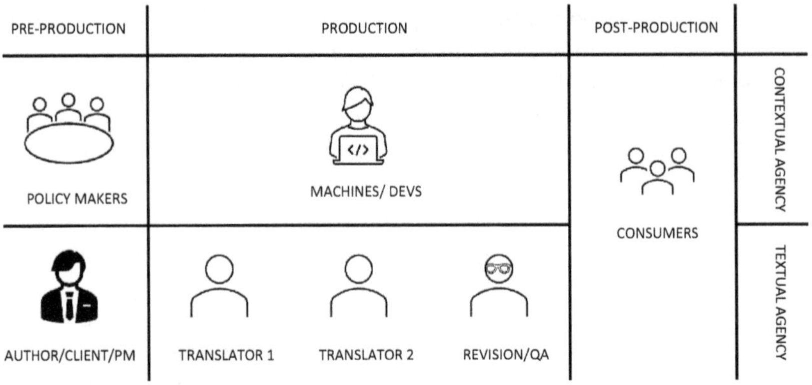

8 Introduction

FIGURE 1.3 Key stakeholders in indirect translation

    maker) who produces the English template for, say, a Polish film for a streaming service provider, such as Netflix. However, a literary translator working from an exotic language may have no way of knowing whether and how her text will be reused.
- The *second translator*, who acts as a **relay-taker**. Again, they may be more or less aware of the translational nature of the text they are meant to translate. For instance, a literary translator who translates a Japanese author from English can figure out that they are dealing with a mediating text, whereas a journalist covering an international event and rewriting a wire dispatch may not be aware of the fact that it contains translated passages because the authorship is not always clear in these situations.
- The **translation buyer**, **author** *(creator)* or **project manager** can ask a translator to work from a specific translated version of the original or can provide a previous translation as support material.
- The *person responsible for* **revision, quality control** or **quality assurance** can introduce changes to a translation after comparing it with other linguistic versions of the same source text.
- *Consumers* (readers, viewers, users of translated products) can express their different tastes, preferences and needs and influence the decision to translate indirectly and/or the choice of the mediating language and text.
- *Policymakers, professional associations*, and *training and research institutions* define the conventions that guide choices to use or not indirect translations, and also to what extent it is disclosed or hidden.
- *Machines* (although it might be more accurate to say "developers") can be instrumental agents in their own right. This is true in scenarios where machines perform one of the stages of indirect translation, playing the role of relayer or relay-taker. As mentioned earlier, it is even possible to witness workflows where the indirect translation is fully automatic and does not involve human performance (at least a substantial one). A workflow in which the written

output generated by a respeaker is fed into a machine translation engine seems to fulfil this condition (Pöchhacker 2022).

Why translate indirectly?

The first reason that is typically given is the complete lack—or temporary unavailability—of translators with the necessary competence to produce a direct translation. It is one thing to translate a highly technical document from Arabic, Hindi or Portuguese into English, but it is quite another to translate a similar document from Swahili into Polish, Korean, or Uyghur. It is not that these languages are too difficult to translate from, or too difficult to translate into. The point is that the number of qualified translators who are able to work with these language combinations is relatively low.

Why else would someone opt for an indirect translation? Here is a summary of possible motivations:

- *Availability of the source text.* The original (or part of it) is nowhere to be found. This can happen for reasons to do with censorship or geographical and temporal distance that separates the source and target cultures (see examples of sacred text translation or the chapter on News Translation).
- *Price.* Translations from lesser-known languages tend to be more costly for the client than those made from well-known languages, as availability and lack of competition influence the rates. Indirect translation can also be more cost efficient for organizations that operate with several languages. Let us suppose a scenario with five different languages. If one language serves as the intermediary (and the other four work into and from this pivot), a project manager will only need enough translators to work in eight directions. Without one language acting as an intermediary, twenty language combinations will be needed to allow communication between every language. (See Chapter 2 on Interpreting for further examples.)
- *Time.* Using a pivot language may boost efficiency. During the Covid-19 pandemic, the World Health Organization's guidance and advice was provided in English (and sometimes five other official languages), then distributed worldwide via many indirect routes, thus becoming a life-saving measure in this crisis situation (Federici and O'Brien 2019). In subtitling, using pre-existing templates (typically English) may save time and effort that would otherwise be spent on cueing, dialogue segmentation, etc.
- *Prestige.* In cases where the mediating culture and cultural models are prestigious within a domain, indirect translation may actually be preferred to direct translation. For example, due to the overarching prestige of English as the language of knowledge, English language translations of foreign works may be preferred as the source of scientific knowledge in different peripheral settings. Apart from being more accessible, the international version of a scientific work may be considered to include the most relevant contributions, and perhaps

even be more in line with the norm of "good" and "accurate" scientific work (Bennett 2007). Also, from the point of view of the source, indirect translation might be viewed as a token of widespread respect or admiration for the ultimate source culture or text. Hung (2014, 75) suggests that, from the standpoint of the ancient rulers of China, indirect translation was actually a sign of prestige: "Since the burden of achieving communication was on the foreigners, the fact that they chose to honour the Chinese government despite such linguistic hurdles was taken as proof of their immense respect".

- *Risk*. Authors, literary agents, publishers, project managers, etc. may ask the translator to use mediating texts, rather than the original, in order to control the translated content. See, for example, Ismail Kadare's work. Since it has no international copyright, a new source text (English translation) ensures the work's survival and authorial control (Washbourne 2013). Indirect translation can also be safer for the client, who may prefer to employ a translator who lacks knowledge of the ultimate source language but who has previous experience and proven reliability.
- *Difficulty*. Recourse to intermediary texts can be quite useful for translators. If the first-hand translation is of good quality, providing a clear and coherent interpretation of the ultimate source text, it can make the second translator's task much easier. Also, if the target text includes different readings of the source text, which would individually require a lot of effort (documentation, approaches, etc.), the final result might be richer. What is more, translated texts tend to be simpler than original texts and, in turn, easier to translate with machine translation (Läubli et al. 2020).
- *Access*. Many speakers of low-diffusion languages live in the world's most impoverished geographic areas. Since not all know English to the required level, indirect translation can help them access important information, be heard on the global stage and thrive. By offering help in overcoming major linguistic hurdles, indirect translation works as a tool for the social, economic and political development of countries, peoples and movements. For accounts on how language becomes a major barrier for development in general, and local NGO's efforts in particular, see, for example, Tesseur and Crack (2020).

What are the consequences of translating indirectly?

Indirect translation is laden with negative connotations. The common perception is that, if something is lost in translation, twice as much is missing in indirect translation. In other words, indirect translation is assumedly linked to poor results. There are three main ways in which indirect translation is viewed as a threat (Pięta 2021):

- *A threat to translation quality*. The reasoning is that mistakes in the pivot versions are necessarily replicated in further translations. Another oft-quoted assumption is that there is always some delay in communication. For example,

when, during a debate at the European Parliament, the Italian prime minister Silvio Berlusconi compared German representative Martin Schulz to a Nazi guard, it took Schulz some moments to realize he was being offended. Also, translating indirectly a source text spoken in a language the translator has not mastered (or does not know) may entail a great deal of additional research (and therefore time) (see Chapter 2 for the specificities of interpreting).
- *A threat to the balance between languages and cultures.* With the English language acting as the main middleman worldwide, there is a danger of economic, cultural and epistemological homogenization, whereby consumer preferences are anglicized, and English mediating is preferred to direct translation from more peripheral languages (Ringmar 2012) (for further reflection on this aspect, see Chapter 3).
- *A threat to the jobs, rights and ethics of translators.* As mentioned, translations from smaller languages tend to be more expensive than translations from larger languages. Translating from a major pivot language may therefore mean that you take translation work away from people who are already marginalized because of the minor language they use. Often, translators are not paid when their work is reused by further translators, which provokes ethical and legal issues (see Chapter 5 for other insights on ethics and indirect translation).

While these arguments are, of course, valid in many situations, they should also be put into perspective because, in many ways, indirect translation leads to positive results. When it comes to quality, the success or failure of indirect translation will, to a large degree, depend on the competence of the translator and on the quality of the translation from which they work. If both are beyond reproach, the result may not be worse than a direct translation. For other merits, see the section "Why translate indirectly?".

Indirect translation in the foreseeable future

Without a crystal ball, it is impossible to foretell what the future holds for indirect translation. However, by looking back and around, we can predict some general trends that are likely to occur in the more or less distant future.

Practice

Indirect translation is unlikely to disappear. Yes, there are more and more professional translators specializing in different languages and text types. However, it is utopic to believe that there will ever be a sufficient number of qualified translators for every language pair in the world who are always available when necessary. Therefore, it stands to reason that, with increasing globalization, there will be more and more situations where there is a sudden need to translate from a given language, but there will not be enough qualified translators working from this language to meet the demand. The alternative, using a lingua franca like English, has serious social and cultural implications. For instance, not everyone knows English well enough to understand how and when to adopt life-saving measures of social distancing, and this lack of knowledge may leave them vulnerable in a sanitary crisis like the Covid-19 pandemic. What is more, if a language is not used to communicate important information, it stops being relevant, which can lead to language death.

Solutions might come from breakthroughs in machine translation. Better outputs between less common language pairs are expected due to changing approaches to the development of neural machine translation for low-resource languages. For instance, in the so-called zero-shot models, a large database of parallel corpora is no longer a prerequisite. Instead, translation solutions come from labelled multilingual quality data (e.g., Johnson et al. 2017; Aharoni, Johnson and Firat 2019). Google researchers are already experimenting with a universal model that handles all language pairs (Arivazhagan et al. 2019). However, it would not be surprising if DeepL, Reverso, Yandex, Tencent or Baidu were to become the leading players in marketing open-domain direct translation for many non-English language pairs. This is because these developers are mainly based outside English-speaking countries, where the demand for direct translation between non-English languages seems higher.

While it could be argued that better quality machine translation might cover some of the growing demand we mentioned above, research suggests this type of translation creates a new demand that is hardly covered by existing translators (Nurminen 2019; Pym and Torres-Simón 2021). Still, improving resources for low-resource languages will probably improve the quality of translations, whether direct or indirect.

While nothing indicates a general decrease in indirect translation practice, the way it is currently perceived is likely to change. Some suggest that, in certain settings, indirect translation may not only be more tolerated but actually preferred over direct translation. This may happen in multilingual governmental organizations (like the European Parliament), where a large number of documents needs to be rendered in various linguistic combinations according to pre-established common standards. It may also be the case in commercially motivated areas, like the film or gaming industry. The use of relay systems resonates well with these commercial imperatives, as it helps streamline production, speeds up turnaround times and solves recruitment issues by increasing the number of available translators (Georgakopoulou 2019). The stigma surrounding indirect translation is relatively recent, dating back to the Romantic period and the sacralization of the notion of originality (Baer 2016). Before this period, a translation from a translation was hardly considered polemical.

Additionally, indirect translation may become increasingly appealing in somewhat less commercially driven areas, such as certain types of literary translation. This is because the overwhelming dominance of English language products (translated or otherwise) on many literary markets can contribute to the anglicization of the general literary taste, leading to situations where Anglo-American mediation will be seen as preferred. In this scenario, non-English authors may first need to pass through the Anglo-American filter to make sure their work is in tune with the readers' expectations (Ringmar 2012). In this context, some authors are expected to write in a translation-friendly style (in a "marketable style"). Then, research already indicates that many non-English authors are strategically translated into English with an eye to translating into a third language (McMartin 2020). Sometimes these authors also write with further translation in mind. This phenomenon may refer to more marketable subject matter, such as magic realism, but also to ready translatability. If this tendency continues and a clear market is defined, more people may specialize in either translating for translation or from secondary sources, thus improving indirect translation quality.

What is more, ongoing research on cross-linguistic plagiarism, particularly promoted in 2020 by the global temporal move to online education, might lead to an easier detection of uncited sources, thus making indirect translation more visible and explicit. Moreover, new developments in corpus studies might provide answers on how to detect the source language(s) of a given text (see Ivaska 2020). If tracking copyright breaches becomes easier, the argument that indirect translation is a threat to translators' rights might lose some power. Moreover, clarity and visibility could help counteract some of the ethical breaches negatively associated with the practice.

Last, increased awareness and better tools to define authorship might encourage more teamwork, where the target language expert has access and collaborates with the original source language expert.

In a nutshell, nothing suggests a reduced relevance of indirect translation in the foreseeable future, rather the opposite. It seems that, as long as there is a need for translation, the demand for indirect translation will be there too. So, we may as well learn how to do it well and make the most of it.

Research

For many years, indirect translation has been marginalized by translation researchers and trainers. This is partly because many traditions of translation reflection have long been anchored in models that prioritize translating from the original. Added to this is the fact that, on many occasions, the indirect status of translations is not put proudly on display. It is often not acknowledged in the texts themselves or in reference materials, which makes researching this practice very time consuming. While statistics may help in identifying instances of this practice with acceptable probability (Ivaska 2020), the problem is only partially solved. This is because, even in the case of simple indirect translation chains, researchers may need to have knowledge of multiple languages and cultural backgrounds.

This might explain why systematic studies on indirect translation are a recent development. For quite some time now, most studies have adopted a historical approach that rarely looks beyond the twentieth century. Traditionally, the emphasis has been on a small range of language pairs and geographic areas (mostly in Asia, Europe and South America), one medium (the printed book) and one text type (literature). Much has been said and written about the negative consequences of indirect translation, adding to the common negative perception mentioned above.

However, in recent years, indirect translation research has experienced a wave of changes. It has grown significantly and evolved in terms of visibility. The most meaningful manifestations of this are the increasing number of academic events, scientific publications (one issued in the 1960s, one in the 1970s, eight in the 1980s, 18 in the 1990s, 32 in the 2000s and over 80 in the 2010s, see Pięta 2017), funded research projects (e.g., the QuantiQual project running at Trinity College Dublin, www.adaptcentre.ie/news-and-events/lost-in-indirect-translation/) and MA and PhD dissertations. Also of note is the founding of an international network of researchers interested in translations from translations (IndirecTrans, www.indirectrans.com).

Indirect translation research is going digital and global: there is an increasing number of studies focusing on digital domains and using digital technologies to identify and study indirect translation (e.g., Ivaska 2020, Oziemblewska and Szarkowska 2021). The range of examined text types, media, regions and language combinations is clearly expanding (see, for example, Van Rooyen 2018 on news translation in South Africa). Most studies deal with translation situations where English is the main pivot language, but increasing attention is being paid to regional pivot languages (Japanese in Asia, Portuguese in Lusophone Africa, Swedish in Nordic Europe, etc.). They also start shifting the focus to the advantages of this practice.

This growth of research on indirect translation has produced results relevant to translation studies, although it is still peripheral to the discipline. On the one hand, by highlighting multifaceted translation processes that break away from a source-target dichotomy, research on indirect translation has led to calls for the revision of fundamental concepts in translation, such as source text, target text, equivalence, etc. (Pięta, Ivaska and Gambier 2022). It has also foregrounded power struggles among languages and cultures, thus opening new perspectives in discussing accessibility, equality and inclusive development (Pięta et al. forthcoming). In this way, indirect translation research is starting to create bridges with myriad other fields that look at issues like ethics, technology and transculturality, thereby feeding the ongoing debate on sustainable growth.

Pięta's critical bibliography lists and comments on research publications published up to 2016 that focus on indirect translation. New additions to the list are mentioned on the IndirecTrans website (www.indirectrans.com/research-publications/updates-to-the-comprehensive-list-of-publications.html). All these different aspects point to the diminishing marginality of indirect translation within the discipline of translation studies.

Training

Although it has evolved in terms of research, indirect translation is still lagging behind when it comes to training. It seems largely overlooked at the institutional level and there are not many opportunities to learn how to translate indirectly, whether within or outside a university.

To begin with, and to the best of our knowledge, there are currently no **university programmes** or **courses** specializing in indirect translation. If hands-on practice in translating from a translation is offered, this typically happens as part of a general translation practicum. Translating for translation is taught even less frequently. Whatever the modality (written or oral), the use of indirect translation in class is unlikely to be mentioned in the official syllabus (Torres-Simón et al. 2021). Professional development courses, continuing education seminars or preconference workshops specializing in indirect translation are also next to impossible to find.

Second, indirect translation is not currently mentioned in the mainstream lists of translation competences, such as the one developed by the European Masters in Translation (EMT 2017). This is problematic because such lists inform curriculum design, indicating which core skills translators need to develop in order to provide a translation service in line with the highest professional and ethical standards.

Third, there is a shortage of ample training advice on how to translate well from a translation and/or with a further translation in mind. This kind of advice is conspicuously missing from a vast majority of published textbooks for trainers and/or self-learners in translation. A few valuable exceptions include Lathey (2015) and Setton and Dawrant (2016), which dedicate a small part of a chapter to a brief discussion of some of the challenges of indirect translation for a child readership and relay interpreting, respectively. There are also journal articles here and there that discuss best practices in creating template files (Georgakopoulou 2019) and drafting contracts for literary pivot translators (Pool 2013). Indirect translators can typically supplement their education by consulting the few guidelines and codes of practices made available by professional associations and the industry. For instance, building and expanding on insights from Pool (2013), the UK-based Society of Authors (2016) provides its members with "Guidance to Relay Translation", Netflix has drafted "Pivot language template guidelines" (Netflix 2020) and AIIC ([2004] 2017) lists some recommendations for pivot arrangements in interpreting (which are developed in Setton and Dawrant 2016). However, more often than not, advice about translating indirectly does not go beyond broad-brush recommendations that it should be avoided. Thus, in situations where translating for/from a translation cannot be avoided or is actually preferred, translators are often left to their own devices.

All this makes the issue of indirect translation a burning one for training providers. More training opportunities and institutional legitimization are desirable as they are likely to have a positive impact on the quality of indirect translations. It would also enhance the recognition and professionalization of this practice, which could materialize into higher fees and better working conditions. We hope this book will be a useful step in this direction.

Further discussion

- *Ezra Pound's "clairvoyance"*. Is it possible to translate without knowing the source language (but with proper documentation)? For an illustrative example, see Yao 2010 (36–39). Is that an indirect translation? How? Why not?

> - *Indirect translation mediated not by language but by other art forms.* Look at the Telephone Art Project (https://phonebook.gallery/about), where one message passes from art form to art form (e.g., from painting to music, then poetry, then dance). Are these trajectories a form of indirect translation?

Activities

Activity 1 Problematize the concept of indirect translation, using appropriate terminology

Activity 1.1 Reflect on the terminology

PART A. List of terms

List all the terms used for different types of indirect translation covered in this chapter. Are these names commonly used across the board? Or are they specific to one linguistic tradition, translation domain or group of translation stakeholders, such as users (viewers, readers, etc.), trainers, translators (professional or non-professional), researchers, critics? Are these terms impartial or do they reflect some kind of judgement? Do different translation stakeholders talk about the same thing when they talk about indirect translation? Consider all of the above and discuss it with a colleague.

PART B. Terms in translation

Do these terms have a correspondence in your language? Which ones? Do they have positive or negative connotations? Summarize the information collected in PART A and PART B in a table. Which term would you prefer to use when talking to a fellow translator? Would you also use it when talking to a client? Or would you rather use a different term? Justify your answers.

Activity 1.2 Indirect translation around us

Look around. On a normal day at home or at work, how many translations can you find that seem indirect? Look in all sorts of places, from your favourite chocolate bar wrapper to the websites you visit, your favourite books, social networks, video games, news channels, TV providers, etc.). How much material is translated from languages other than English? Do you think they are direct? How can you tell? How sure are you? If using linguistic cues, be aware that, in some cases, foreign-ness might not result from poor practice but from an intentional communication strategy. Then, how recent can this direct trend be?

Activity 1.3 Indirect translation awareness

Ask around. Are your friends, family and colleagues aware of indirect translation? Do they consume it? What do they have to say about it? You can use the examples you have identified in your own experience to illustrate what you mean by indirect translation. Try to understand if there is an area in your cultural or linguistic environment where indirect translation is tolerated or perhaps even preferred to direct translation.

Activity 1.4 Indirectness in MT

Do some fun detective work to prove that there is an English hack in a machine translation system of your choice. The fact that many machine translation engines use English as a bridge when asked to translate between two low-resource languages is not exactly a secret. However, it is fun to prove it to ourselves. Have a look at the images contained in Figure 1.1. Can you guess the ambiguous English words that caused the surprising translations in these examples?

Can you find other translations that expose this hack? Please bear in mind that different machine translation systems (DeepL, Google Translate, Yandex, etc.) can offer different solutions and the results can change with time (machine translation engines learn from every input they get).

As a disclaimer, we want to stress that machine translation systems are not trained to be used as dictionaries. So, it is only natural that such mistakes occur if we use the engine to translate one word only. You may want to try using a machine translation engine to translate a whole sentence with this word, to see if the engine yields a more correct output. We are not saying that machine translation will not work if it uses a bridge method. We only stress that machine translation should be used critically and with careful consideration, especially in connection to low-resource languages.

Activity 2 Discuss common misconceptions associated with this practice

Activity 2.1 Rates and availability

PART A. Rates

Check translation directories (e.g., https://the-poool.com, www.proz.com) and other relevant webpages to find out the rates for:

a) Translating from a **supercentral language** into another.
b) Translating from a supercentral language into/from English.
c) Translating from a peripheral language into/from English.
d) Translating from a peripheral language into a supercentral language.
e) Translating from a peripheral language into another peripheral language.

Compare the results. What seems cheaper? What is the most expensive combination? Would indirect translation (via English) be a less costly option in any situation?

PART B. Availability

Now, consider how easy/difficult it was to find out the rates and how many translators are listed for different linguistic combinations. Think how all this impacts the time spent on finding a professional with relevant language expertise. Could it mean a delay in locating available experts?

Once you have gone through all these tasks, critically reread the different statements from this chapter. To what extent is indirect translation easier, cheaper, marginal? To what extent does it read or sound differently from a direct translation? Should it be avoided? Justify your answer.

Activity 2.2 Professional associations

Look for professional translation associations in your area and check their codes of good practice and statements about ethics. If possible, find a national association and a domain-specific association. (You can find a list of several associations on FIT's website: www.fit-ift.org). Look for mentions of indirect translation. What do they say? Do they offer any advice that could be helpful if you had to translate indirectly (for or from a translation)? Are there differences between the codes of ethics for general translation and for specific domains (legal translation, interpreting, etc.)? To complete the picture, try to find mentions of indirect translation in threads on translator mailing lists and forums. What new insights do they provide?

Activity 2.3 Training

If you have ever received training in translation, try to recall if indirect translation was ever mentioned in your classes. Was it something that you only discussed or something that you actually did? Skim through translation textbooks you used to check whether they mention indirect translation. To what extent do they echo the ideas mentioned in this chapter? What other insights do they provide?

If you have never received training in translation, check translation courses in your area to see if they teach how to translate for/from a translation. You can also check translation textbooks to see if they teach how to translate for translation and/or from a translation.

Resources

List of competencies linked to indirect translation. Link to a constantly updated list of research publications on indirect translation. Academic and professional videos and blogs on indirect translation.

Activities

Consideration for Activity 1. Extra activities.

References

Aharoni, Roee, Melvin Johnson, and Orhan Firat. 2019. "Massively Multilingual Neural Machine Translation." In *Proceedings of the 2019 Conference of the North American Chapter of the Association for Computational Linguistics: Human Language Technologies* 1: 3874–3884.

AIIC (International Association of Conference Interpreters). [2004] 2017. "Practical Guide for Professional Conference Interpreters." https://aiic.org/document/547/AIICWebzine_Apr2004_2_Practical_guide_for_professional_conference_interpreters_EN.pdf [Accessed December 12, 2019].

Arivazhagan, Naveen, Ankur Bapna, Orhan Firat, Dmitry Lepikhin, Melvin Johnson, Maxim Krikun, Mia Xu Chen et al. 2019. "Massively Multilingual Neural Machine Translation in the Wild: Findings and Challenges." https://arxiv.org/abs/1907.05019.

Assis Rosa, Alexandra, Hanna Pięta, and Rita Bueno Maia. 2017. "Theoretical, Methodological and Terminological Issues Regarding Indirect Translation: An Overview." *Translation Studies* 10 (2): 113–132. DOI: 10.1080/14781700.2017.1285247.

Baer, Brian James. 2016. "De-sacralizing the Origin(al) and the Transnational Future of Translation Studies." *Perspectives* 25 (2): 227–244.

Bennett, Karen. 2007. "Epistemicide! The Tale of a Predatory Discourse." *The Translator* 13 (2): 151–169. DOI:10.1080/13556509.2007.10799236

Biscaye, Elizabeth. 1993. "Problems in Interpretation." *Meta* 38 (1): 101-103. https://doi.org/10.7202/002085ar.

Borges, Jorge Luis. 1997. "Los traductores de las 1001 noches." In *Obras Completas*, 397–412. Barcelona: Salamandra.

Boulogne, Pieter. 2015. "Europe's Conquest of the Russian Novel: The Pivotal Role of France and Germany." *Iberoslavica*: 167–191.

Davier, Lucile. 2022. "Translational Phenomena in the News: Indirect Translation as the Rule." *Target: International Journal of Translation Studies* 34.

Davier, Lucile, and Luc Van Doorslaer. 2018. "Translation without a Source Text: Methodological Issues in News Translation." *Across Languages and Cultures* 19 (2): 241–257. DOI:10.1556/084.2018.19.2.6.

Dollerup, Cay. 2000. "Relay and Support Translations." In *Translation in Context: Selected Contributions from the EST Congress*, edited by Andrew Chesterman, Natividad Gallardo and Yves Gambier, 17–26. Amsterdam: John Benjamins.

Dollerup, Cay. 2014. "Relay in Translation." In *Cross-linguistic Interaction: Translation, Contrastive and Cognitive Studies*, edited by Diana Yankova, 21–32. Sofia: St. Kliminent Ohridski University Press. Original edition, http://cay-dollerup.dk/publications.asp.

EMT (European Masters in Translation). 2017. "EMT Competence Framework." https://ec.europa.eu/info/sites/info/files/emt_competence_fwk_2017_en_web.pdf.

Federici, Federico and Sharon O'Brien, eds. 2019. *Translation in Cascading Crises*. London: Routledge.

Gambier, Yves. 1994. "La retraduction, retour et détour [Retranslation, revival and detour]." *Meta* 39 (3): 413–417. DOI:10.7202/002799ar.

Gambier, Yves. 2003. "Working with Relay: An Old Story and a New Challenge." In *Speaking in Tongues: Language across Contexts and Users*, edited by Luis Pérez González, 47–66. València: Universitat de València.

Georgakopoulou, Panayota 2019. "Template Files: The Holy Grail of Subtitling." *Journal of Audiovisual Translation* 2 (2): 137–160. DOI:10.47476/jat.v2i2.84.

Halme-Berneking, Riikka. 2019. "Translation Traditions in Angola." In *World Atlas of Translation*, edited by Yves Gambier and Ubaldo Stecconi, 271–286. Amsterdam: Benjamins.

Hung, Eva. 2014. "Translation in China—An Analytical Survey: First century B.C.E. to Early Twentieth Century." In Asian Translation Traditions, edited by Eva Hung and Judy Wakabayashi, 67–108. London: Routledge.

Ivaska, Laura. 2020. "Identifying (Indirect) Translations and their Source Languages in the Finnish National Bibliography Fennica." *MikaEL* 13: 75–88.

Johnson, Melvin, Mike Schuster, Quoc V. Le, Maxim Krikun, Yonghui Wu, Zhifeng Chen, Nikhil Thorat et al. 2017. "Google's Multilingual Neural Machine Translation System: Enabling Zero-Shot Translation." *Transactions of the Association for Computational Linguistics* 5, 339–351.

Landers, Clifford E. 2001. *Literary Translation: A Practical Guide*. Clevedon: Multilingual Matters.

Lathey, Gillian. 2015. *Translating Children's Literature*. London: Routledge.

Läubli, Samuel, Sheila Castilho, Graham Neubig, Rico Sennrich, Qinlan Shen, and Antonio Toral. 2020. "A Set of Recommendations for Assessing Human–Machine Parity in Language Translation." *Journal of Artificial Intelligence Research* 67. DOI:10.1613/jair.1.11371.

Liu, Chao-Hong, Catarina Cruz Silva, Longyue Wang, and Andy Way. 2019. "Pivot Machine Translation Using Chinese as Pivot Language." In *Machine Translation: 14th China Workshop*, edited by Jiajun Chen and Jiafun Zhang, 74–85. Singapore: Springer.

Maia, Rita Bueno. 2021. "The Picaresque Novel as Eclectic Translation: Composing Heteroglossia." In *Iberian and Translation Studies: Literary Contact Zones*, edited by Esther Gimeno Ugalde, Marta Pacheco Pinto and Ângela Fernandes 137–152. Liverpool: Liverpool University Press.

McMartin, Jack. 2020. "Dutch Literature in Translation: A Global View." *Dutch Crossing* 44 (2): 145–164. DOI:10.1080/03096564.2020.1747006.

Netflix. 2020. Pivot Language Template Guidelines. https://partnerhelp.netflixstudios.com/hc/en-us/articles/219375728-Timed-Text-Style-Guide-Subtitle-Templates#h_01EXJ1B1VSKZP6HAM6SW1F480V.

Ng, Michael. 2014. *Legal Transplantation in Early Twentieth-century China: Practicing Law in Republican Beijing (1910s-1930s)*. London: Routledge.

Nurminen, Mary. 2019. "Decision-making, Risk, and Gist Machine Translation in the Work of Patent Professionals." In *Proceedings of the 8th Workshop on Patent and Scientific Literature Translation*, 32–42. European Association for Machine Translation.

Oziemblewska, Magdalena, and Agnieszka Szarkowska. 2021. "The Quality of Templates in Subtitling. A Survey on Current Market Practices and Changing Subtitler Competences." *Perspectives* 30. DOI:10.1080/0907676x.2020.1791919.

Pięta, Hanna. 2017. "Theoretical, Methodological and Terminological Issues in Researching Indirect Translation: A Critical Annotated Bibliography." *Translation Studies* 10 (2): 198–216. DOI:10.1080/14781700.2017.1285247.

Pięta, Hanna. 2021. "Indirect Translation." In *Handbook of Translation Studies* (vol. 5). Amsterdam: Benjamins. Online.

Pięta, Hanna, Laura Ivaska, and Yves Gambier, eds. 2022. "What Can Indirect Translation Do for Translation Studies?" Special Issue, *Target: International Journal of Translation Studies* 34.

Pięta, Hanna, James Hadley, Jan Buts, and Laura Ivaska, eds. Forthcoming. "Indirect Translation and Sustainable Development." Special Issue, *Translation Spaces* 12 (1).
Pool, Kate. 2013. "Relay translation: Some guidelines." *In Other Words: The Journal for Literary Translators* 42: 62–66.
Pöchhacker, Franz. 2022. "Relay Interpreting: Complexities of Real-Time Indirect Translation." *Target: International Journal of Translation Studies* 34.
Pym, Anthony, and Torres-Simón, Ester. 2021. "Is Automation Changing the Translation Profession?" *International Journal of the Sociology of Language* 270: 39–57. DOI:10.1515/ijsl-2020-0015.
Ringmar, Martin. 2012. "Relay Translation." In *Handbook of Translation Studies*, edited by Yves Gambier and Luc van Doorslaer, 141–144. Amsterdam: John Benjamins.
Setton, Robin, and Andrew Dawrant. 2016. *Conference Interpreting: A Complete Course*. Amsterdam: Benjamins.
Society of Authors. 2016. Guidance on Relay Translation. Originally published as Pool, Kate. 2013. "Relay translation: Some guidelines." *In Other Words*. 42: 62–66. www2.societyofauthors.org/wp-content/uploads/2020/05/Guidance-on-Relay-Translations.pdf [Accessed November 19, 2020].
St. André, James. 2019. "Relay." In *Routledge Encyclopedia of Translation Studies*, edited by Mona Baker and Gabriela Saldanha. London: Routledge.
Tesseur, Wine. 2015. "Institutional Multilingualism in NGOs: Amnesty International's Strategic Understanding of Multilingualism." *Meta* 59 (3): 557–577. DOI:10.7202/1028657ar.
Tesseur, Wine, and Angela Crack. 2020. "'These Are All Outside Words': Translating Development Discourse in NGOs' Projects in Kyrgyzstan and Malawi." *Journal for Translation Studies in Africa* 1: 25–42.
Torres-Simón, Ester, Hanna Pieta, Rita Bueno Maia, and Catarina Xavier. 2021. "Indirect Translation in Translator Training: Taking Stock and Looking Ahead." *The Interpreter and Translator Training* 13 (1): 260–281. DOI:10.1080/1750399X.2020.1868173.
Toury, Gideon. 2012. *Descriptive Translation Studies and Beyond*. Amsterdam: John Benjamins.
Van Rooyen, Marlie. 2018. "Investigating Translation Flows: Community Radio News in South Africa." *Across Languages and Cultures* 19 (2): 259–278. DOI:10.1556/084.2018.19.2.7.
Washbourne, Kelly. 2013. "Nonlinear Narratives: Paths of Indirect and Relay Translation." *Meta* 58 (3): 607–625. DOI:10.7202/1025054ar.
Witt, Susanna. 2013. "The Shorthand of Empire: 'Podstrochnik' Practices and the Making of the Soviet Literature." *Ab Imperio* 3: 155–190. DOI: 10.1353/imp.2013.0080.
Witt, Susanna. 2017. "Institutionalized Intermediates: Conceptualizing Soviet Practices of Indirect Literary Translation." *Translation Studies* 10 (2): 166–182. DOI:10.1080/14781700.2017.1281157.
Yao, Steven G. 2010. "Translation." In *Ezra Pound in Context*, edited by Ira B. Nadel, 33–42. New York: Cambridge University Press.

2
INTERPRETING

Introduction

This chapter focuses on oral translation, including both conference interpreting and interpreting in community settings (such as courts, police and social services). It tackles particular challenges for pivots and relay-takers deriving from the fact that the original speaker, the pivot and the relay-taker typically share one physical or virtual location; and the enunciations are separated by a relatively small time lag.

Learning outcomes

Upon successful completion of this chapter, you will be able to:

- Analyse an already translated source text to identify potential translation difficulties, such as the presence of domesticated cultural items (measurements, currencies, historical references, legal terms, names of places, reference titles, etc.) or displaced indexicality (here, there, now, then, etc.).
- Summarize, rephrase, restructure, adapt and shorten rapidly and accurately in at least one target language, using written and/or spoken communication, and keeping the most relevant features.
- Process multimodality.

> **Warm-up activity**
>
> Consider how different booths work together in the multilingual environment presented in Figure 2.1. What challenges will the pivot and the relay-taker face when giving and taking relay, respectively?

FIGURE 2.1 Interpreter booths

Relay in the history of interpreting

The best-known historical examples of relay interpreting concern the consecutive mode. For example, in the sixteenth century, to conquer the Aztec Empire for Spain, Hernán Cortés relied on communications between Spanish and Nahuatl. This communication was initially enabled by two interpreters working in a consecutive relay: Jerónimo de Aguilar worked from Spanish to Maya, and Malintzín (La Malinche) worked from Maya to Nahuatl (and back). In areas where other languages were spoken, indigenous interpreters worked with Malintzín and translated from Nahuatl to the local language, thereby engaging in the so-called **double-relay** (Karttunen 2015). Another historical instance of consecutive relay interpreting relates to the League of Nations. Here, a speech in, say, Italian would first be rendered into French (the official language, on a par with English), then onwards to other languages (for example, German).

When it comes to relay in the simultaneous mode, according to Chernov (1992, 149), a relay system with a so-called "lead language" was used for the first time in the early 1950s, during an international conference held in Moscow. Six working languages were used during this event, with Russian serving as the pivot language. Apparently, this event got the ball rolling. As stressed in Pöchhacker (2004, 21), "relay interpreting in the simultaneous mode was standard practice in what used to be the Eastern bloc countries, where Russian served as the *pivot* language in the multilingual Soviet empire".

Relay interpreting today

Working modes and settings

As should be clear from the above, relay interpreting can be performed both in **simultaneous** and **consecutive interpreting**. Relay arrangements are also verifiable in a range of settings, as summarized in Figure 2.2.

- *Diplomatic, conference settings*. At the United Nations, relay interpreting is standard practice for rendering delegates speaking Arabic and Chinese. These two languages are rendered via French or English into other official languages (Čeňková 2015, Pöchhacker 2022). Many congresses in China use not only Chinese but also English and Japanese, thus creating a systematic need for relay arrangements (Setton 1994, 185). To promote multilingualism, all delegates at the official institutions of the European Union (EU) (the European Council, the European Commission, the Council of the European Union and the European Parliament) can use their own native language. The idea is to ensure that all twenty-four official languages are treated on the same footing. Without relay, the internal communication would be extremely time, resource and cost consuming, as there are 552 possible language combinations (calculated using the formula: n languages × (n languages−1). This is why trainee interpreters who want to work for one of the official EU institutions should receive training in how to give and take relay. They are particularly likely to work in relay arrangements, possibly much more often than other professionals on the market (DG interpretation 2019, 4).
- *Crisis settings*. For example, a rescue team from Finland can render aid to Turkish citizens who need help after an earthquake. A Finnish member of the rescue team who also knows English can liaise with a (professional or ad hoc) English interpreter on the scene who knows both English and Turkish, thereby guaranteeing basic communication between the Finnish rescue team and the local community.
- *Business settings*. In a business meeting, the CEO of a Japanese corporation can talk to a roomful of European investors in Japanese. The first interpreter

FIGURE 2.2 Settings where relay interpreting is most common

can interpret the CEO's speech into English. The English language version is listened to by the delegates who speak English. However, it is also listened to by other interpreters, who translate the English rendition into other languages that are understood by the remaining investors in the audience.
- *Legal settings*: Mikkelson (1999) discusses how, to deal with the lack of proficient English-speaking interpreters from indigenous Mexican languages (Mixtec, Zapotec), courts in California use consecutive relay. Speakers of indigenous Mexican languages receive basic training in how to interpret between their languages and Spanish. The Spanish output is then interpreted by professional Spanish-English interpreters.
- *Asylum settings*: Shlesinger (2010) describes a situation of an NGO in Tel Aviv, where Tigrinya speakers from Eritrea who have basic knowledge of Arabic serve as ad hoc interpreters. Ad hoc interpreters interpret from Tigrinya into Arabic, then professional interpreters render this pivot version into Hebrew to allow communication between the medical team and the patient.

Languages

Although the common belief is that English is the most frequent go-to solution when it comes to relay languages in interpreting, the reality is more complex and constantly evolving. An illustrative example can be found in Aguirre (2022), who zooms in on the experiences of Spanish booth professionals working for European Union institutions. According to her findings, Spanish interpreters frequently needed to take relay right after Spain joined the European Union (in 1986). The typical pivot languages for the Spanish booth were French and German. In those early years, Spanish interpreters acted as pivots mainly in situations where Portuguese needed to be translated into other languages. However, in time, the number of language combinations and directionalities increased substantially. In 2020, the most common pivot languages for the Spanish booths were English and French, followed by German, Italian and Portuguese. At the same time, Spanish interpreters give relay for Portuguese, Italian and French units whenever Bulgarian, Romanian and Croatian are spoken and, for colleagues working into languages added after the so-called "Eastern enlargement", whenever Portuguese, German, Dutch, Greek or Italian are spoken.

In consecutive interpreting, a pivot language is often known as a **bridge language**. Relay arrangements do not involve only spoken languages, as **sign languages** are also an important part of the equation. These sign language contexts can involve both simultaneous or consecutive modes and occur in all sorts of settings (from doctors' appointments to court hearings, business meetings and international conferences).

A deaf relay interpreter can be part of an interpreting team for the sake of (i) deaf home-sign users, e.g., a deaf-blind person, a deaf person who is linguistically or socially isolated, a deaf individual whose proficiency in standard sign language is limited (Bontempo and Levitzke-Gray 2009), (ii) foreign sign language users and (iii) sign language users in international settings.

An example of deaf relay interpreting is outlined in Dellamont (2021), where we can see this modality integrated in regional Covid-19 briefings that are broadcast for viewers in Nova Scotia (Canada). A hearing interpreter listens to what the premier of Nova Scotia and the chief medical officer have to say about the current health situation in the province. The hearing interpreter conveys the message to the deaf interpreter in one sign language (American Sign Language), then the deaf interpreter translates this input into another sign language—one that is regionally more specific (Maritime Sign Language). Viewers are unaware of this relay configuration because, unlike the deaf interpreter who is visible on screen, the hearing pivot is working behind the camera.

In scenarios involving international audiences, a given sign language (say, Polish Sign Language) may first be rendered into the spoken language of that country (Polish) and from there into other spoken languages, or the communication can pass through International Sign Language. Also, in this alternative solution, deaf interpreters work in relay with hearing colleagues.

Technology

Simultaneous interpretation needs specialized sound and transmission equipment. Relay mode may require additional capabilities—for example, a console with high functionality.

Technological advances are reshaping interpreting, and relay interpreting is no exception. Videoconferencing in particular has taken relay interpreting to a different level, adding an extra layer of complexity (as described in more detail below; see also Pöchhacker 2022). For instance, when focusing on **remote interpreting** in immigration settings, Braun (2015) foregrounds a case of remote relay interpreting that was used to overcome the low number of interpreters available for asylum interviews involving peripheral languages. The immigration officer, the interpreter speaking the immigration officer's language and the applicant were all on site (in a shared location), whereas the interpreter speaking the applicant's language was in another country, rendering the applicant's utterances via videoconferencing.

Challenges

In Altman's (1990) survey among European conference interpreters, most professionals indicated that relay impacts negatively on the communication process. The majority of respondents also reported that they avoid taking relay. Similar responses were found among Korean interpreters (Lim 2002). This negative attitude seems to be reflected in AIIC guidelines, which discourage the systematic use of pivot configurations (AIIC [2004] 2017, 9). Oft-quoted traps connected to pivot interpreting relate to two aspects: spatial and temporal immediacy.

Regarding spatial immediacy, in relay interpreting, the pivot, the relay-taker and the other participants of this situated interaction (speakers and listeners) typically share one location, be it physical or virtual. The extent of this co-presence may vary according to mode. For example, it is more limited in simultaneous interpreting, where the two interpreters work from separate booths. This spatial co-presence contrasts with what happens in written indirect translation, where a translator and the audience have no (or very limited) access to the process of the original text production and to the producers of the original source text (Pöchhacker 2022).

This spatial co-presence in interpreting means that the interpreter and the audience have visual and auditory access to the process/situation of the original text production and to the producers of the original source text (Pöchhacker 2022). Therefore, the audience can see and/or hear the speaker as well as the interpreters.

Regarding temporal immediacy, unlike in written translation (where the transition from the original to the mediating text and then the target text can take weeks, years or even decades), in relay interpreting the enunciations are necessarily separated by a relatively small time lag. In certain situations, the production of the original, relay and final product can largely overlap.

These two characteristics bring about traps that may be particularly challenging for pivots and relay-takers, as outlined below.

Incomplete multimodal perception

The original speaker and other interactants communicate through a range of meaning-making, semiotic resources, as summarized in the box.

Semiotic resources

verbal auditory: dialogue, monologue, comments, reading.
non-verbal auditory: vocal noises like shouting, crying, coughing, and paralinguistic code like tone and pitch.
verbal visual: script, slides with written text.
non-verbal visual: still or moving images, kinesic code including body posture, hand gestures, head movement, facial expression, gaze, object manipulation, clothes, etc.

To fully understand the meaning that the original speaker wants to convey, interpreters and listeners need to have access to (and a full understanding of) all these expressive signs (visual, auditory, verbal and non-verbal), including their cultural specificity. As discussed in Pöchhacker (2022), problematically, in relay interpreting, some interactants may not have (visual and/or acoustic) access to all these resources. And even if they do, they may not fully understand all of them (for lack of semiotic resources, for example) or the access to these elements can be delayed.

A case in point is consecutive interpreting performed in relay mode in community settings, where all interactants (two speakers and two interpreters) are on site. As outlined in Pöchhacker (2022):

> a) In such configurations, non-verbal visual and non-verbal auditory signs (kinesics and paralanguage) are, typically, accessible to all. In principle, everyone has auditory and visual access to non-verbal elements used in communication (everyone is heard and seen by everyone else).
> b) However, the verbal acoustic signs (the verbal component of utterances) are only understood by the two interpreters in their shared language (the pivot language).

This means that, while the relay-taker and the final listener can understand the original speaker's tone and some gestures, they do not understand what the original speaker is actually saying (they do not have perceptual access to the verbal auditory elements). When combined with the pivot's rendering, the original speaker's tone and gestures can help the final listener understand the original meaning more fully. The pivot's own tone and gestures can also help in conveying this meaning (Pöchhacker 2022).

Another example is relay in simultaneous conference interpreting, where all participants are on site and simultaneous interpreting equipment is used. According to Pöchhacker (2022), in this scenario:

> a) The pivot has access to the full range of the speaker's semiotic resources (verbal, non-verbal, auditory and visual), at least in principle.
> b) The relay-taker has access to the visual resources with which the original speaker communicates (hand gestures, head movements, images in slides) and sometimes also understands the verbal-visual elements (e.g., slides are in English, although the speech is a different language).
> c) However, the relay-taker does not have access to the speaker's verbal and non-verbal acoustic signs.

This is because the relay-giver occupies the audio channel that is available to the relay-taker. The presence of the relay-giver thus makes it impossible for the relay-taker to access auditory components of the original speech (similar to dubbing in media settings). So, even if the original speech is delivered in a high-pitched tone, the relay-taker will only have access to the voice of the pivot, which has its own expressiveness and which does not necessarily correspond to the expressiveness of the original speaker (Pöchhacker 2022). This problem can be exacerbated in remote interpreting where all the information comes through the headphones only. In on-site interpreting, this problem (pivot blocking the audio channel) can be mitigated to some extent, since imperfectly soundproof booths can provide some access to original non-verbal cues.

This lack of access to the original sound is inconvenient because the relay-taker cannot rely on the original speaker's prosody and other non-verbal cues that could otherwise aid his or her comprehension of the main message. This leads to the feeling of estrangement between the different elements of the relay (Seleskovitch and Lederer 1995).

Increased time lag

Any time lag between the enunciations will be compounded by the relay process. This is aptly illustrated in Dollerup (2000), who describes a situation from a plenary session of the European Parliament where a Dutch speaker is rendered into Danish through a double relay:

> if [...] a Dutch delegate cracked a joke, the Dutch delegates would laugh; after 5–10 seconds, the French and German would get the point; after some more seconds, the English, the Irish and the Italians would catch on, and then, finally, the Danes would join in the general merriment.

This time shift also seriously hinders the multimodal processing of the speaker's message, causing a mismatch between what the relay-taker and his or her listeners see, and what they hear. More specifically, "the cumulative time lag deprives the relay-taker, and even more so his or her audience, of the full benefits of visual stimuli (such as gestures or slides) synchronized with the source speech" (Čeňková 2015, 340). This delayed perceptual access further exacerbates the feeling of being disconnected from the original speaker.

Cumulative time lag can barely be overcome in situations "when there is a quick code switching from the speaker or the chairperson and the management of the relay cannot be quickly rearranged accordingly" (Gambier 2003, 60–61).

Increased time in consecutive

Using relay interpreting in consecutive settings means that the whole exchange will take longer. Having two interpreters increases the number of steps required in a fluent conversation. If interpreters need to clarify terms or ideas, the time will increase, too. This needs to be planned for in advance.

Hybrid audience

The interpreters taking relay are fully dependent on the interpreter giving relay. This means that, apart from catering for the needs of their speakers and listeners, the pivot must also attend to the needs of the relay-taking booths and their audiences. In some cases, the pivot might interpret only for the sole purpose of relay interpreting (i.e., to enable interpreting into other languages and not for the benefit of the audience). All this causes relay interpreting to be a particularly difficult and stressful configuration for interpreters taking relay, and even more so for pivots.

Retour

It is not uncommon for pivots to be working into their B language. They can thus be faced with certain linguistic limitations (they are not translating into their strongest language) and technical issues (they are transmitting on a language channel with which they are not comfortable or familiar). All this can be an additional source of stress for pivots and sometimes also for relay-takers, who can distrust the quality of the output before they even hear it. This distrust can be explained by the fact that "in the central languages of Western Europe, translation into language B has long been considered inferior to translation into language A" (Pokorn 2011, 37), although evidence for this presupposed inferiority has not been given.

Positioning and turn-taking

In simultaneous interpreting, both pivot and relay-taker are placed in separate booths. Listeners (and occasionally also the speakers) may not be able to see the interpreters' booths. They may often be unaware of the fact that they are listening to a relayed output. Speakers may also be unaware that their utterances are being interpreted in relay mode. However, in consecutive interpreting in community settings, the indirectness of the interpreting process is visible to all participants and may cause additional tension and confusion for all interactants. Speakers and interpreters may be unsure who is who, whom to speak to, with whom to keep eye contact and where to stand/sit to facilitate interaction.

A sense of disconnect from the original culture

Čeňková (2015, 340) argues that relay is more prone to mistakes and may be characterized by a more incomplete rendition due to the additional link that exists in relay chains. Since relay-takers do not speak the ultimate source language, they will often mispronounce names related to the original source culture. Moreover, since relay-takers may not know the cultural, political, or economic situation of the speaker's country, they may be more likely to ignore or misunderstand culture-specific allusions or nuances.

Silver linings

Relay interpreting is hard, but there are positives too. Some interpreters argue that relay interpreting is not necessarily more difficult than interpreting without relay. The rationale is that some pivots may provide a well-organized input that can bring order and clarity to the original speaker's confusing utterance (Aguirre 2022). Moreover, some conference interpreters stress that giving relay impacts positively on their overall performance (Altman 1990). Here, the rationale might be that with great responsibility comes better quality. It is also worth noting that, as shown in Mackintosh's empirical research (1983, cited in Čeňková 2015), when it comes to precision, there is hardly any difference between relay and direct interpreting. The study seems to suggest that the only noticeable differences are mistranslated numbers and omissions, which are more frequent in the relay mode.

Above all, relay interpreting often makes communication possible. In the context of languages of limited diffusion, relay interpreting might be a better option than requesting a person with weak language skills to interpret alone (Romero 2008, 30).

Tips on how to deal with pivot interpreting situations

Below you will find a list of tips for interpreters giving and receiving pivot. They are meant to help you mitigate some of the challenges outlined above. When compiling this list of tips, we drew largely on the guidelines provided by the International Association of Conference Interpreters (AIIC [2004] 2017)—a professional association that defines internationally recognized standards for the profession. Tips related to consecutive interpreting (in community settings) are mainly based on Allen et al. (2018). We complement these recommendations with insights provided by practitioners and researchers (Aguirre 2022; Belisle 2020; Giambagli 1993; Chouc and Conde 2018; Pöchhacker 2022; Seleskovitch and Lederer 1995; Setton and Dawrant 2016).

Guidelines for relayers in simultaneous interpreting

As per AIIC ([2004] 2017, 11–12), when giving pivot:

> all the principles of quality interpreting apply, […] and a good pivot is, first and foremost, a good interpreter. However, the pivot must also make a special effort to interpret with the needs of colleagues in mind, and to be maximally clear and helpful.

In a similar vein, Seleskovitch and Lederer (1995) stress that, to increase the quality of relay interpreting, pivots need to be mindful of the interdependency that exists between the different participants of the relay process. The authors also stress that a pivot's interpretation needs to be instantly identifiable as trustworthy. According to Aguirre (2022), this trustworthiness is linked to the following quality factors:

- Message clarity and concision.
- Dynamism and speed.
- A sense of receiving a pre-analysed, re-organized message.
- Perception of completeness.
- Natural prosody and fluent pace.
- Form-content balance.
- Pivot status awareness.

In other words, the relay must closely follow the original speech but, at the same time, be mindful of the dual audience (final users and other interpreters).

Share the speaker's text

If you have received a copy of the speaker's text or slides before the meeting, make sure that the interpreters taking relay from you can access it too. You can try providing them with details on key ideas, figures, specialist terminology and unfamiliar names in the text (AIIC [2004] 2017). If providing such details is not possible, relay-takers may sometimes be able to run the text through a machine translation system for **gisting**. This can give them a general idea of the main points and take aways. Previous access to the text in the original language can be especially useful for relay-takers if this text is packed with lists, acronyms, tables, numbers, references (e.g., to treaties, standards, legislation), etc.

Ask for an extra pair of ears

The AIIC's practical guide recommends against leaving a pivot alone in a booth ([2004] 2017, 11–12). It also makes suggestions on how to help a boothmate who is giving relay. These include:

- Verifying that the pivot's microphone is switched to the right language channel (this aspect is particularly important after retour).
- Locating relevant documents on the floor as they are used and offering them to the pivot (without distracting him or her).
- Helping the pivot find the excerpt in the text that the speaker is reading from or commenting on.
- Noting down numbers, unfamiliar names, specialist terminology, acronyms and other useful information in a clear and legible manner (for easier retrieval); if you type fast, then technology may also be helpful (e.g., a tablet can be used like a paper notebook).

Get familiar with the technology

Make sure you know how to use the console. Combining relay with retour can be particularly tricky, and this is why it is particularly important to know how to switch back to the right channel after another booth has borrowed it (e.g., the English channel to do Czech into English, which could not be covered from the English booth) (AIIC [2004] 2017, 11–12). Run a sound check and do not forget to verify if microphones and the mute option are working as should be. Remember that the mute button can be used strategically for editorialisms, communication with boothmates, etc.

If you occupy the relay channel for too long, relevant parts of the next speech may get lost. To clear the channel as soon as the speaker has finished speaking, you need to work with very little decalage towards the anticipated end of the speech.

Articulate clearly

Make a special effort to pronounce clearly, especially when it comes to numbers, acronyms, and the names of people, products, places, organizations, etc. If time allows, consider articulating these elements more slowly, or even repeating them (AIIC [2004] 2017). Furthermore, many interpreters tend to pronounce names as proficiently as possible, to the best of their linguistic skills (like a native language speaker of the original language would pronounce them). Since relay-takers do not speak the original source language, they will often find it impossible to pronounce these names in an equally fluent, near-native manner. To make these elements easier for a relay-taker to repeat, when you are doing pivot from, say, Hungarian into English, consider toning down your Hungarian accent. Instead, consider articulating unfamiliar Hungarian names similarly to the way speakers of the English language would pronounce them (Belisle 2020). In other words, consider opting for what Setton and Dawrant (2016) call a "mild domestication".

Always keep an eye on the time (aim for synchrony)

Any time lags will be compounded by the relay process. Therefore, it is often good to start speaking right away (see AIIC [2004] 2017). If necessary, consider using the first few instances of time lag to say something objective (e.g., "Let's start", "As I was saying", "So, then", etc.). This way, you will subtly reassure your relay-takers that their equipment is working fine and they are using the appropriate relay channel. Moreover, try to avoid long pauses in your interpretation. Do your best to finish interpreting at the same time the speaker has wound up his or her speech, or at least as soon as possible afterwards (AIIC [2004] 2017). If you get too far behind the speaker, then, by the time the relay-takers have finished their rendering of your rendering, a new speaker may have already started talking and they may already be way ahead in their speech (Belisle 2020). This means that you may need to be more concise closer to the end so as to release the occupied channel in order to minimize delays (Song and Cheung 2019).

Know when to compress or gist

As stressed in AIIC ([2004] 2017), synchronicity is particularly important when the speaker is referring to accompanying visuals (e.g., presentations with slides, tables, photographs, etc.). In such situations, the whole audience needs to be literally on the same page, i.e., they need to have visual access to the visual material that accompanies the ideas they are listening to. Indeed, as remarked by an anonymous interpreter surveyed by Aguirre (2022): "a good relay is like good dubbing: what you are listening to needs to keep up with what you are seeing". If the time lag is too long, the relevant slide is likely to disappear before the relay-taker is done with it, and this may cause serious problems in communication.

To minimize the chances of this happening, the pivot needs to interpret fast enough to let the relay-takers produce a relevant rendering before the speaker flips slides. This calls for some drastic prioritizing. Such prioritizing involves, first and foremost, a rigorous hierarchization of information based on its relative relevance in context, and considering the extent to which information is amenable to expression through paralinguistic signs (AIIC [2004] 2017). More to the point, the pivot needs to sort key new information from information that is already known, can be conveyed by paralinguistic signs, or is comparatively less significant.

Such radical prioritizing also requires a skilful use of linguistic devices for compressing (AIIC [2004] 2017) and sometimes even abstracting (e.g., in the case of factually dense material delivered at a fast pace). However, this last strategy is high risk and may not always be acceptable (Setton and Dawrant 2016, 334). Here we understand compression to be "an act of syllable-shrinking," (Viaggio 1989/1991, 14), a maximal concision that entails editing for relevance (Setton and Dawrant 2016). By abstracting we mean reducing the speaker's input down to its essentials (Setton and Dawrant 2016), an extreme way of summarizing while retaining only key ideas as bullet points, drastically reducing the length (to even 5% of the original). According to Setton and Dawrant (2016), both compressing and abstracting require linguistic proficiency and readiness, knowledge of the subject matter and an awareness of the meeting situation.

Language proficiency and readiness can be achieved by previous, extensive research and practice, followed by a recapping of key terms and ideas immediately before entering the booth (Setton and Dawrant 2016). To acquire knowledge and grow awareness of the meeting context and the listeners' needs, interpreters often ask clients for relevant information about the event's schedule, logistic details, speakers' and participants' languages and origins, the company's departments, key competition, etc. and try to locate parallel documents (e.g., how a given subject matter was covered in the news). When on site, interpreters also carefully consider visual, vocal and environmental clues, as these help better understand the communicative event and situation.

If possible, before the event you or your team leader can also ask the speaker to pause before she moves on to the next slide (AIIC [2004] 2017). This deliberate breathing space will allow your relay-takers to catch up. Such requests for extra pauses may be more efficient if made indirectly, e.g., through the chairperson or organizers.

In principle, pivots should prioritize what they hear over what they see on the slides.

Condense judiciously

Opinions regarding the desirability of having a speech pre-analysed and/or re-organized by the pivot are divided. Significantly, most respondents in Aguirre's study (2022) expected to receive a relay with smooth and regular delivery. Therefore, knowing when and how to synthesize the original speech seems to be a crucial component of every pivot's skillset. Indeed, when acting as pivots, many professional interpreters seem to keep in mind that less is more. They thus try to be as efficient as possible, even if this means changing the message's form (Aguirre 2022). Admittedly, such a practice may go against the general recommendations to capture every nuance and avoid adding or omitting. However, here the issue is mostly pragmatic. Why capture slips of the tongue, unless it is a courtroom setting, etc.? The larger communicative purpose overtakes the imperative to be complete.

To synthesize the original speech, professional interpreters quickly and efficiently analyse the information, then provide an output that can be structured differently from the original speech (Belisle 2020). Since we have to use the simplification method, it is important to practice simplifying the contents of our different questions without losing the exactness of their meaning.

This approach is very much in line with Pym, who argues that omissions do not necessarily lead to lower quality (2008, 90). Obvious candidates for omission are the speaker's slips of the tongue or false starts (AIIC [2004] 2017). There is often no need to render them, nor is it always necessary to faithfully replicate the speaker's digressions (Belisle 2020).

Condensing may be particularly needed in situations where the original speech is extremely fast paced. In such scenarios, there is little worth in keeping up with a speaker's fast pace and density. For the sake of colleagues downstream (and often also the general audience), it makes more sense to reorganize the content. Apart from compressing the text, such adjusting for very fast speakers often entails adding cohesive devices (Belisle 2020). However, some interpreters would still rather have all the information at their disposal, and they dislike synthesized, re-organized messages (Aguirre 2022).

Prioritize clarity

According to Giambagli (1993), clarity is the bedrock of a quality pivot. As aptly put by an anonymous trainee interpreter: "when you are working from relay, you don't want a flowery and convoluted language. You just want a clear, calm delivery so that you can work with this" (Chouc and Conde 2018, 69). Indeed, when it comes to quality indicators in assessing a pivot's performance, many professionals seem to prioritize message clarity and concision over dynamism and speed, completeness, natural prosody or form-content balance (Aguirre 2022).

All this suggests that priority should be given to rendering the core of the message as clearly as possible. To do that, avoid local slang expressions or rare, extravagant, or literary formulations (AIIC [2004] 2017). Furthermore, make conscious efforts to simplify syntax and deliver complete sentences. Remember that, depending on their language, some of the relay-takers may need to hear the main verb of the sentence as early as possible. Therefore, if you are to render a very long sentence, do your best to "split it into several shorter sentences that all have a main verb that the other interpreters can work with" (Belisle 2020). Since, in relay scenarios, it is key to communicate in a clear, concise and well-organized manner, some principles of plain language may be applicable here. These are discussed in greater detail in Chapter 3.

Context is everything

Constantly provide context (even textual or visual). If the speaker mentions specific technical, administrative, political, etc. concepts that only apply to their culture or language (e.g., bidonville, Reichstag, Sejm), relay-takers might need a brief explanation of the main characteristics of this concept. This way, they will be able to find a proper corresponding terminology in their target languages. Moreover, you can try to compensate for the relay-taker's lack of perceptual access to the original speaker's intonation, gestures and pauses, etc. If you realize that you have not been clear or precise enough, try briefly paraphrasing and reformulating the main idea (AIIC [2004] 2017). Do not shy away from self-correcting, but do it succinctly.

Indicate any change of speakers

As a pivot, you occupy the full capacity of the audio channel that is available to the relay-taker. This means that, in principle, the relay-taker cannot hear the speakers from the floor and may not realize when the speaker or a language spoken on the floor changes. This lack of knowledge is problematic because it can easily lead either to a channel conflict or a relay interpreting that is actually redundant (AIIC [2004] 2017). For instance, a Dutch speaker may follow a Polish speaker. If the relay-taker knows Dutch, there is no need for an English pivot, although it was necessary for the Polish speaker.

To minimize this risk, make sure to announce any change of speakers, if necessary, by giving their name and role, rank, etc. (e.g., Jan Kowalski, Polish Minister of Foreign Affairs). In some cases, it may be equally important to name the new language that the new speaker is using (AIIC [2004] 2017)—for instance, when the speaker switches between Portuguese and Spanish to address different parts of her audience.

Also, make sure to contextualize interventions ("The speaker says…") in order to compensate for the relay-taker's lack of access to the text (or slides). For example, if the speaker makes a mistake, corrects himself or herself and apologizes, or when they make other remarks about their own intervention, consider adding the words "The speaker says…." to avoid confusion (AIIC [2004] 2017).

Guidelines for relay-takers in simultaneous interpreting

Although much of the responsibility for the final output lies on the shoulders of the pivot, there is also a lot that relay-takers can do to significantly contribute to a satisfactory outcome.

Get familiar with the technology

Ensure that you know how to use the console. It is key that you know how to switch back and forth between the input channel from the floor and the adequate relay channel. If you are providing *retour*, you should also learn how to switch the output channel to that of your *retour* language (and back again as well).

If you are doing remote simultaneous interpreting (a modality which became common during the Covid-19 pandemic, when meetings moved online), make sure that you are familiar with the platform you will be using. In remote configurations, it is vital to ensure that every participant is using suitable equipment, internet connection and settings. For instance, built-in computer microphones hardly ever deliver the frequency range that interpreters need. Unlike the unidirectional microphones used in professional conference rooms (designed to pick up only the speaker's voice), built-in computer microphones tend to be omnidirectional, picking up all background noises. Some of these noises may be sudden and jarring, and thus very painful and potentially harmful to interpreters' health, causing auditory disorders (Brady and Pickles 2021). Likewise, constant breaking of the audio due to slow internet bandwidth will almost inevitably lead to a substandard rendition, which, in turn, will have repercussions for the entire relay interpreting. To address these challenges, it may be a good idea to raise the client's awareness about how important the quality of the equipment, the connection and the settings is for the performance of the pivot and the relay-takers. Short videos or other instructional documentation that can be shared with clients can be particularly useful here (Brady and Pickles 2021).

Build trust with your pivot

Professional interpreters tend to choose or avoid pivots based on lessons learned from their own previous experiences with colleagues (Aguirre 2022; Seleskovitch and Lederer 1995). Interpreters seem more confident when they take relay from someone whom they already know and who has successfully acted as pivot. According to Aguirre (2022), this personal experience seems to have higher weight in pivot-takers' decision-making process than factors like language or directionality (mentioned below).

Knowing what to expect from a given pivot is said to diminish the feelings of uncertainty and tension, at least to some degree (Aguirre 2022). Of course, such a degree of familiarity is not viable in all workflows. Regular working environments allow for some stability and hence also predictability. In the absence of one's own personal experience, relying on peers' experience with certain pivots may also come in handy. Since professional bonds are not built overnight, it is important to actively and constantly invest in expanding our network (e.g., becoming a member of professional associations, participating in conferences and training sessions, etc.).

Choose the pivot language judiciously (know your language preferences)

For some relay-takers, the language of the relay is also an important factor to consider when looking for a pivot, although it may have lesser weight than prior knowledge of the interpreter doing pivot (as mentioned above).

Some interpreters prefer taking relays from a pivot language that is close to their A language (their native language or best active language, see AIIC 2019). For example, when confronted with the choice of an English or Spanish pivot, an interpreter working into Portuguese may be more inclined to take relay from a Spanish colleague. The rationale is that this trajectory (translating between cognate languages) entails less message modification, thus minimizing the potential diversion vis-à-vis the original speech. This is, of course, not applicable to all language combinations. Take, for instance, Hungarian and Finnish. Although they are cognate languages, it will probably be difficult to find a Hungarian interpreter who prefers to take relay from Finnish over English. Finnish speakers cannot understand Hungarian without additional study and vice-versa. Apart from a handful of basic words, the vocabulary differs immensely, etc.

Other interpreters give equal priority to pivot renditions done in their strongest C language(s), i.e., a "passive" language of which they have a "complete understanding", over others (AIIC 2019). This preference seems to be justified by the desire to strengthen the feelings of control over possible challenges that may arise from the relay process (Aguirre 2022). So, to use the above example as a starting point: when choosing between an English or Spanish pivot, an interpreter working into Portuguese and whose strongest C language is English may be more inclined to take relay from an English language colleague.

There are also those interpreters whose decision about which relay to choose depends not so much on their strongest working language but on the language in which the meeting documents are written. Following this train of thought, if listeners and interpreters only have access to the English language version of the meeting agenda or draft document to be discussed, some interpreters see advantages in prioritizing English when choosing a relay. However, as suggested in Aguirre (2022), this factor may have a comparatively low significance.

Be mindful of the directionality

Interpreters providing relay may be working into their A (native language) or their B language (second active language, often non-native). The general understanding is that, for spoken language conference interpreters, it is better to work into one's A language (Seleskovitch and Lederer 1995; Pokorn 2011). However, when it comes to the **directionality** of the pivot, this preference does not necessarily hold. In studies conducted by Chouc and Conde (2018) and Aguirre (2022), there is practically no difference in the number of interpreters who prioritize pivots interpreting into their native language over pivots doing retour. All this suggests that, from the standpoint of relay-takers, there is much to gain and lose in both modalities.

An attractive benefit of pivots working into their B language (relay in retour) is that they are more likely to have a full understanding of the original message and, in particular, its culture-specific elements (Aguirre 2022). Another upside is higher chances for increased concision and simplicity of vocabulary and syntax, which, in turn, make the output more accessible and easier to work with. These characteristics relate to the pre-processed nature of relay renditions that some relay-takers expect from pivots (see above).

This is evident in the testimonial provided by an anonymous participant of Chouc and Conde's study (2018, 67):

> Sometimes it [relay] is very good, even when it is not done by a native speaker, because the pace is slower and because of that, they go straight to the point and use less complicated vocabulary.

The oft-quoted drawbacks of retour pivots include limited expressiveness (Pöchhacker 2022), the strong foreign accent of pivots working into their B language (Chouc and Conde 2018, 67) and a supposedly higher potential for incoherent delivery (Seleskovitch and Lederer 1995). For their part, pivots who are interpreting into their A language may be prioritized because they are more likely to produce a coherent output (Seleskovitch and Lederer 1995) and one that is in a richer, more nuanced language (Aguirre 2022).

Ask the relay for a pre-event brief

Repeating names after a pivot can be hard if you do not know the original language. To minimize chances of stumbling over pronunciation, be sure to familiarize yourself with the final list of participants and final versions of other relevant documentation (e.g., culture-specific terminology in a draft legislation to be discussed). Select **names** that may be difficult to pronounce and check their pronunciation with colleagues or use a machine translation system to check the correct pronunciation (like Google Translate). To do that, tap the speaker icon to hear the name or term you have typed in.

Be quicker than usual

Since relay results in additional delay, your audience is, by default, further behind than the audience who is listening directly to the pivot. To minimize this discrepancy, make sure that you have as short a lag as possible, at least towards the end of the speaker's statement (Belisle 2020). This way, you maximize the chances of finishing your interpretation shortly after the relay has ended. Here, resorting to the compensation and bullet-pointing techniques outlined above can be particularly useful.

Be constructive and appreciative (debrief)

Even if the pivot's feed did not meet your expectations, avoid firing complaints about their performance (AIIC [2004] 2017). Instead, take a deep breath and try to be constructive. Objectively pinpoint aspects that could have gone better and brainstorm ways in which these aspects could be improved in the future. Above anything else, be mindful of the difficulties that are inherent to pivot-giving. Always remember that you are compounding these difficulties by needing to take relay. After all, the pivot's task is particularly demanding because you are also missing competences in the original language.

If you are content with the pivot's performance, be sure to let them know, ideally specifying which aspects were particularly helpful. Such tokens of appreciation are not only professionally gratifying, but they also help reinforce good practices.

Guidelines for consecutive interpreters

Several tips listed for simultaneous interpreting are equally valid for consecutive interpreting, such as information related to sharing documents beforehand and building trust with the other interpreter. Also, one must be aware of positioning, as indicated in the initial challenges. Other recommendations are summarized below.

Plan ahead

Adequate planning in consecutive relay sessions is the first step to success (see Chapter 8 for a summary on tips for project managers). Before the meeting, interpreters should agree on "how to handle introductions, where you will sit or stand and how you will manage turn-taking, mediation and sight translation" (Allen et al. 2018, 368). Agreeing on a pause gesture is also recommended in such configurations.

The client should provide relevant documents and be reminded of the importance of pausing for the interpreter to do their work.

Explain the situation clearly to all the parties

In consecutive interpreting, the unfamiliar setting might be particularly stressful for the participants. Therefore, before the assignment starts, you and the other interpreter should introduce yourselves, stating which language combination each one has and explain why you are both there. Normally, you will address the person with whom you share a language.

Remind both parties that interpreting happens between the pause. Therefore, communication is clearer if participants do not rush but instead express only one idea at a time. Inform the participants that, if you come to require any linguistic clarification during the event, you will indicate this explicitly.

In court interpreting, you might want to check if and how you can inform the judge of the need for pauses and clarifications. Please note that, in some countries, this will not be possible. If you are unfamiliar with court protocols, you might want to request instructions on how to manage those interruptions respectfully. It might be useful to also stress the need for slower communication. Court protocols and expectations tend to be very different in any given national setting. Therefore, the interpreter should evaluate whether the previous recommendations would be welcomed or not in their host situation. In some cases, there is a liaison in charge of informing interpreters, so this can be addressed before the hearing starts.

Positioning

Allen et al. (2018, 379) mention how it can sometimes be hard to know where to sit or stand in a relay interpreting situation due to lack of room.

In principle, positioning must first and overall respect the client's needs: you and your fellow interpreter will choose your positions after the client chooses theirs. Usually, each interpreter will stand next to the person with whom they share a language, so they can hear them (see Figure 2.3). This way, you will ensure that clients have a direct line of sight of each other. Such a configuration will also help guarantee that you can hear your colleague (and vice versa) and you can work together. For sign language, sign language users must be able to see each other easily.

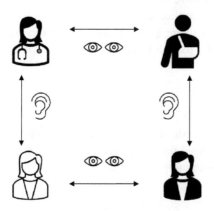

FIGURE 2.3 Positioning in relay consecutive interpreting

In court interpreting, follow the judge's instructions. If the position does not allow the interpreter to clearly see the client and the other interpreter (in case of sign language interpreting), indicate this to the judge.

Turn-taking and strategic mediation

In relay interpreting, both you and your colleague must make sure that interventions do not last too long. When needed, ask the parties or the other interpreter to pause. You are also responsible for requesting clarifications when necessary.

Bancroft et al. (2015, 237) list the various steps needed for a successful strategic mediation. These are summarized in the box.

> 1. Interpret the last thing said.
> 2. Identify yourself as the interpreter.
> 3. Mediate briefly with the other speaker.
> 4. Tell the other speaker what you said.
> 5. Go back to interpreting.

In a relay interpreting setting, all the parties must be informed of a clarification underway, so that they know why the communication pattern has been modified. For example, if you request clarification from the other interpreter before starting to discuss what needs to be clarified, each of you should indicate to their client that, as an interpreter, you are uncertain about one part of an earlier intervention, and you want to confer with your colleague about it.

Handling documents and forms

If possible, sight translation should be avoided in relay interpreting. However, sometimes you must assist their clients so that they can understand documents or fill in forms. If the document is very technical, you can ask the client to explain the form and then relay the information. Finally, you will show the parties where to sign.

Debrief

Evaluate the session with the other interpreter and try to pinpoint any misunderstandings or need for clarification. If possible, also debrief with the provider. The objective is to improve the process for future sessions, so all suggestions should be welcome.

Further discussion

- *Respeaking and relay interpreting.* In respeaking, the respeaker listens to the original input and simultaneously dictates the message to a speech recognition software that, in turn, converts the respeaker's speech into a written text (Romero-Fresco 2011). In a way, the respeaker serves as a pivot for the consecutive, intralingual-cum-intermodal rendition (Pöchhacker 2022). What challenges will the respeaker face when adjusting their pivot text to the constraints of the machine? Think about lexis, tempo, rhythm, intonation, pitch, inflection, pauses, etc. How are these challenges different from the challenges discussed in this chapter?
- *Policy and accessibility (rights).* Relay interpreting policy and arrangements affect the rights and interests of particular social groups, be they linguistic minorities or disabled individuals. Consider relay in the context of indigenous interpreting (read McDonnell 1997) and sign language interpreting (see, for example, D'Angelo 2021 and Dellamont 2021).

Activities

Activity 1 Analyse an already translated source text to identify potential translation difficulties, such as the presence of domesticated cultural items (measurements, currencies, historical references, legal terms, names of places, reference titles, etc.) or displaced indexicality (here, there, now, then, etc.)

Activity 1.1 Identifying potential difficulties (textual vs. oral)

PART A. Speech selection

Select a transcription of a speech. Jamesclear.com provides samples of famous speeches (https://jamesclear.com/great-speeches). You can also use Charles Michel's speeches compiled on the European Council's website. These speeches are available in twenty languages (www.consilium.europa.eu/en/european-council/president/speeches/#).

Then, read the text you selected and mark potential difficulties.

PART B. Pre-event brief

Ask a colleague to come up with a communicative situation for the speech you selected. Then ask them to prepare a pre-event brief. Check which elements need clarification.

PART C. Interpreting

Play the text and try to interpret as you hear the speech. To do this, you can use the Read Aloud tool in Word's accessibility options on your computer or even the audio option in Google Translate. Try to interpret as you hear the speech. You may want to record yourself as you do this. Mark the times when you get stuck. You can pause the reading and continue, but do not invest time in trying to provide a correct utterance: only pause to mark that there was a difficulty. Compare the difficulties marked in Part A to those felt in Part B. Were they the same? What could explain the differences?

Activity 1.2 Identifying potential difficulties (content vs. context)

Interpreting deals with a specific challenge: utterances are normally presented only once and cannot be reviewed or replayed. This task proposes a variation of the telephone game (Chinese whispers) focusing on potential translation difficulties.

PART A. Speech selection

Select a source text, either a video or a podcast, that contains challenging characteristics for interpreting. You can also record someone ad hoc for the task (but do mind confidentiality issues and copyright). Some of the characteristics you can consider are:

- Genre: specialized source text with difficult terminology. You can use EU recordings or podcasts/online videos with technical content (pseudoscience is well known for overusing technical terms out of context). Recordings of conferences held at your university/workplace can be a possibility, too.
- Domesticated cultural items: source texts with names of places, reference titles or measurements. Talks on travel, anthropology or palaeontology could be a good place to start.
- Decontextualized exchanges: conversations without explicit background or intertextual references that might be unclear to you. TikTok videos, excerpts from monologues in soap operas or political discourses in settings that the participants do not know well could work here.
- Speed: the speaker's speed is moderate or fast.

The text does not need to be long, as the activity will only require one or two sentences.

PART B. Telephone game

In the telephone game, participant 1 interprets a selected fragment from a source text to participant 2 (one or two sentences is enough). Then, participant 2 relays the same information to participant 3. This continues until the message has been relayed consecutively to all the participants. The last participant compares their notes (what they understood) to what participant 1 originally said. What was retained? What was left out? Did the key information survive the telephone challenge? Can you find out where the information was lost?

PART C. Content modifications

Repeat Part B with a different type of source text. Optionally, if you are working in a classroom setting, you can have different groups working in different types of original source texts. Were there differences as to when the message was best conveyed? Was there any trend related to the information that was retained or left out? Please reflect on how this affects interpreting performance.

PART D. Context modifications

Find another source text with the most challenging characteristics. Try the activity again but this time modify some variables: adjust speed, provide better context or give time to the participants to pause, think and then translate. Compared to the previous results, which variables imply a higher challenge?

Activity 1.3 Identifying potential difficulties (direct vs. relay)

PART A. Relay

Participants are divided into groups of three. Ideally, they will share two languages. Participant 1 improvises a short speech in language 1, which is interpreted by participant 2 in language 2. Participant 3 interprets from the relay back to language 1 (if languages are shared) or to language 3 (if languages are not shared). The process is recorded. If there are only two participants, they can work from a video. See Figure 2.4 for a visual diagram.

PART B. Revision

Looking at the recording, the group discusses the best solutions proposed in the first relay and what can be improved. Then, they do the same for the second relay. Last, if participant 3 went into language A, they look at the source text and the last

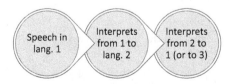

FIGURE 2.4 Proposal for relay interpreting process (Activity 1.3)

translation. Would the solutions listed as "best" or "improvable" still be in the same category? List the topics that you would cover in a debrief meeting.

Activity 2 Summarize, rephrase, restructure, adapt and shorten rapidly and accurately in at least one target language, using written and/or spoken communication, and keeping the most relevant features

Activity 2.1 Summary as documentation of interpreting

PART A. Preparation

Select one speech (see possible sources in Activity 1.3) and divide the class into 3 groups: group 1 will be half of the class, groups 2 and 3 the other half. Group 1 summarizes the text, trying to keep it relevant. Group 2 uses the summary to absorb key ideas, then does a short interpreting practice with the initial text. Group 3 does the interpreting with the initial text without having accessed the summary.

PART B. Evaluation

Using a rubric (see the Routledge Translation Studies Portal), group 1 evaluates and takes notes on the performance. Group 2 evaluates how useful/cumbersome using the summary was. All the participants compare their notes: did group 2 find the summary useful? Was the performance of group 2 and group 3 comparable? Was the summary effective? Reflect on whether using the text to absorb key ideas was positive and whether even those who had the summary still reproduced the speaker's speech and not the summary.

Activity 2.2 Sight translation from a summarized translated text

Ask a colleague to summarize a short speech and translate it into another language. Try to do a sight translation from the text: did you detect any specific difficulty? You can consider missing, pragmatic or density of information as factors to bear in mind.

Activity 3 Process multimodality

Activity 3.1 Multimodality and relay interpreting (conference setting)

When reflecting on simultaneous relay interpreting, Pöchhacker (2022) presents different relay scenarios and asks the following two questions.

> Scenario 1: "If the speaker's slides are in a language accessible to the relay-taker, to what extent can or should they be referred to in the interpretation?"

Scenario 2: "And what if this is done by the pivot but the relay interpreter's target language audience has no linguistic access to what is being shown (with more or less delay)?"

PART A. Individual evaluation

Individually, consider the answer to these questions. Reflect on how your strategies change depending on the scenario and how these strategies affect the listener's perception.

PART B. Simulation

Working in a group of at least four people (speaker, pivot, relay-taker, listener), play out these two small scenarios that can occur in a conference setting. After the simulation, does your answer to the previous questions change? What did you notice in the simulation that you hadn't considered?

PART C. Group reflection

Based on Pöchhacker (2022) and your experience in the simulation, try to explain how the relay-taker's rendering is affected by the relay-taker's delayed perceptual access to the slides that are being presented and to the original speaker's facial expressions, gestures, etc.

Activity 3.2 Multimodality and remote consecutive interpreting

In groups of two, explore the Speech Repository from SCIC, the Directorate-General for Interpretation of the European Commission (https://webgate.ec.europa.eu/sr/).

Each of you should select one "real-life speech" to interpret for a relay-taker. Make sure to mark "consecutive" in the Use field. You can also select a suitable level of progression (Beginner, Intermediate, etc.).

PART A. Watch and interpret

Watch the video and interpret it to your partner, taking into consideration the presence of non-verbal signs and other speakers that may also be communicated to the relay-taker.

PART B. Watch and evaluate

Watch the video with your partner and take notes on the non-verbal signs and the presence of other speakers that could be relevant to communicate in consecutive interpreting.

PART C. Work in pairs

Discuss in pairs if the relay interpreting was successful in conveying non-verbal signs and think of ways to improve the management of multimodality in consecutive interpreting.

> **Resources**: Links to speech repositories mentioned in the chapter. Links to short videos on relay interpreting in international organizations.
> **Activities**: Extra activities and adaptations.

References

Aguirre Fernández Bravo, Elena. 2022. "Indirect Interpreting: Stumbling Block or Stepping Stone? Spanish Booth Perceptions on Relay." *Target* 34.

AIIC (International Association of Conference Interpreters). [2004] 2017. "Practical Guide for Professional Conference Interpreters." https://aiic.org/document/ 547/ AIICWebzine_Apr2004_2_Practical_guide_for_professional_conference_interpreters_ EN.pdf [Accessed December 12, 2019].

AIIC (International Association of Conference Interpreters). 2019. "Profession." https://aiic. org/site/world/about/profession/abc. [Accessed November 12, 2021].

Allen, Katherine, Victor Sosa, Angelica Isidro, and Marjory A. Bancroft. 2018. *The Indigenous Interpreter. A Training Manual for Indigenous Language Interpreting*. Salinas, CA: Natividad Medical Foundation.

Altman, Janet. 1990. "What Helps Effective Communication? Some Interpreters' Views." *The Interpreters' Newsletter* 3: 23-32.

Bancroft, Marjory A., Katharine Allen, Sofia Garcia Beyaert, Giovanna Carriero-Contreras, Denis Socarrás-Estrada, and Hank Dallman. 2015. *The Community Interpreter: An International Textbook*. Columbia: Culture and Language Press.

Belisle, Annika. 2020. "Relay Interpreting." www.mehrsprachige-kommunikation.de/relay-interpreting/. [Accessed November 12, 2021].

Bontempo, Karen, and Patricia Levitzke-Gray. 2009. "Interpreting Down Under: Sign Language Interpreter Education and Training in Australia." In *International Perspectives on Sign Language Interpreter Education* edited by Jemina Napier, 149–170. Washington, DC: Gallaudet University Press.

Brady, Amy and Martin Pickles. 2021. "We Miss Being Able to Understand Voices in our Heads." [online] UN Today. October, 1. https://untoday.org/we-miss-being-able-to-understand-the-voices-in-our-heads/. [Accessed February 19, 2022].

Braun, Sabine. 2015. "Remote Interpreting." In *The Routledge Handbook of Interpreting* edited by Holly Mikkelson and Renneé Jourdenais, 352-367. London/New York: Routledge.

Čeňková, Ivana. 2015. "Relay Interpreting." In *Routledge Encyclopedia of Interpreting Studies* edited by Franz Pöchhacker, 339-341. London/New York: Routledge.

Chernov, Gelij V. 1992. "Conference Interpreting in the USSR: History, Theory, New Frontiers." *Meta* 35 (1): 149–162.

Chouc, Fanny, and José María Conde. 2018. "Relay Interpreting as a Tool for Conference Interpreting Training." *International Journal of Interpreter Education* 10 (2): 58–72.

D'Angelo, B. 2021. *Nic Zapko, ASL Interpreter for Minnesota Gov. Tim Walz, Goes Viral.* [online] KIRO 7 News Seattle. www.kiro7.com/news/trending/nic-zapko-asl-interpreter-minnesota-gov-tim-walz-goes-viral/REFGCKKFZFCZHMSWSXQEJRZASA/ [Accessed October 19, 2021].

Dellamont, Kieran. 2021. "'We're Using Debbie's Ears, and Then My Hands': Meet the COVID-briefing Deaf Interpreter Team." HalifaxToda.ca. www.halifaxtoday.ca/helpers/were-using-debbies-ears-and-then-my-hands-meet-the-covid-briefing-deaf-interpreter-team-4177897 [Accessed October 19, 2021].

DG Interpretation. 2019. "Annual Activity Report." https://ec.europa.eu/info/publications/annual-activity-report-2019-interpretation_es [Accessed December 1, 2021].

Dollerup, Cay. 2000. "Relay and Support Translations." In *Translation in Context: Selected Contributions from the EST Congress, Granada 1998*, edited by Andrew Chesterman, Natividad Gallardo and Yves Gambier, 17-26. Amsterdam: John Benjamins.

Gambier, Yves. 2003. "Working with Relay: An Old Story and a New Challenge." In *Speaking in Tongues: Language across Contexts and Users* edited by Luis Pérez-González, 47-66. València: Universitat de València.

Giambagli, Anna. 1993. "L'interprétation en relais: une perte d'information? Un essai expérimental." *The Interpreters' Newsletter* 5: 81-93.

Kartunnen, Frances. 2015. "Malinche." In *Routledge Encyclopedia of Interpreting Studies* edited by Franz Pöchhacker, 242–244. London and New York: Routledge.

Lim, Hyang-Ok. 2002. "Relay Interpretation: A Necessary Evil?" *Conference Interpretation and Translation* 4 (2): 149-171.

McDonnell, Patrick J. 1997. "Group Calls for Indian-language Interpreters." *Los Angeles Times*, March 14, 1997. http://articles.latimes.com/1997-03-14/news/mn-38155_1_spanish-interpreters [Accessed December 19, 2019].

Mackintosh, Jennifer. 1983. *Relay Interpretation: An Exploratory Study*. MA dissertation, Birkbeck College, University of London.

Mikkelson, Holly. 1999. "Relay Interpreting: A Viable Solution for Languages of Limited Diffusion?" *The Translator* 5 (2): 361-380.

Pöchhacker, Franz. 2004/2016. *Introducing Interpreting Studies*. London/New York: Routledge.

Pöchhacker, Franz. 2022. "Relay Interpreting: Complexities of Real-Time Indirect Translation." *Target* 34.

Pokorn, Nike K. 2011. "Directionality." In *Handbook of Translation Studies*, vol. 1, edited by Yves Gambier and Luc van Doorslaer, 37–39. Manchester: St Jerome Publishing.

Pym, Antony. 2008. "On Omission in Simultaneous Interpreting: Risk Analysis of a Hidden Effort." In Efforts and Models in Interpreting and Translation Research, edited by Gyde Hansen, Andrew Chesterman and Heidrun Gerzymisch-Arbogast, 83–105. Amsterdam/Philadelphia: Benjamins.

Romero, Bruno G. 2008. *Interpreters in the Judicial System: A Handbook for Ohio Judges*. Columbus, OH: Supreme Court of Ohio and Columbus State Community College.

Romero-Fresco, Pablo. 2011. *Subtitling through Speech Recognition: Respeaking*. Manchester: St Jerome.

Seleskovitch, Danica, and Marianne Lederer. 1995. *A Systematic Approach to Teaching Interpretation*, translated by J. Harmer. Paris: Didier Érudition. Silver Springs, MD: RID Publications.

Setton, Robin. 1994. "Experiments in the Application of Discourse Studies to Interpreter Training." In *Teaching Translation and Interpreting 2: Insights, Aims, Visions*, edited by Cay Dollerup and Annette Lindegaard, 183–198. Amsterdam: John Benjamins.

Setton, Robin, and Andrew Dawrant. 2016. *Conference Interpreting: A Complete Course*. Amsterdam: Benjamins.

Shlesinger, Miriam. 2010. "Relay Interpreting." In *Handbook of Translation Studies* Vol. 1, edited by Yves Gambier and Luc van Doorslaer, 276-278. Amsterdam: John Benjamins.

Song, Shuxian, and Andrew Cheung. 2019. "Disfluency in Relay and Non-Relay Simultaneous Interpretation: An Initial Exploration." *Forum* 17 (1): 1-19.

Viaggio, Sergio. 1989/1991. "Teaching Beginners the Blessing of Compressing (and How to Save a Few Lives in the Process." In *The Coming of Age: Proceedings of the 30th Annual Conference of the American Translator*, edited by Deanna Lindberg Hammond, 189–203. Medford: Learnt Information.

3
SCIENTIFIC-TECHNICAL TRANSLATION

Introduction

In this chapter, we discuss scientific and technical translation as a domain where English is often the language of reference and therefore also a default pivot. We look at specific challenges brought by indirect translation, such as stylistic ambiguity, the influence of English academic discourses and adapting to discourse fields. We consider how indirect translation can be integrated into translation workflows as part of quality assurance procedures so that it can help improve the final output.

Learning outcomes

Upon successful completion of this chapter, you will know how to:

- Develop and implement quality assurance and quality control strategies to produce a mediating text, using appropriate tools and techniques (including writing for translation).
- Develop and implement quality control and quality assurance strategies to produce indirect translations, using appropriate tools and techniques.
- Check, revise and/or review your own work and that of others (including machine translation) according to standard or work-specific quality objectives to mitigate the chance of errors reaching the final translation.

Warm-up activity

Consider the language options in Figure 3.1. Try to think of possible pivot arrangements. Which challenges and opportunities does indirect translation

52 Scientific-technical translation

> create for pivots and for further translators who work in multilingual contexts that convey technical or scientific knowledge?

Indirect translation in scientific-technical translation

As discussed in the introductory chapter, we can find many historical examples of scientific and technical texts that were translated indirectly. Over centuries, Greek, Latin, Arabic, French and German were used as the *linguae francae*—and therefore the main mediating languages—of science and technology. Today, an important part of the international exchange of scientific and technical knowledge happens in the English language or through the English language (see Montgomery 2009) and sometimes involves indirect translation.

In this chapter, our theoretical considerations will be organized around the technical and scientific genres for which indirect translation is most likely to be commissioned—the division by domain as followed, for example, in Olohan (2015) seemed appropriate. When approaching the technical translation domain, we will focus on patent specifications and instruction manuals. To discuss indirect scientific translation, we will zoom in on specialized scientific research (in particular, articles in scientific journals and their abstracts) and popular science reporting (Wikipedia entries and communicating science in crisis situations). This is because, in these genres and settings, indirect translation may happen with considerable frequency.

The focus of this chapter will be on written texts with a heavy verbal component. However, scientific and technical knowledge is communicated through a wide range of modes, platforms and media. Technical illustration, text callouts, screen captures and figures are an important part of textual production in this domain. Moreover, currently,

FIGURE 3.1 Language options for the Wikipedia article "Translation"

TED Talks, podcasts, social media posts and even news reports on the radio and TV disseminate all sorts of specialized knowledge (suggestions on how to incorporate these into classes on indirect translation can be found on the Translation Studies Portal).

Scientific and technical translation is a wide and productive field within the translation profession. Thus, significant research has been carried out on this type of translation between an array of languages and English, but also between languages other than English. Cross-linguistic comparisons indicate differences that are relevant for translation, whether direct or indirect. We can identify linguistic differences, such as the tendency to highlight the distance between text producer and reader; the formulation of directive speech acts (Baumgarten 2008; Schreiber 2004); writing conventions, such as measurements and legal warnings (Göpferich 1998; Schmitt 1999; Fleischmann 2001; Dias 2004); and cultural conventions, such as the use of illustrations or comic strips (Horn-Helf 2005; Li, Menno and Karreman 2021).

Importantly, the role of indirect translation as an information generator is also key in the dissemination of scientific and technical knowledge. This is why, in this chapter, we offer some insights into how indirect translation can be used as an effective tool in some modes of technical and scientific translation.

In order to help you produce the best translation possible, we start by looking at the importance of quality, both as quality control and quality assurance. We also consider how pivot translations interfere in the process.

Quality control and quality assurance and how they relate to indirect translation

"Quality" might be defined differently, depending on the purpose of the text. For information mining, a translation that is understandable but not fluent might be useful enough to be considered a "good translation". For certain types of patent translation, where the target text could be used to determine patent infringement, or lack thereof, only accurate, unambiguous wording would be good enough. In Wikipedia translations, a free translation might be considered of quality because it helps other users to expand an article.

"Quality assurance is a full set of procedures that can be applied before, during and after the translation production process, by all members of a translating organization. The aim is to ensure that the final output meets quality objectives that are important to clients" (Mossop 2020, 131). Quality control—that is, the identification and resolution of problems (often taking the shape of text revision)—and quality assessment—that is, the evaluation of the quality of a translated fragment—are, in part, contributions to quality assurance. However, while quality assessment is business oriented (it does not deal with the text itself but with the translation process), quality control is text oriented and post factum.

Traditionally, indirect translation has been linked to a lack of quality. As explained in the Introduction, the practice is often perceived as a necessary evil, and its positive value has often been ignored. Against this backdrop, we would like to argue that indirect translation can be integrated into quality assurance to improve the final outcome. This is because it provides yet another reading and rendering of a source text. If one has access to the whole process (to all relevant language versions generated from one ultimate source text), indirect translation may reveal differences that, in turn, might point towards a lack of clarity in the original or misreadings in (one of) the final target text(s). More specific suggestions on how exactly this can be done can be found in the sections that follow and also in subsequent chapters. Of course, in the professional world, clients might have implemented their own quality control systems, which shall prevail.

Indirect translation in international patenting activity

In this section, we zoom in on the first technical genre to be considered in this chapter—namely, patents. A patent is a form of technical document written by specialists for specialists, and the wording can have legal consequences regarding industrial or intellectual property (Olohan 2015). Patents describe an original invention and grant the patent holder some rights over the intention. These rights seek to prevent other parties replicating the invention without first seeking the patent holder's explicit go-ahead. Like many texts that are generated in institutional settings and have specific legal status (such as birth certificates or business contracts), patents make recurrent use of formulaic expressions and follow a relatively fixed structure. This fixed structure makes patents easier and faster to read for expert users. This means that, once the translator is familiar with the subject matter and format, the translation process should be relatively straightforward. However, given that the wording of the document is key for later patent claims, it can become one of the most challenging professional endeavours.

There are quite a few instances in the patenting process where indirect translation occurs. Before submitting a patent application, inventors (or their representatives) need to make sure that their invention has not already been invented. To do that, they need to consult the different patents and patent applications available in dedicated search databases (e.g., EPO, SIPO). Many patents are in English, but there are also quite a few that are in a vast array of other languages. If the inventor's command of these other languages is insufficient, they often resort to machine translation because it gives them the gist of a patent or related files. Several patent databases already incorporate machine translation in their systems.

Inventors might also read other patents to make sure that others are not infringing on their patents (or vice versa), to keep up with recent progress in their field, or to check on the intellectual property rights of other companies. A similar modus operandi is sometimes used by examiners who evaluate patent applications. This helps them decide about the novelty and patentability vis-à-vis pre-existing patents in other languages.

Usefulness of machine translation

One challenge related to indirect patent translation is the usefulness of machine translation. As mentioned, when translating a patent translation, second translators may want to use machine translation to grasp some sense of the ultimate source text for which they lack language competence. Let us consider a hypothetical situation where a Portuguese translator is commissioned to translate a patent from German that was originally written in Polish. Since the Portuguese translator does not know Polish, they can use machine translation to translate the Polish patent directly into Portuguese. However, they can also use machine translation to translate indirectly, in which case they first run the Polish source text through an engine to receive an output in English. Then they run the English output to receive an output in Portuguese. The results obtained through the direct and indirect approach may be quite different. Some find it worthwhile to do a joint reading of the direct and indirect translation outputs in order to have an enhanced understanding of the original.

However, for many purposes, this is simply insufficient. Patent structure has core parts that are summarized below.

Parts of a patent

Front page
    Title and abstract.
    Processing info: filing date, people, etc.
Drawing set
Specifications
    Background (current state of the art).
    Summary of the invention.
    Description of the drawings.
    Detailed description of the invention.
Claims (set the limits of what the patent covers)

In some cases, the translation of a title and abstract will not be sufficient—for example, in cases where the patent is to be used in a court hearing. In those instances, the claims (which set the limits of what the patent covers) and specifications will also be needed. Moreover, the quality of a machine translation system, even when trained on patent documentation, may simply not be enough to allow for a thorough comprehension of how a specific invention works. A translation generated mostly by a human translator may be a safer solution.

Concepts without an equivalent in the ultimate target language

One must also be aware of possible terminological misuses introduced by machine translation. In general, terminology plays a key role in patent translation, and multilingual glossaries help avoid mistakes.

However, translators might have to deal with concepts that do not have an equivalent in the target language. In this case, information on both the source text and the mediating text might be of help. In principle, translators should avoid disambiguating terminology. It may be counterproductive to use terms from technologies that are already on the market. In the context of patents, ambiguity might be legally strategic: it might be a way to avoid other patent infringements (Olohan 2015).

If this is a feasible option, final translators may also try to use cognate forms in their terminological choices. In legal contexts (e.g., litigation), indirect translation may assume an important role, as it can serve as evidence to support arguments related to infringements.

Mistakes in the mediating text

The last challenge we would like to highlight in the context of patent translation is errors in the mediating texts. As mentioned above, an indirect translation of a patent may also be commissioned in the context of litigation. In such contexts, an indirect patent translation should not be approached as an instrumental translation, as it does not serve a full-fledged communicative purpose in the target culture (Nord 1997). Rather, an indirect translation should be approached as an example of documentary translation (Nord 1997), where the final translation is meant primarily to record the details of the communication between the mediating text author and the mediating text receiver. In other words, in this type of rendering, readers of the final translation can learn more details about the communicative event of the mediating text.

Documentary translation foregrounds features of the text that are being translated. For instance, you can opt for a documentary translation that is close to the mediating text in terms of lexis so that the reader can have access to the lexical nuances of the mediating text (e.g., for the purpose of their linguistic analysis).

If you are translating from a patent translation that contains apparent mistakes, you should try to mirror these issues in your final translation. For example, patents often include complex images that are accompanied by descriptions. Due to this complexity, chances are that the original author or the first translator made a mistake or were inconsistent in their terminological choices. There can be mislabellings or inconsistencies between the written text and the images in the original, in the first translation or in both versions. If you spot such a mistake, it may be advisable to highlight it with a translation note. This note will enable those using the final translation for their purposes to decide how significant the error is from their perspective. This way, they may also be able to ask the translator for clarification. Even more importantly, it will help them understand where the problem first appeared: in the source text or in the mediating text.

Since the final translation will often be visible and used together with the original and the pivot text, the client will need to be able to identify the original sentence structures while they read the pivot version and the final version. Depending on language combination, this often means that it may be a good idea to avoid splitting or merging sentences. If possible, you should also do your best to mirror the punctuation of the mediating text.

Indirect translation as part of instructional text production

In this section, we move on to a different technical genre—namely, instructional texts. Written by specialists for users, instructional texts come in a plethora of formats, such as user guides, operating instructions and manuals (Olohan 2015). Whether they are about how to bake a cake, install subtitling software or rebuild a respirator, instructional texts are meant to teach someone something they do not yet know.

In the early days, it was relatively easy to determine who this someone was. Based on specifications from the product team (e.g., engineers), a technical writer wrote a manual for one clearly identified and culturally homogenous audience: the product end user (e.g., medical doctors working in Great Britain or middle-aged German female consumers). After closely analysing their target group, technical writers typically had a clear idea of how to communicate their message—in what language, tone, style, register, etc.

Today, however, things are quite different. In the increasingly global economy, a product is often scheduled to launch in dozens of different markets. This means that subsequent translations are often planned from the very outset of the manual writing process. This is because, today, instructional texts are often subject to localization and thus need to be first prepared for internationalization. (Both localization and internationalization will be discussed in the next chapter.) Many companies are aware that their technical documentation needs to address the needs of non-native English speakers and future translations (see Franco-Aixelà 2001 for an overview of the dramatic increase in the growth of publications related to technical translation in the 1980s and 1990s).

Thus, rather than writing specifically for end users, technical writers often write for further translators, keeping their different audiences in mind. What is more, when drafting their documentation, technical writers draw on specifications and hand-scribbled notes originally written by engineers, sometimes in different languages, in a process situated somewhere between translation and multilingual writing. All this makes it possible to consider the technical writer as the first translator. After all, they translate multilingual data into one language, knowing that their text will be reused by further translators. It also makes it possible to consider indirect translation as part and parcel of the production of instructional texts. In this context, the revision process, both regarding quality assurance and quality control, can be highly informative for translation.

The fact that technical writers translate for further translation involves specific challenges. This is because it implies targeting primarily subsequent translators, while, at the same time, anticipating the needs of different language audiences for whom the subsequent translators are translating. Many of these challenges can be addressed by using a translator-friendly style of writing during the production of the mediating text. This process might somewhat resemble **pre-editing**, with some caveats. It is also part of a quality-assurance process because it diminishes the chances of problems occurring in the transition from the mediating text to the final translation.

Below we outline aspects that you may want to keep in mind when writing and translating in a translator-friendly style. Indirect translation is always challenging, and it will be much more challenging if the mediating material (pivot text) is confusing and ambiguous. This is why, in indirect translation, the most convenient basis for a final translation of high quality is an accurate, easy-to-read and unambiguous pivot text.

Therefore, when you are in the position of translating for translation, it is important to adopt a translator-friendly style of translation. Many of the aspects we outline below draw on guidelines for writing for translation—from Sanderlin (1988) to the recent Translation Centre for the Bodies of the European Union (2019)—and the emphasis is on writing that uses simple and plain language.

Our guidelines use examples in English. This is because, in terms of scientific and technical translation, English appears to be the main pivot language worldwide. However, translators who are preparing a translation in a different language will likely benefit from a similar approach. A translation that is written in any plain language will serve as a more convenient stepping stone than a translation that is not adhering to plain language guidelines.

Please note that, with these guidelines, we are not trying to impose a strict, one-size-fits-all style of translating on technical (or scientific) translators around the world. We recognize that these guidelines are not recommendable in every single setting. Instead, we want to promote a mindset where, as a translator, you are aware of (and are trying to address) the potential challenges that await other translators who may come to use your translation as a starting point for their translation.

Some may argue that translating in this way will result in a dull, unappealing text. And they may be right! However, if the first aim of a translator is to communicate technical knowledge in a way that helps the second translator rather than entertain readers, then a dull style may not be harmful and, at times, may even be preferable. The terminology may not be exciting, but the concepts that these terms label might as well be. If the first translator wants to make the subsequent translator's task easier, then they need to produce a translation that is written in an accessible, translator-friendly style. Readability formulas can be used to measure friendliness. Take, for instance, the formula that helps word processing software (e.g., Word) provide a readability score. However, do not forget that these formulas will not consider a correct logical flow or content meaningfulness, which are also key for a translator-friendly text. Don't try to dumb the text down for the second translator. Just do your best to make it accessible and clear.

Global English (mind your language!)

It is important that your translation into English is understandable to all English language speakers, not only the native speakers of one of the many varieties of the English language. It may thus be a good idea to avoid idiomatic expressions, metaphors that draw on culture-bound references and other elements that are specific to only one culture and not used internationally. If, for some reason, you must include these elements, it is always good to carefully vet your text for global readiness. Try tagging culture-bound references for local adaptations and explaining what they mean. This can be done in text (e.g., in brackets) or in a supplementary document (e.g., annotations).

One way of ensuring that your translation is translator friendly is to ask a translator working into a different language to have a fresh look at your text. This will be different to the final user's experience because the final user is interested in the subject matter, not the language.

Use of technical terminology

To avoid confusion, use the same term for the same concept throughout. Do not replace terms with synonyms. If you use four different labels to refer to one and the same concept, the second translator will likely do the same, particularly if they cannot check with you the intended meaning. Moreover, the second translator may not always understand which terms are consolidated in the field and which are still in flux and thus subject to change. It will be easier for the second translator to find an equivalent if you italicize or place consolidated specialist terminology within quotation marks.

Of course, using a synonym can sometimes be helpful because it makes the second translator aware of an alternative way of describing the concept. In such a case, identify the synonym early on, i.e., the first time that the concept is introduced, but avoid using synonyms interchangeably throughout the document.

Instead of:

This *blender*, or *liquidizer*, takes the effort out of your daily tasks in the kitchen. The *liquidizer* comes with a handy storage bag. Read this manual carefully before using your *blender* for the first time, and keep them for future reference. When using this *liquidizer*, please follow these basic safety precautions.

Try:

This *blender*, or *liquidizer*, takes the effort out of your daily tasks in the kitchen. The *blender* comes with a handy storage bag. Read this manual carefully before using your *blender* for the first time, and keep them for future reference. When using this *blender*, please follow these basic safety precautions.

You can also make the translator's job easier by providing the source language equivalent in brackets. Moreover, it may be worthwhile to make sure the glossary includes a brief definition. It is also good practice to clearly mark specialist terms that need to be left untranslated because they belong to the client's list of DNT ("do not translate") terms. This can be done in a "Comments" section in your glossary. In this sense, remember that clients might provide specific style guides for translators and writers to follow.

Lexical considerations also apply to acronyms. Use short forms only when absolutely necessary, as further translators may find them difficult or even impossible to decipher. They can thus easily lead to mistakes in the final translation. If the short form is absolutely unavoidable, then, the first time you mention it in the text, make sure you write the acronym in brackets and precede it with the noun in full.

It is also good practice to accompany your translation with a bilingual list of the abbreviations and acronyms used so that the second translator will have a better idea of what they mean.

Ambiguity in sentence structure

Make the sentence structure as straightforward as possible to remove ambiguities. For instance, think twice before you join various clauses together in one sentence that begin with *which*, *who* or *that*. Such complex sentences may be difficult to process because it is often unclear what each relative clause refers to. For instance: "Of particular relevance is the regular maintenance of the central parts of the engine of the left wing of the lower part of the deck and the cooling system of the upper deck." Can you tell how far *maintenance* stretches?

If you cannot understand your translation without reading it twice, or without consulting the source text, chances are that the second translator will not understand it either. In this case, a correction is definitely necessary.

Shorter sentences help avoid confusion. A good trick for keeping sentences brief is to aim for sentences that have no more than 25 words. This is, of course, a general principle, as clarity is more important than brevity. To keep the sentence length reasonable, it is good to read the text aloud. Do you need to take various breaths when reading a sentence? Do you need to read a sentence more than once to understand how its various components fit together? If yes, then your translation is likely to cause problems downstream during the further translation process.

Instead of:

> The multi-optic device (MOD) is a very easy-to-use device that enables enhanced sensorial access to complex images that are otherwise inaccessible to most viewers and is made of innovative materials created only from natural ingredients and by certified manufacturers, thus being durable, easy to recycle and environmentally friendly.
>
> *(48 words)*

> **Try:**
>
> The multi-optic device is a very easy-to-use device that enables enhanced sensorial access to complex images that are otherwise inaccessible to most viewers. This device is made of innovative materials created only from natural ingredients and by certified manufacturers. It is thus durable, easy to recycle and environmentally friendly.
>
> *(23 + 16 + 10 = 49 words)*

Lengthy combinations of nouns

Noun strings make text more concise but also more difficult to translate into the vast majority of languages. This is because, when connecting elements are omitted from noun strings, translators are left to their own devices, and they must deduce the relationship between the words. Translators may thus misinterpret the intended meaning or translate too literally.

In most cases, these lengthy series of nouns need to be broken down in a way that is semantically and grammatically logical. All this will help clarify the relationship between the various nouns. Take, for example, the noun string *efficiency verification of material filtering and cleaning elements*. It will be much easier to translate if you separate the words that form meaningful segments, as in *verifying the efficiency of those elements which filter and clean the material*. It is often preferable to go for intelligibility over conciseness. So, do use relative pronouns such as "that" and "which" if you think they will improve understanding.

In this sense, if you need to include supplementary information, avoid including it between words that belong together. Instead, try placing this supplementary information at the beginning or end of the clause. As an alternative, consider splitting the information and organizing it vertically, i.e., in a list where each point is introduced separately, for example with bullet points.

> **Instead of:**
>
> *Metal parts of an engine* that has been properly assembled following steps 1 and 2 and that has been successfully dismantled in line with steps 4 and 5 *can be reused* in other devices produced by this manufacturer.
>
> **Try:**
>
> *Metal parts of an engine can be reused* in other devices produced by this manufacturer if the engine
>
> - has been properly assembled following steps 1 and 2, and
> - has been successfully dismantled in line with steps 4 and 5.

Active voice vs. passive voice

In a passive sentence, the thing that is acted on is specified first, and the person who is performing the action is specified at the end or sometimes not at all. In an active sentence, the person who is performing the action is specified first. This makes sentences easier to understand and, therefore, more translation friendly. A sentence from a translation that uses the active voice is thus more likely to yield a better final translation.

> **Instead of:**
>
> What happens if the red button is accidentally pressed?
>
> **Try:**
>
> What happens if you accidentally press the red button?

However, please note that some cultures and genres identify the use of passive discourse with an objective view of the world. For instance, since objectiveness is an inherent quality of science, some scientific discourses prefer passive forms, even if passive forms hinder communication. So, this specific recommendation may be applicable to many instructional texts but not necessarily to all technical and scientific texts.

Nouns vs. personal pronouns

The use of a pronoun can make a text sound less repetitive. Indeed, a text without pronouns may not read well in English. However, sometimes repeating the initial noun will help to improve the second translator's understanding of the mediating text. It will also help those languages that create cohesion through the repetition of keywords rather than the use of pronouns.

This is very much the case when translating via a non-gendered language, such as English, into a language that uses grammatical genders, such as Polish, Portuguese or Greek. For example, the English pronoun "it" can be translated into Polish in three different forms: as the masculine "on", the feminine "ona", or the neuter "ono", depending on the gender of the noun to which it is referring. It is thus useful to keep this challenge in mind and think twice before using pronouns. If you use the incorrect gender for a pronoun, the message from the original will be transferred incorrectly, and this will likely lead to mistakes in the final translation. Of course, we are not saying that your mediating text should be deprived of pronouns. Rather, we stress that one of the keys to a translator-friendly translation is to find a balance between pronouns and nouns.

Scientific-technical translation **63**

> **Instead of:**
>
> Safely place the buffer sachet in the plastic waste bag. It is only designed for human use and cannot be reused.
>
> **Try:**
>
> Safely place the buffer sachet in the plastic waste bag. The sachet is only designed for human use and cannot be reused.

In this example, replacing the pronoun with a noun helps to address ambiguity.

Multimodality and culture (mind your images!)

Non-verbal visuals (images, symbols, icons, colours, artwork, etc.) are frequently used in technical instructions. They help cut down on the word count and reinforce the meaning conveyed by verbal elements (words). Non-verbal visuals can also draw readers' attention to important details. There is, however, a warning to the practice, as non-verbal visuals are not universal. Take, for instance, a cross. While in many cultures it means a plus or a target, in East Asian languages it is the symbol for ten. Likewise, in English, a tick (check mark) beside an item on a list indicates that something is done or correct. However, Japanese and Korean use a circle for similar purposes and a tick may not convey the intended meaning. This is why, when translating from a translation, the second translator should pay close attention to how the accompanying non-verbal component relates to the message conveyed through the verbal component.

If there is any mismatch, it may be worth using search engines like Google Images to double check the intended meaning of the graphic elements. In turn, when translating for translation, it is useful to accompany graphic elements with concise, descriptive captions that reflect the images' context and intent. Consider, for instance, these images and their accompanying captions:

> **Examples**
>
> Caption: A triangular warning sign used in traffic to warn drivers to be extra cautious.
>
> Caption: A thumbs up, used in chats to indicate that the user has achieved the expected result.

For more information on how processing multimodality can be problematic when translating for or from a translation, see Chapters 2, 4 and 6.

Of course, as mentioned, we do not claim that the above list of recommendations is complete or applicable in all circumstances where you are translating for or from a scientific or technical translation. We only stress that it is important to take the time to look at your translation from the point of view of a second translator, i.e., someone who will be accessing and processing your translation not for their own benefit, but rather for the benefit of other users. If your translation will be reused to create a further translation, even a tiny effort on your part to make the translation more translation friendly can yield a huge payoff for the second translator and, by extension, for the second translation's users.

Indirect translation in international scientific publishing

In this section we zoom in on professional science—in particular, abstracts and research articles published in scientific journals (i.e., scientific texts written by specialists for specialists, see Olohan 2015). First, we briefly refer to differences in academic discourses. We will pay particular attention to the implacable hegemony of English in scientific publishing and to its consequences for other discourses worldwide. Then, we will consider different ways of dealing with quotations and examples stemming from previous works. We zoom in on these two elements of scientific texts written for specialists because these elements seem most likely to be subject to indirect translation.

Status of English as the language of science

The hegemonic status of English in all areas of scientific publishing is unquestionable. In fact, if we take translation studies as a case in point, it becomes clear that leading international journals in this field favour English over other languages, and, despite better acceptance of international English, highlight the importance of the American and British varieties. This may seem somewhat surprising considering that multilingualism and hybridity are central, foundational notions of this scientific discipline.

Bennett (2011; 2014a) theorized how these hegemonic practices are leading to the impoverishment of the semi-periphery and its languages, both in economic and epistemological terms. This impoverishment is particularly visible in university curricula, for example in Poland, where the focus is placed solely and prescriptively on essay writing in English, without paying proper attention to training in mother tongue conventions, or to exploring what brings Polish and English academic traditions together and what sets them apart (Gonerko-Frej 2014, 80). Even when research is not written directly in English, some authors adapt their local language academic works to academic English conventions in order to make the text look more scientific by mimicking Anglo-Saxon textual expectations (see Baumgarten, House and Probst 2004). For instance, Bennett (2014b, 21) acknowledges that, in her career as a Portuguese-English translator, she has worked with both Portuguese source texts written in the Portuguese academic style and with intermediary versions produced for translation.

Some publishers and journals try to counteract the effects of English hegemony, either by establishing quotas in languages other than English or by publishing different language translations of the articles on their online platforms. Moreover, many journals publish abstracts and keywords in several languages to facilitate global circulation. This diffusion might then encourage further translation in non-publishing contexts (research groups, institutions or organizations conducting research, think-tanks, etc.). Arguably, a model that adapts academic English conventions or at least supports the use of plain language versions of academic texts would make the task of the translator easier, faster and, probably, more affordable.

Within this context, the indirect translation of academic discourse could help fight the epistemological impoverishment of languages, but it risks encouraging an English language-based discursive model. Therefore, it is still important to include quality control and quality assurance strategies to preserve academic writing in peripheral languages. In this context, we encourage efforts to compile a list which aims at distinguishing discourse features or "a sort of comparative grammar between academic discourse conventions" (Dontcheva-Navratilova 2014, 60) in the tradition of contrastive rhetoric, even though this can raise barriers for translation in general and for indirect translation in particular. So, training in both local and international discourse conventions should not only be expository but should also include studying and editing actual academic texts.

Somewhat ironically, we feel that, to a certain extent, this book contributes to perpetuating the English hegemony in scientific discourse. In this chapter, we provide tips on how to prepare a text for further translation using English language conventions. In an effort to counterbalance this approach, we will also propose strategies and examples applicable to other languages and contexts.

Quotations from already translated texts

Research in the humanities draws heavily on past discourses. This seems to be particularly the case in disciplines like history or philosophy, but it is definitely not restricted to these fields. Many such works often report and engage with previous research and, for this, they cite and discuss quotations that are generally taken from articles or books by other researchers. Such quotations may stem from overt or covert translations, and they may equally require further translation. For example, an article written in French may include translations of quotations taken from a Latin text, which, in turn, need to be translated into English for publication in an English language journal. Similarly, it could also provide examples taken from other non-scholarly sources (e.g., poems, treatises), which can also be translations from other works that can become a starting point for further translation. For instance, a French article that needs to be translated into English can contain examples showcasing how a Polish translator rendered a Chinese poem.

All this means that indirect translation can play an important role in international scientific research, particularly when it comes to quotations and examples. Now, put yourself in the shoes of an indirect translator who needs to translate into English the above-mentioned French article containing quotations and examples originally written in a third language. How will you approach this task? At this point, it may be useful to, once again, resort to Nord's distinction between instrumental and documentary translation.

If the quotations based on previously translated texts are meant to support arguments put forward in the article, you may prefer producing an instrumental translation. Translating such argumentative quotations may therefore give rise to terminological problems. To address this challenge, it may be a good idea to first consult Google Scholar and Google Books, searching for any previous argumentative quotations and paraphrases from the same source into English. This way, you may check if specific terms have already been translated into English by other researchers. If the quoted work has not been translated into English, you will need to coin a new term.

On the other hand, if the quoted work has already been translated into English, then resorting to the published translations may be a way to avoid terminological confusion. In this case, you should check with the author of the article you are translating. The author might prefer that you transfer the quote verbatim from their article, completely ignoring other published versions, or they might prefer to include a citation to the English language article. In this case, the English language translation will have to be included in their list of references, and the source of the translation will have to be indicated in text.

When it comes to examples contained in a research article, you may prefer adopting a documentary (word for word) translation, also known as a gloss. This way, you will provide readers with access to the third-language texts that your author is analysing. In this case, you may have to rely on the author's first translations and glosses because you may not know the original language of the analysed examples.

Indirect translation in popularizing science

In this section we consider instances where indirect translation is used in the context of sharing scientific knowledge with non-specialists. Incidentally, the process of popularizing science itself could be considered an intralingual translation, and thus the first step in an indirect translation process. However, we are not applying this broad focus in this section. We consider the popular scientific text to be the source text. In other words, we understand there are three languages at play.

Characteristics of a scientific text for non-specialist readers

Non-specialist readers may find it difficult to understand scientific texts written by specialists for specialists. Such texts seem inaccessible due to textual and linguistic choices. For this reason, when popularizing science, defining the target audience might be challenging as it needs to estimate previous knowledge and might require argumentation skills to fulfil a persuasion purpose (Olohan 2015).

Let's consider an exhibition in a science museum. Museums are open to visitors with different backgrounds. Exhibits might target concrete age groups or education levels either by the selection of artifacts they exhibit or by the paratextual elements accompanying the display (guides, instructions, tags, etc.). Their purpose is to create an interest in a certain topic and sometimes encourage sustainability landmarks. For example, the ArtScience Museum in Singapore (www.marinabaysands.com/museum.html) offers information in six different languages with exhibits for all ages. Certain concepts might be more comprehensible through similes and comparisons, but those are not necessarily international. Rather, they tend to be more effective when they are more culture specific. If translation into Indonesian happens via English, some cultural references might need to be modified.

Science is also presented to the general public through news websites such as Science Daily (www.sciencedaily.com). To be more appealing to a vast array of readers, these sites build their news from press releases and use a vast range of communication modes (see Chapter 7 for more information on news translation). If the underlying scientific research was published in other languages, often these press releases will be in English (or sometimes French), and these translations will serve as source texts for further translations. These types of press releases often comprise fixed structures, including a headline and a lead paragraph with "pseudo quotes" that are used to engage readers (see Strobbe and Jacobs 2005; Sleurs, Jacobs and Van Waes 2003). As happens in scientific publishing, quotations are often used for the sake of credibility.

Popular science might have more room for multilingualism and thus for indirect translation. For example, television documentaries on scientific themes tend to include locals speaking different languages, and these are translated through English into various other languages to reach global audiences. Moreover, popular science discourses are in constant contact with other public discourses, following the norms and limitations of the media they are presented in. In the previous examples, interactive exhibits might have to take into account the specificities of museum translation; documentaries will encapsulate their messages within audiovisual limitations (see more in Chapter 6); and science news websites work as most news reporting websites (see Chapter 7). However, in all cases, quality procedures should include content revision.

Open access: curating content through indirect translation

One realm where knowledge reaches a wide non-specialist audience and indirect translation plays an important role is the curation of Wikipedia content. In Wikipedia articles, translation is often a tool to expand knowledge, so the concept itself is loose and it often combines with further content writing. Wikipedia articles are often written independently, without an editor-in-chief who checks that content in one language corresponds to content in other languages. Since a translator interface was incorporated in 2014, sections of well-written articles might be added to stubs or they can be used to create new articles. However, this is a choice made by volunteer editors according to the best of their knowledge, and such knowledge includes linguistic competence.

All in all, even translated articles often combine information from other intralingual and interlingual sources (see Shuttleworth 2018 for the role of translation in Wikipedia creation). This is even more the case in articles based on breaking news. Omnipedia was a short-lived project that encouraged the visualization of language-specific information selection (see Bao et al. 2012 for a visual summary). It made it easier to pinpoint information gaps in articles written in different languages. Manypedia (Massa and Scrinzi 2012) had a similar approach, but it focused on articles with a strong political bias that other nations might have found controversial (e.g., the status of Malta, the retelling of wars, the classification of languages, etc.).

Why are these differences in content relevant here? Given that English is the primary source language for content translation, the translation of articles into English is often a first step towards global outreach (Warncke-Wang et al. 2012). This fact is problematic as it works against the concept of a decentralized Wikipedia (which allows for the content-wise differences we have already mentioned). However, English is in no position to effectively work as a hub language. On the one hand, it discourages non-English language sources (thus requiring rewriting or the identification of new sources). Incidentally, this does not happen when translating from English, as the acceptance of sources in English is more common in the other Wikipedias. On the other hand, articles might not meet the notability threshold in the new locale. That is, some articles that might be locally important might be equally known in other peripheral languages, but they lack relevance in English (see, for example, the entry 사랑한다 말해줘, which has a Korean, Chinese and Japanese wiki page only). In this sense, each Wikipedia article has its own bias or "linguistic point of view" (Massa and Scrinzi 2012). This bias influences decisions on what information should be translated, and how it should be presented to readers.

Irrespective of the preferred viewpoints—i.e., those in favour of the decentralization of knowledge (Warncke-Wang et al. 2012) or those supporting policies aiming at translation justice (McDonough Dolmaya 2017)—the truth is that (a) while there is a huge demand for English language articles, the number of English native speakers has not managed to meet this demand, and (b) Wikipedia can help us reflect on knowledge transfer networks as well as multilingual interactions that are operated via multiple indirect translations.

While the use of other linguistic versions in fields like literary translation might bring about ethical challenges (see Chapter 5), the open-access characteristics of Wikipedia call for the evaluation of indirect translation as a support translation. The rationale is that other language versions might help expand or detail information on specific aspects mentioned in Wikipedia articles. In this sense, free access to parallel multilingual versions can be an important step in quality procedures. Moreover, this approach may enhance our understanding of how even encyclopaedic information is spontaneously tailored to local needs and discourses. We would like to link this to another aspect of popularizing scientific knowledge—namely, (health) crisis translation.

Health crisis: science must reach the population

In the scenarios mentioned above, scientific discourse is not merely simplified in order to be more accessible to a lay public. It also tends to be articulated with local public discourses (whether economic, political or cultural), which may be quite different in the source, mediating and target cultures. This articulation can be challenging for translators. This is because the translator responsible for the final translation needs to consider the knowledge and opinions of audiences located in a different part of the world. Moreover, they need to situate the scientific discourse in the context of other public discourses. At the same time, an indirect translator, in their role as a cultural mediator, might be asked to decide which part of the information needs to be foregrounded, which one needs to be explained in more detail, and also which one should stay untranslated. See WHO (2015) on how privileging certain information over a discourse more specific to a particular culture impacted on the spread of the Ebola epidemic in Africa.

What happens when it is crucial to communicate scientific information in every language on how to be safe? During the Covid-19 pandemic, vital information has reached diverse linguistic communities through pivot machine translation or relay interpreting. A case in point is the "Translation Initiative for Covid-19: TICO-19", which brought together partners from NGOs, academia, language services and major tech companies like Amazon, Facebook, Google and Microsoft. The partners helped in various ways: funding or generating urgent translations, creating terminologies in local languages, creating translation memories (to help professional translators), and collecting data to improve the way in which machine translation systems handle the new, constantly evolving terminology related to Covid-19. The main idea was to translate data (from different domains, including medicine) from English into over thirty different languages. In some cases, this was achieved through pivot languages. The English content was first translated into the pivot language (e.g., French, Farsi) and from there into a number of target languages (e.g., Congolese Swahili, Dari) (https://tico-19.github.io/data/paper/ticopaper.pdf).

Another example related to the Covid-19 crisis is the international trajectory of guidance proposed by the World Health Organization (WHO). WHO operates through six official languages. This means that important health guidance generated by this body is disseminated worldwide through many ad hoc indirect trajectories. For example, vaccine guidelines or outbreak reports were written in English and then translated into Portuguese, which served as the pivot for other local languages spoken in Angola. For other examples of potential indirect trajectories see Lees (2021), who presents a case study in Greece; Luo (2021), who discusses examples in China; and Marshall (2021), who addresses the situation in Vancouver.

In such crisis situations, information is transmitted rapidly. The stakes are high and so is the risk of excessively universalizing the ultimate source culture's (or the mediating culture's) local point of view. Therefore, it is key to approach all argumentative information critically and apply modulation or domesticating strategies whenever relevant. Given that translation might be speedy, it is highly recommended that the final target text be revised (or even delivered) by an external expert with a thorough knowledge of the final language and culture. Alternatively (and perhaps even more realistically), indirect translation can possibly be integrated into translation workflows that are put into practice in earlier or later phases of crisis management. While in the Covid-19 pandemic many indirect translation trajectories seem to have been devised and operationalized in the phase of crisis response, indirect approaches may be better suited to translation workflows that are put in place during the phases of crisis mitigation, crisis preparedness or crisis recovery.

Further discussion

- *Translating for translation and pre-editing.* In the first part of the chapter, we provide some indications on how to improve translation to facilitate the work of subsequent translators. How do these recommendations compare to strategies for pre-editing?
- *English as the lingua franca of science.* When discussing international scientific publishing, we argue that international scientific publishing tends to lead to the epistemological impoverishment of languages. What is your stance on this? Do you see any consequences of this established use of English as a *lingua franca*? Are there any strategies to counteract this influence?
- *Technical writing, multilingual writing and indirect translation.* What do these practices have in common? What sets them apart? Think about the processes, texts and agents they involve, as well as the professional status of these practices.

Activities

Activity 1 Developing and implementing quality assessment strategies to produce indirect translations using appropriate tools and techniques

This activity focuses on quality assessment techniques for indirect translations produced using machine translation. You will need to have knowledge of two languages other than English (A and B) that are supported by a machine translation system of your choice. If you do not have such language skills, you will be able to complete this activity with the help of a third-language expert from your language network.

PART A. Pre-translation

Start by selecting a scientific or technical text fragment of around 150 words. The text should be written in your B language (your weaker language) and should be on a topic that you find appealing. Instruction manuals, Wikipedia entries and abstracts in academic journals may be particularly useful.

PART B. Direct translation

Now we will translate directly. Using the machine translation system you selected, translate the selected excerpt from your B language into your A language (i.e., the language in which you can write/edit most easily).

PART C. Indirect translation

Now we will translate indirectly. Using the same machine translation engine, translate the same excerpt from your B language into English. Once you are done, translate the raw English language output into your A language using the same engine.

PART D. Post-editing

Post-edit the outputs from steps B and C **to publishable quality**. This means you will have to correct the text in terms of both accuracy (is the content complete and correct?) and adequacy/fluency (does it read like a natural text free from errors in lexis, grammar, register, etc.?). For helpful tips on how to post-edit, go to www.taus.net/academy/best-practices/postedit-best-practices/machine-translation-post-editing-guidelines. While editing the outputs, measure the total time spent on editing.

Take note of the additional reference works you need to use to check if a term, grammatical choice, etc. is correct. These works may include dictionaries, terminology databases, corpora, websites, etc.

PART E. Translation quality assessment

Evaluate the final outputs. To do that, reflect on:

- The quality of the raw machine translation outputs (which translation seems completer and more correct: the direct translation or the indirect one? Which one seems more adequate and fluent? Is there a clear winner?)
- What kinds of errors you needed to correct.
- How difficult it was to post-edit the two outputs (can you find any noticeable differences?).
- The type of reference works you needed to use.
- How long it took to bring the machine translation output to publishable quality.
- How useful the indirect translation approach was.

Activity 2. Developing and implementing quality control and quality assurance strategies to produce a mediating text using appropriate tools and techniques

PART A. Identifying translation problems

This particular activity builds and expands on Bowker and Cyro (2019).

Take a look at the research abstract below. It is one of our own abstracts, translated from Polish into English. Your aim is to revise the English translation to facilitate the work of the second translator who will be rendering this text into your language. The English translation was not translated with further translation in mind, so there is plenty of room for improvement.

> This research is meant to analyse the most common pros and cons related to combining qualitative and quantitative methods used in identifying indirectness in Polish-Portuguese literary translation. Two sets of texts resulting from direct and indirect translation strategies were jointly used. The analysis was conducted as a collaborative effort between experts in discourse analysis, scientific translation, and ISS. For each set of texts, a single set of key variables was proposed, a single comparative model was developed, and a single comparative method was implemented. Initial data seems to suggest that the joint use of qualitative and quantitative methods can be said to be yielding novel insights with regard to the long-standing, historical patterns researchers want to trace in inter-peripheral transfers as well as in terms of micro-structural modifications indirect translations often undergo. Based on these results, five guidelines for ways in which a combined quantitative and qualitative comparative analysis can be set up for success are proposed. Moreover, our results suggest that joint methods not only help streamline the analysis but also allow researchers to generate more systematic knowledge which the publishing industry and grammar schools may be more willing to implement for translation workflow improvement. Finally, they can be used as a springboard for future studies in the area of cross-cultural communication.

Imagine this English language translation is meant to be translated into your language. Identify and briefly explain the problems in this first translation that are likely to make the second translator's task more difficult.

PART B. Revision

Revise this English language translation so that it is more translator friendly. Essentially, you should improve the text in a way that will reduce ambiguity and complexity with the goal of making the text easier to translate. For a reminder about how this can be done, consult our tips on translator-friendly writing (in the section "Indirect translation as part of instructional text production").

When you are done, you may check the portal for a key to this part of the activity: a sample on how the improved version could look (and our rationale behind specific improvements).

PART C. Comparison

Have another translator translate both versions, starting with the non-revised translation (i.e., the raw, non-translator-friendly text). When they are done, ask them which version they found more helpful and why.

Compare the two translations created by your fellow translator. To what degree have the problems that you initially identified in the first translation been resolved thanks to your edits? In other words, try to evaluate whether or not your revisions made the text more translator friendly. Do some of the original problems remain? Have any new problems appeared?

PART D. Quality checklist

Based on this activity and on what you have read in this chapter, create your own checklist of different aspects that need to be verified before submitting the text for further translation into your working language.

If possible, compare your list to those prepared by colleagues working into other languages. This way, you will be able to see if and how the checklists change depending on the specific language combination used.

PART E. Optional follow-up

Ask a non-translator (a lay user) to read the two translated English language versions. Which one do they prefer and why? You can also try running both English versions through a machine translation engine of your choice to see which version generates a better output. Reflect on the outcome: apart from facilitating the work of fellow translators, are there any other payoffs to using plain language in your translations?

Activity 3. Check, revise and/or review your own work and that of others (including machine translation) according to standard or work-specific quality objectives to mitigate the chances of errors reaching the TT

Have a look at the Wikipedia entry "Wikipedia: Writing better articles". This wiki page is available in 40 languages.

Choose three languages you can read in. It is best if they have a similar amount of information (some will clearly be stubs). If you are not fluent in three of the ones available, you can work in groups and share information or you can use machine translation for gisting.

PART A. Quality criteria

Compare the information highlighted in each of the three wiki pages. Pay attention to language-related criteria (grammar, terminology, etc.) and discuss your results on the following:

- Is any recommendation mentioned in all three versions?
- Is there any recommendation which is clearly language specific?
- Do any two versions provide the opposite recommendation (e.g., one recommends the use of active verbs and another the use of passive forms?).

PART B. Applicability to indirect translation

Drawing on the previous answers, can you improve the recommendations in the first part of the book so that they are more language specific? Can you draw any other recommendation for those who write and translate texts that will definitely be translated?

PART C. Apply recommendations

C.1. Look for an article in the category "Articles needing cleanup". (If you search for those specific words, you will land on the English wiki page and can then navigate from there to the other 44 available languages.) Improve the article by applying the specific recommendations. Which ones are easier to apply? Which ones are more difficult or time consuming?

C.2. Now select an article in the category "Articles needing cleanup after translation" (https://en.wikipedia.org/wiki/Category:Wikipedia_articles_needing_cleanup_after_translation). Improve the article by applying the specific recommendations. Which ones are easier to apply? Which ones are more difficult or time consuming?

C.3. Compare the results of C.1. and C.2. Were there any relevant differences?

Activity 4. Culturemes

PART A. Culture-specific items

Think about one culture-specific item in your language which is often considered to be untranslatable. Here are some possible examples:

- Hygge (in Danish)
- Morriña (in Galician)

- 风水 (feng shui in Chinese)
- Polot (in Polish)
- Saudade (in Portuguese)
- Spleen (in French)

Imagine you are to write a scientific article in which your chosen word is a key concept. Write up to five keywords for your article in your language.

PART B. Translate keywords

Now translate those five keywords into English and another language and consider the following questions:

- Concerning the English version, did you keep the selected keywords untranslated or did you manage to translate them?
- Did you add a different keyword to the translated versions (maybe an approximate translation)? If so, what other keyword did you drop to give room to the translation?
- How did the translation of the keywords influence the structure of the article you previously imagined?
- About the second translation: was it done directly or indirectly? Why?
- Read the three versions once more. Which one feels more scientific and accurate? Why?

PART C. Evaluate word choice

Use Google Scholar to look for results which include the first keyword you selected. Reflect on:

- Which languages are presented?
- Did you find direct mentions of the keyword?
- What does this search tell you about the international reach of culture-specific items such as the above?

Still using the keyword selected before, write the first sentence (in your language) of your article or abstract and try to engage the reader. Then, perform an intralingual translation in order to prepare this article for subsequent translation into English.

- What changes did you perform?
- Do you feel your aim/argument endured the changes? Why?

Look up the word on Wikipedia and look at the discussion section (tab not available in phone view). Are there any arguments supporting a specific use?

> **Resources**: Expanded bibliography on intercultural comparison of technical production. References for clear writing. List of online machine translation engines.
> **Activities**: Resources and follow-ups for Activity 1. Extra activities and adaptations for group work and multilingual classrooms. Key to Activity 2 (Part B).

References

Bao, Patti, Brent Hetch, Samuel Carton, Mahmood Quaderi, Michael Horn, and Darren Gergle. 2012. "Omnipedia: Bridging the Wikipedia Language Gap." In *Proceedings of the SIGCHI Conference on Human Factors in Computing System*s, 1075–1084.

Baumgarten, Nicole. 2008. "Writer Construction in English and German Popularized Academic Discourse: The Uses of We and Wir." *Multilingua* 27: 409–438. https://doi.org/10.1515/MULTI.2008.019.

Baumgarten, Nicole, Juliane House, and Julia Probst. 2004. "English as *Lingua Franca* in Covert Translation Processes." *The Translator* 10(1): 83–108. https://doi.org/10.1080/13556509.2004.10799169.

Bennett, Karen. 2011. "The Scientific Revolution and its Repercussions on the Translation of Technical Discourse." *The Translator* 17(2): 189–210. https://doi.org/10.1080/13556509.2011.10799486.

Bennett, Karen. 2014a. "Introduction: The Political and Economic Infrastructure of Academic Practice: The 'Semiperiphery' as a Category for Social and Linguistic Analysis." In *The Semiperiphery of Academic Writing. Discourses, Communities and Practices* edited by Karen Bennett, 1–9. London: Palgrave Macmillan.

Bennett, Karen. 2014b. "The Erosion of Portuguese Historiographic Discourse." In *The Semiperiphery of Academic Writing. Discourses, Communities and Practices* edited by Karen Bennett, 13–38. London: Palgrave Macmillan.

Bowker, Lynn, and Jairo Buitrago Cyro. 2019. *Machine Translation and Global Research: Towards Improved Machine Translation Literacy in the Scholarly Community*. Bingley: Emerald.

Dias, João Roque. 2004. "Translating Technical Manuals: What Are They? What Are They Used for?" *Translating Today Magazine* 1 October 2004: 17–19.

Dontcheva-Navratilova, Olga. 2014. "The Changing Face of Czech Academic Discourse." In *The Semiperiphery of Academic Writing. Discourses, Communities and Practices*, edited by Karen Bennett, 39–61. London: Palgrave Macmillan.

Fleischmann, Eberhard. 2001. "Kulturfaktor Schukosteckdose." In *Kultur und Übersetzung. Methodologische Probleme des Kulturtransfers*, edited by Gisela Thome et al., 57–73. Tübingen: Narr.

Franco-Aixelà, Javier. 2001. "The Study of Technical and Scientific Translation: An Examination of its Historical Development." *JosTrans* 1: 29–49.

Gonerko-Frej, Anna. 2014. "Teaching Academic Writing for the Global World in Poland: The ELF Perspective." In *The Semiperiphery of Academic Writing. Discourses, Communities and Practices* edited by Karen Bennett, 75–90. London: Palgrave Macmillan.

Göpferich, Susanne. 1998. *Interkulturelles Technical Writing. Fachsprachliches Adressatengerecht Vermitteln*. Tübingen: Narr.

Horn-Helf, Brigitte. 2005. "Visualized Information in Multilingual Translations." *MuTra Conference: Challenges of Multidimensional Translation. Saarbrücken*.

Lees, Christopher. 2021. "'Please wear mask!' Covid-19 in the Translation Landscape of Thessaloniki: A Cross-disciplinary Approach to the English Translations of Greek Public Notices" *The Translator*. DOI: 10.1080/13556509.2021.1926135.

Li, Qian, Menno de Jong, and Joyce Karreman. 2021. "Cultural Differences and the Structure of User Instructions: Effects of Chinese and Western Structuring Principles on Chinese and Western users." *Technical Communication* 68(1): 37–55. www.ingentaconnect.com/content/stc/tc/2021/00000068/00000001/art00004.

Luo, Xuanmin. 2021. "Translation in the Time of COVID-19." *Asia Pacific Translation and Intercultural Studies* 8 (1): 1–3. DOI: 10.1080/23306343.2021.1903183.

Marshall, Steve. 2021. "Navigating COVID-19 Linguistic Landscapes in Vancouver's North Shore: Official Signs, Grassroots Literacy Artefacts, Monolingualism, and Discursive Convergence." *International Journal of Multilingualism*. DOI: 10.1080/14790718.2020.1849225.

Massa, Paolo, and Federico Scrinzi. 2012. "Manypedia: Comparing Language Points of View of Wikipedia Communities." In *Proceedings of the Eighth Annual International Symposium on Wikis and Open Collaboration*, 1–9.

McDonough Dolmaya, Julie. 2017. "Expanding the Sum of All Human Knowledge: Wikipedia, Translation and Linguistic Justice." *The Translator* 23(2): 143–157.

Montgomery, Scott L. 2009. "English and Science: Realities and Issues for Translation in the Age of an Expanding Lingua Franca." *JosTrans* 11: 6–16.

Mossop, Brian. 2020. *Revising and Editing for Translators*. London: Routledge.

Nord, Christiane. 1997. *A Functional Typology of Translations*. Amsterdam and New York: John Benjamins.

Olohan, Maeve. 2015. *Scientific and Technical Translation*. London: Routledge.

Sanderlin, Stacey. 1988. "Preparing Instruction Manuals for Non-English Readers." *Technical Communication* 35 (2): 96–100.

Schmitt, Peter A. 1999. *Translation und Technik*. Tübingen: Stauffenburg.

Schreiber, Michael. 2004. "Sprechakte in Bedienungsanleitungen aus Sprachvergleichender Sicht." *Lebende Sprachen* 49 (2): 52–55.

Shuttleworth, Mark. 2018. "Translation and the Production of Knowledge in 'Wikipedia': Chronicling the Assassination of Boris Nemtsov." *Alif: Journal of Comparative Poetics* 38: 231–263.

Sleurs, Kim, Geert Jacobs, and Luuk Van Waes. 2003. "Constructing Press Releases, Constructing Quotations: A Case Study." *Journal of Sociolinguistics* 7 (2): 192–212.

Strobbe, Ilse, and Geert Jacobs. 2005. "E-releases: A View from Linguistic Pragmatics." *Public Relations Review* 31(2): 289–291.

Translation Centre for the Bodies of the European Union. 2019. *Writing for Translation*. https://cdt.europa.eu/sites/default/files/documentation/pdf/writing_for_translation_en.pdf [Accessed July 2020].

Warncke-Wang, Morten, Anuradha Uduwage, Zhenhua Dong, and John Riedl. 2012. "In Search of the ur-Wikipedia: Universality, Similarity, and Translation in the Wikipedia Inter-language Link Network." In *Proceedings of the Eighth Annual International Symposium on Wikis and Open Collaboration*, 1–10.

WHO. 2015. "Factors that Contributed to Undetected Spread of the Ebola Virus and Impeded Rapid Containment." In *One Year into the Ebola Epidemic Report*. www.who.int/news-room/spotlight/one-year-into-the-ebola-epidemic/factors-that-contributed-to-undetected-spread-of-the-ebola-virus-and-impeded-rapid-containment [Accessed July 2020].

4
LOCALIZATION

Introduction

In this chapter we outline the challenges of pivot localization workflows that are particularly relevant for digital content originally developed in languages other than English. To complete the picture, we also consider how translating for translation relates to the global distribution of digital content, as well as to internationalization.

Learning outcomes

Upon successful completion of this chapter, readers will know how to:

- Work in multiprofessional and plurilingual teams where the translators are not competent in all the working languages, and collaborate to produce a translation with recourse to a third common language.
- Use the most relevant software to translate from multiple source texts and languages.
- Pre-edit source material for the purpose of potentially improving further translation using appropriate pre-editing techniques.

Warm-up activity

If you were to prepare the webpage in Figure 4.1 for a further translation and adaptation into your locale, what challenges would you face? What challenges would you face if you were to localize this website? Pay particular attention to

DOI: 10.4324/9781003035220-4

both verbal and non-verbal elements, such as reading direction, images, space allocated to specific segments of texts, names (their connotations in your language/culture), and colours (for this, visit the website online).

Indirect translation and localization

Localization (often abbreviated to "L10n") means "taking a product and making it linguistically and culturally appropriate to the target **locale** (country/region and language) where it will be used and sold" (Esselink 2000, 3). As a process, localization is applied to digital products (e.g., websites, video games, software) that will be displayed on digital platforms (e.g., smartphone, tablet, computer, game console, etc.) (Schäler 2010).

In many translation domains, the original—and also the mediating—text is often not designed with a further translation in mind. In conference interpreting, speakers hardly ever consider how to simplify the task of the relay-giver and the relay-taker. Sometimes, even the relay-giver is unaware that they are acting as a pivot and so they do not try to adjust their rendering to the relay-taker's needs. Likewise, when creating a movie, filmmakers very rarely try to minimize the challenges that the template maker or the pivot subtitler will face (Romero-Fresco 2019). In principle, translation and indirect translation are an afterthought in these workflows. They are usually considered to be something that happens later, once the work on the original and the mediating text has been completed (Pym 2014, 119).

Against this background, the way indirect translation is often handled in localization represents a drastic shift from what happens in other translation domains. This is because, in this branch of industry, final translations need to be thought about and planned for from the very outset and at every stage of a product's development. This is particularly

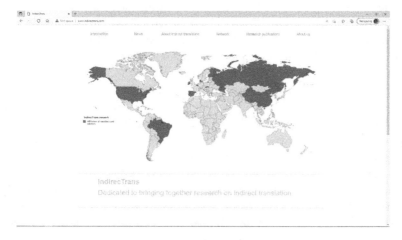

FIGURE 4.1 The landing page of www.indirectrans.com

evident in the process known as **internationalization**, which we will discuss later in this chapter. Internationalization takes place before the actual localization—i.e., at the stage of content design and document development—and this stage essentially corresponds to the creation of the original (or at least an interim version thereof). This is when a product and the accompanying documentation (i.e., the original) is generalized "so that it can handle multiple languages and cultural conventions without the need for re-design" (LISA definition, cited in Esselink 2000, 2).

These characteristics make localization a potentially fertile area for professionals with skills in indirect translation. Although translation is at the centre of localization, (pivot) translators usually join the party almost at the end of the process. Here we want to promote a mind frame, in line with Pym (2013) and others, which suggests that, in localization workflows, translators can do much more than just translate. Their competences are useful at different stages of the localization process, before localization proper begins and after it ends. When consulted in the early stages of the localization process, professionals with skills in indirect translation may help anticipate and avoid challenges downstream, thus helping to make the final product more successful. For this to happen, indirect translators need to know how to work in multiprofessional and plurilingual teams. They also need to be aware of different stages of pivot translation workflows and the challenges they bring about. While, in certain companies, translators are the first to be contacted to think about internationalization and localization, this practice is not as widespread as it deserves to be.

Indirect translation in the history of localization and today

Localization as we know it today is young. It was born in the mid-1980s (Schäler 2010) and was triggered by the need to adapt software and hardware to different languages and cultures.

The historiography of localization is still a largely uncharted territory. Indirect translation has not generated substantial research foci within localization itself. See Mangiron (2017 and 2018), Maylath and St. Amant (2019), Pym (2011) and Jiménez-Crespo (2021) for examples of literature reviews of research on localization. See also O'Hagan (2022) and Peng (2021) for very recent studies that start to counter the lack of scholarly interest in pivot localization.

Therefore, it is difficult to pinpoint the exact moment when translating via a third language became a go-to solution in this domain. The extent to which pivot approaches were used largely depended on the type of content being localized. In video game localization, the earliest instances of pivot translations can probably be traced back to the 1980s, when Japanese companies entered the (until then) US-dominated video game industry. Japanese games were first localized into English for the North American region (considered a top priority for Japanese developers). Other localized versions were based on these English pivots and released on further markets with some delay, as part of the so-called **post-gold model** (O'Hagan and Mangiron 2013).

In turn, resorting to indirect translation might have been a later development in web localization, considering that websites were, for quite some time, almost exclusively created in the Anglophone world and originally in English (Pym 2011). Traditionally, website localization goes from English to the languages of the world's major markets. However, languages such as Chinese, Japanese and Korean have become important players in web-based industries. Increasingly, websites in those languages are localized into English and other globally important languages (so the traditional directionality is often reversed, see Schäler 2006 for early reflections on this process). These localized versions may serve as start texts from which other locales are generated.

Moreover, the very nature of localization makes it possible to theorize that indirect translation (broadly defined as a translation of a translation and not just a translation via a third language) has become part and parcel of localization since the early 1990s. It was then that many software developers stopped seeing localization as an afterthought when creating their products and the internationalization and reuse of previous translations became increasingly common (Schäler 2010), allowing for the simultaneous localization of content in a number of different locales (known as the **simship model**). Our rationale behind this proposal is that the constant reuse of previous translations can be treated as translating from translations: bits from previous translations are reused to make localization more efficient. For its part, internationalization, which is very much about preparing an intermediary version, can be treated as translating with a further translation in mind, whereby the subsequent translation needs to be thought about very early on in the process. This preparation for (further) translation does not only happen at the level of verbal components (e.g., writing the source text in a way that facilitates the work of subsequent translators). It also happens at the level of non-verbal components (e.g., graphics and layout need to be readily adaptable to further contexts).

Localization processes

Localization is often described as a multi-step process that includes more than just translating words (Schäler 2010; Pym 2013). Every localization project has its own specificities, but most projects share core stages. How these stages are labelled and classified varies substantially. Here, we are adopting and expanding on the terminology and taxonomy from Valdez (2019), and we complement it with insights from Esselink (2000), Google (n.d.), LISA (2003), O'Hagan and Mangiron (2013), Pym (2013) and Schäler (2010).

Pre-translation phase or pre-localization phase

In this phase, the pre-localization team develops the product and writes the source text. Before they send them for actual localization, the product and the source text are analysed and prepared with internationalization in mind. The aim is to anticipate and address challenges that can appear during the later stages of localization into many different languages so that the product can be successfully used in languages other than the original. Key aspects to be considered and sorted out at this stage are summarized below.

Market analysis

The pre-localization team needs to decide which markets to launch products into. Local markets are therefore analysed to understand if a particular product will be appealing to a particular group of users in a given territory. For instance, if we want to launch a tablet app for teenage girls, at this stage we might want to check if teenage girls typically have access to a tablet in a given locale. They may only use smartphones or they may not have access to electronic devices at all. Market analysis is tightly linked to the development of the product.

Language tiering

Based on marketing insights, decisions are made about the languages into which a product will be translated. This is called language tiering, whereby languages are grouped and ordered hierarchically depending on how important a particular market is to a given product at a given time. If a hierarchy includes five tiers, Tier 1 will correspond to languages with the highest priority for a given product. Factors considered at this stage often include the number of speakers, the number of potential internet users, how big and wealthy the local economy is, etc. For instance, Portuguese has many more speakers than Danish, but the Danish economy is wealthier, hence potentially more lucrative than the economy of some regions where Portuguese is spoken. The internet connection may also be problematic for certain users of Portuguese localized versions (e.g., in Lusophone Africa or in Brazil). So, a profit-driven company that wants to launch a web-based app may prefer to prioritize Danish over Portuguese (or a particular variety of Portuguese). However, for a freelance photographer based in Colombia who has a chance of offering her services in Brazil (where Portuguese is the official language), Brazilian Portuguese is more likely to be Tier 1 (not Danish).

The decision about which language to use as a pivot can be taken at this stage, and Tier 1 languages may be likely candidates to serve as mediating languages. At present, indirect translation is most commonly applied to content developed in a language other than English (LOTE for short) so that this content can be localized into multiple languages with the English version typically serving as the pivot. For many Japanese game developers/publishers, American English has traditionally been Tier 1 and, at the same time, the most common mediating language because this market tended to make the largest revenue. However, the situation is starting to change, and American English may stop being the default pivot for Japanese gamers (O'Hagan 2022). This is because China has recently surpassed the US as the largest game consuming market (2020 Newzoo report, cited in Wijman 2020). The increasing prominence of Chinese may lead to a change in the traditional language hierarchy of the game localization ecosystem. For Asian games commercialized in Asia, this may entail less indirect translation and a shift away from English as the main pivot language (O'Hagan 2022).

The degree to which a product is localized may also be decided at the pre-translation phase. Localization into languages considered of lesser commercial importance can be partial or non-existent, thereby potentially minimizing users' access to a given content (Pym 2011; Schäler 2010). This, in turn, can exacerbate the imbalance between globally more central and less peripheral languages. For instance, if English language content is to be localized, often the first-tier languages are the so-called FIGS (French, Italian, German and Spanish). This can mean that, for the (European) French, Italian, German and Spanish locales, all content will be localized. If Polish, Greek and Slovak are the Tier 2 languages for this product, they may not be entirely localized because they are not considered a priority. The users in these locales may be forced to use a product where a part of the text to which they have access is in the pivot language and other parts are in their own language. A case in point is a Japan-designed software that has Help Files and FAQs available only in Spanish (the pivot language) and system messages in Portuguese (the final language). This can mean that the user experience in these more peripheral locales will not be entirely satisfying and/or the product may not be accessible to all in its entirety.

Internationalization

To minimize the risk of having to expensively redevelop their product for every locale, pre-localization teams (engineers/user interface designers) need to make sure that the product is flexible enough to adapt to different (mediating and final) languages. They therefore write code and create layouts that support different languages. In a sense, they create an intermediary, internationalized version (Pym 2014). Essentially, this version is to be as language and culture neutral as possible. It is supposed to be independent from such features as specific language/character set encoding (e.g., writing direction), specific cultural conventions (e.g., formatting, see Example 4.1), grammar rules (e.g., plurals, gender, etc., see Example 4.2) because those are the features that are most likely to cause issues downstream. The rationale is that, later in the localization process, references, colours, images, etc. can be added so as to render the internationalized content more appealing to users from given locales (Pym 2014).

Example 4.1

English: The song "Yellow Submarine"
Polish: Piosenka „Yellow Submarine"
Portuguese: Canção «Yellow Submarine»

> **Example 4.2**
>
> English: Do you like summer?
> Spanish: ¿Te gusta el verano?

At this stage, all data is stored in a language and country neutral format. To handle language/culture-specific differences, internationalization teams/programmers use special programming toolkits, which are often termed internationalization libraries. These libraries store all localization data (e.g., about formatting, script writing, grammar rules, etc.). Thanks to these libraries, the content can be automatically adapted to the rules and conventions of the different languages in the pivot workflows.

Controlled language

Controlled languages are rules that apply when the aim is to write source content with localization in mind (O'Brien 2003). These rules aim to avoid lexical ambiguity and complex grammatical structures and are very much in line with the recommendations on translator-friendly writing outlined in the chapter on scientific and technical translation. The ultimate goal of a controlled language is to make sure that the source content is more translatable into various languages and easy to understand, thus also easy to be processed by a machine translation system or translation memories. This way, content creators help maximize consistency and the reuse of different text segments, thus minimizing translation costs and facilitating quality control. Controlled language is often applied at the level of vocabulary and grammar. It is aimed at specific fields or companies and is closely related to pre-editing (O'Brien 2003).

Pre-editing

Apart from fixing typographical errors or mistakes in the source content, pre-editing is about splitting long sentences, using simplified word orders and consistent terminology, and marking terms that need to be kept in the original form in all locales (for instance, concept names). Pre-editing can be done entirely by human translators or it can be done automatically by specialized software (e.g., Acrolinx). Such software helps pre-edit by adding terminological, grammatical or stylistic rules to a database that is then run in the source text (e.g., gender inclusive language that is inviting to all applicants) (Koponen 2016).

All the previous considerations should affect the way the source text is produced and usually precede the preparation of the translation project.

Testing internationalization

Once the pre-localization team (e.g., engineers/programmers) has designed their product with internationalization in mind, their work is tested. One way of testing if the internationalized version can be successfully translated into further languages is called pseudotranslation (sometimes also pseudolocalization). In pseudotranslation, engineers/programmers replace strings within digital content with strings that contain the characters of the different target languages (ideally, both the pivot and final languages). This strategy makes it possible to detect and fix problems that have not been sufficiently foreseen and addressed during the design of the internationalized version (e.g., a part of the text may have been left in the original language or there may not be enough space to display the translated version). When these issues are fixed, the product is sent to the localization project manager.

Localization kit

The localization project manager prepares the project for actual localization, often in collaboration with the product team and different language managers. They review the project specifications and assign team members. They also create a localization kit that will be sent to the translators and reviewers producing both the pivot and final translations. Typically, such a kit contains all the material to be translated/reviewed as well as extensive reference material, such as:

- *Style guides*. These documents include general guidelines on how to translate a specific project. For instance, a style guide can specify the register and tone that the translation needs to use in a specific content. These can differ across languages. For example, an English language user may expect to be addressed in a semi-formal register, so the pivot version will try to adhere to this expectation. However, the users of a Slavic language version of the same product may expect to be addressed more formally, and the guidelines should include this indication. Style guides may also include specifications on how to improve the content (including the pivot source text) to facilitate further translation.
- *Source references*. Other documentation that helps provide context for translators (screenshots, demo versions, app descriptions, mocks).
- *Terminology databases*. If the client does not provide their own glossary, the language project manager creates a multilingual glossary for all the languages involved. This glossary includes terminology that needs to be consistent throughout and in all locales (e.g., industry-specific terminology). The glossary may also indicate terms that need to be left in the original language or in the mediating language (also called DNTs, as in "do not translate"). All terms are accompanied by a short definition. The glossary is typically in a spreadsheet, and it is uploaded to a terminology management tool.
- *Translation memories*. These are databases that contain all the previously translated segments for a given product. If properly prepared, such memories help translators work more efficiently (minimizing time spent on searches for a good match) and keep consistency throughout the translated

content. Translation memories are usually bilingual only, but some CAT tools allow for the inclusion of multiple languages in a project, with indications on what languages work as pivots.
- *Source files prepared for localization.* Test plans, project outline and milestones: these provide details on the workflow, the deliverables, stakeholders' responsibilities, relevant contact details, etc. They often include tips for translators and revisers on how to share feedback on problems found during the testing phase. Sometimes they provide indications on how to work around these issues. In localization, changes in certain pivot localized versions that were not planned ahead might lead to changes in other, subsequent locales. Therefore, translators have to know clearly whether they can intervene and what the process for feedback would be.

Brainstorming session

Before finalizing the localization toolkit, the localization project manager may want to schedule a brainstorming session with translators and revisers. Such a session may help break the ice and clarify who is who—for example, who creates and revises the pivot version(s) and the final language versions. It can also be used to finetune terminology, anticipate translation challenges, share good practices, and explain the scope of the project.

Translation phase or localization phase

After all this preparation, the localization project is finally being executed. The translators can finally start translating. They do that according to the guidelines specified in the instructions, in the project order document, or simply in an email.

Translatable elements

In localization projects, these are the elements that may require translation.

> **Translatable elements**
>
> - Main body of the text (also known as content text): for example, the narrative passages in a video game or the description of a product displayed on a website.
> - Text embedded in graphics.
> - Audio and cinematic assets: for instance, videos within a game, video tutorials for a specific tool. These may need to be subtitled, dubbed, voiced-over, audio described, etc.

- Materials for marketing: materials that promote the service or product (in the gaming industry these are collectively called box and docs): game boxes, adds, newsletters, banners.
- Instruction manuals and HELP files (i.e., instructions on how to install software, FAQs, troubleshooting manuals).
- User interface (typically abbreviated as UI), as specified below.
- Website title (visible at the top of the web browser).
- Keywords and descriptors, i.e., elements that briefly describe the aim of localized content so that it is more likely to be found by search engines. This process is termed search engine optimization (SEO). As part of SEO, target language options are tested (in terms of their visibility in search engines) with, for example, Google Analytics. The most efficient results are chosen as keywords for specific locales. It is risky to assume that a keyword that proved successful for a pivot locale will be equally effective for a later locale, as these will differ depending on the culture.
- Hyperlinks and menus (which help navigate online content, leading to other locations, websites, images).
- System messages (e.g., "Autosave has been disabled". Typically, these are very platform specific).
- Dialogue windows (small boxes that communicate information to the user and prompt their response (e.g., "Press OK to continue").

Degrees of localization

The degree of localization varies, as does the way we classify this degree. According to Chandler (2005), there are four levels of video game localization.

Degrees of video game localization

No localization: a game is not localized at all. For instance, it can be very specific to its original market and will not be appealing to other language audiences. It may also be that a game cannot support the features of other language systems. The localization of such a game would entail substantial rebuilding, which, in turn, could be unsustainable from a financial point of view.

Box and docs localization: the marketing materials and packaging are localized but the game itself is not.

Partial localization: for example, when labels on images (e.g., maps) are not translated and they appear in the original or pivot language. Therefore, the language of the original (or the mediating language version) can be visible to the user of a different language version.

Full localization: e.g., spoken dialogues are re-voiced (using voiceover or dubbing) and images are created from scratch or adapted to the locale.

In turn, when considering websites, Singh and Pereira (2005) outline five degrees of localization.

> **Degrees of website localization**
>
> *Standardized*: one version of a website for all users worldwide.
> *Semi-localized*: one website displays several translated sections (e.g., the contact page) to cater for the needs of different language communities.
> *Localized*: for each locale, there is one translated site where most of the content is localized.
> *Highly localized*: not only has the content been translated but the website structure has also been adapted to the target market (for example, a URL is country specific or locally important content is foregrounded).
> *Culturally customized*: the culture-specific adaptations are extensive and deep, bordering on a complete regeneration (e.g., the product display and campaign make the website look as if it was a local business).

To what degree the product is localized depends on various factors and is closely related to language tiering and market analysis. The degree of localization may also result in different types of indirectness for different locales. For example, the game *Final Fantasy XV* (Square Enix 2016) was originally developed in Japanese. As explained by O'Hagan (2022):

> the game was voiced in Japanese, and English, French and German, which were all directly translated from Japanese with Korean and Chinese (Simplified and Traditional) subtitled based on the Japanese VO. The English voice scripts were used to subtitle into Russian, Brazilian Portuguese, Italian, European Spanish (non-voiced assets were translated directly from Japanese into these languages) […]. However, non-voiced texts for Italian and European Spanish were directly translated from Japanese.

For more details, see Tobe (2018).

A constantly evolving original

Just because translation has started, it does not necessarily mean that the original version is complete. Both the original, the mediating translation and the final translation are subject to constant change. This can be illustrated by situations where publishers release games knowing there are bugs that need to be corrected. After the game is launched, publishers fix these games through the so-called day-one patches that correct the bugs and reach all users who purchased the initial product in a given language.

Another example of constantly evolving content is situations where a game developer markets their game in several languages and, afterwards, releases an updated version. When preparing an updated version, the game developer will not rewrite or translate the entirety of the content (all the narrative passages, the audio and cinematic assets, the game boxes, the installation instructions, the FAQ, etc.) (Pym 2014; Schäler 2010). This would be too time consuming and financially unviable. Instead, the game developer needs to identify and isolate all the modifications that need to be translated. For this, the content is divided into small bits that can be modified later. In further translations, these bits are then reassembled and translated accordingly. The project manager needs to keep track of what has been added, erased or modified, making sure that all these changes are reflected downstream so that all language versions can be updated accordingly. For instance, if any string is modified in the original, the content in the pivot language and the different target languages needs to be modified, too. Subsequent translations also contribute to the instability of the original. For instance, when one of the translators detects problems in the source (e.g., at the level of grammar or visuals), the original (and other translations) may need to be corrected accordingly.

Tools

In some workflows, translators can work on a simple word processor or spreadsheet. However, they often use advanced, dedicated technologies, which ensure that the final translation complies with the style guide and terminology requirements. These technologies include machine translation engines, terminology databases or translation memories, which help generate raw translations (semi-)automatically. Instead of creating a translation from scratch, translators need to accept translation suggestions or post-edit the raw output.

Some technologies make it possible for translators to access the communication act using preview (e.g., where exactly and how their translations will appear on the screen). However, this access cannot always be taken for granted. In some configurations, the translation is blindfolded (see below).

To keep track of all the modifications (and the rest of the content that is reused almost intact), content management systems are used. There are many such systems currently available on the market, and many are still struggling to propose solutions that facilitate the handling of the pivot localization process. Ideally, if any changes occur in the original language, such a system should automatically signal changes that might also be needed in the pivot language and in all the subsequent target languages. Otherwise, pivot localization processes can become very confusing to handle. For an example of a content management system with such a pivot language functionality, see Figure 8.2 in the chapter on project management.

Essentially, content management systems provide translators with isolated sequences of words (e.g., phrases, sentences) that are meant to be translated. These sequences are often called "translatables" or "translatable strings". This is why an important part of translation work within the localization industry is about rendering bits that represent additions, modifications or updates, rather than rendering the entire internationalized versions of websites, games, software, etc.

In many workflows, the target text segments on which the translators will be working are already automatically pre-filled by matches from a translation memory and/or raw machine translation outputs. If needed, translators can edit these pre-filled segments (e.g., they can split or merge with surrounding segments). However, such editing might be seen as counterproductive if the text in the pre-filled segments was previously approved. With raw machine-translated segments, there is often a need for post-editing to achieve the desired quality. However, post-editing might not be suitable for scenarios involving low-resource languages. Low-resource machine translation is still in its infancy. The quality of raw output may be so low that post-editing is not worth the effort and translation will be of higher quality and produced faster if done from scratch. What is more, it is important to have access to the source text when post-editing, especially when it comes to translation accuracy (Koponen 2016; Nitzke and Hansen-Schirra 2021). This is because, in neural machine translation (the mainstream paradigm currently used in the industry), content errors are difficult to identify, as the raw output is fluent and therefore seemingly correct. Post-editing combined with indirect translation thus represents an extra risk.

Raw machine translation outputs might also be substandard in the case of creative texts such as video games. As suggested by Guerberof-Arenas and Toral (2020), creativity is highest when translation is carried out by professional translators without the involvement of machine translation. However, the same study indicates that, when it comes to the audience's enjoyment, the difference between a human translation and a post-edited machine translation is marginal. All this means that, in the case of creative content (e.g., video games) originally developed in (or localized into) low-resource languages, post-editing may be an acceptable solution, but it needs to be approached with extra care.

Translatable strings

Sequences of words that are meant to be translated are surrounded by a computer code (e.g., HTML), which takes the form of words or strings of characters, etc. (as per Example 4.3). These are called tags. Tags define where a text appears on screen, what colour it is, whether it is accompanied by an image, whether it appears as a link, etc. In turn, placeholders are bits that are to be replaced by fixed strings of text. They temporarily replace the final data that will be displayed to the user. For instance, in the string in Example 4.3, both %1 and %0 are placeholders. %1 represents the total number of pages to be printed and %0 represents the exact page that is being printed when this UI string goes live. Both placeholders are replacing the final information (precise value numbers) that the user will see on their screen.

> **Example 4.3**
>
> Printing page %0 / %1

If the tag is modified, then the way the final product (webpage, software, game) looks and functions will be modified too. Therefore, a wide range of tools can be used to separate "translatables" from the "untranslatables".

The text surrounding the placeholder will often need to be modified, depending on the input of the user. For example, if, in an online booking form, a placeholder replaces a number in a string of text (e.g., the number of rooms being booked), the translator will need to correctly translate the noun that follows the placeholder, using the correct plural pattern: in English, "1 room", "2 rooms"; in Polish "1 pokój", "2 pokoje"; in Portuguese "1 quarto", "2 quartos", etc. The aim is to ensure that the final product is grammatically correct in the final locale.

Parallel work

In an ideal scenario, translations into different language sets are carried out at roughly the same time. This simultaneous work by different translation teams helps maximize coherence between different language versions. This parallel work also contributes to the streamlining of marketing efforts so that the product can be launched and promoted without large time gaps in different locales. However, it may be that, in certain pivot configurations (post-gold models), some language versions take longer to be produced and released, often to the frustration of users. For example, as shown in O'Hagan and Mangiron (2013, 233) and O'Hagan (2022), in the case of *Final Fantasy XIII*, the Japanese version was released in December 2009, the North American versions and FIGS (French, Italian, German and European Spanish) versions (with subtitles translated from the American English voiced text) were released in March 2010, and the version in traditional Chinese (with subtitles translated directly from the Japanese voiced text) was not released until May 2010.

Revision

Once the translation is complete, the translator self-revises the files. Then, it is time for a reviser to check the target text against the source text(s). The reviser's job is to ensure that the quality of the translations meets the client's expectations. In cases where translators and revisers work for different language service providers, consultancy with in-house language specialists (sometimes called language consultants or managers) may be needed. Self- or third-party verification often focuses on the translation's accuracy and its contextual and cultural appropriateness (Valdez 2019). In the case of pivot translations, it is important that the mediating translation is continually revised in order to reflect changes introduced in the later versions or in the original. An open channel between the revisers of different language versions may also be helpful in guaranteeing a certain level of coherence between different locales.

After all the revisions, the translator submits the translation to the project manager. Apart from the actual target text, the translator also delivers the output file of the computer-assisted tool in which the source and target text are saved (the so-called bilingual file), an updated translation memory and a quality control report (Valdez 2019, 120). These additional materials will help enhance further work on the source texts, the pivot version and further translations.

Post-translation phase or post-localization phase

This final stage focuses on quality control procedures and can entail substantial engineering and testing. After the different language versions are revised, the content is reassembled and holistically tested (Schäler 2010). The focus is now on the complete product (not only the translations). This is when the different locales are thoroughly checked for appearance, linguistic and functional bugs, etc. The rationale is that even the best internationalization cannot foresee and avoid all the problems that the translations may potentially cause (Jiménez-Crespo 2009). According to Valdez (2019, 120–121), this phase consists of four stages, which are summarized in the box.

1) *Linguistic quality inspection.* A language specialist revises content or files in terms of terminology, country standards, project guidelines, customer-specific requirements, etc.
2) *Build or desktop publishing.* If the translation is to be displayed on a website, software, app, or is part of another type of non-static, online-based content, it undergoes a process called "the build". During this process, the translated content is adapted into the software program by an engineer for each locale (Valdez 2019, 121). Alternatively, the target text can undergo a process called desktop publishing, whereby a master copy is created in portable document format (PDF). This process is deployed in the case of target texts that are meant to serve as a printable file (a leaflet, packaging material) or web or online-based content (e.g., online manuals).
3) *Localization testing* (sometimes called engineering quality assurance or linguistic sign-off). Following the build or desktop publishing, the translated content is verified in its final media, such as a PDF file or on the actual app. If the translated content is to be published in the form of a leaflet, then the focus during this stage will be on problems related to language, layout, and consistency between what we see on the leaflet and on the corresponding online product. If the target text is to be part of a video game, the translation may be checked for language quality, formatting

problems (including truncation or incorrect mirroring), synchronization between the image and audio, etc.
4) *Country-approval validation.* At the very end of the post-localization phase, a linguist (e.g., an in-house reviser working closely with the client) needs to approve the final version of the translated content. For this, they check the detailed specifications provided by the client and consider them against the specific requirements of the locale (Valdez 2019, 121). For instance, in Europe, using the term "free" is now forbidden for many digital services (such as cloud services or social media) (EC 2018). This is because, even if consumers do not need to pay for these digital services, they need to provide their personal data. Service providers then use these data to make money. So, to have "free" access to these digital services, consumers "pay" with their data. This is a legal matter that affects the way the term is translated into many European languages. It is the legal team who decides how "free" can be translated into these languages, and the reviser needs to validate this translation.

During all these substages, except for the build and desktop publishing, quality control is done directly in the translated files. Alternatively, quality control can be done on a scorecard, i.e., a file where all modifications are marked (Valdez 2019, 121). In an ideal scenario, the translator's approval should be sought for each revision throughout this stage (as per Figure 4.2). If the translator rejects a revision, they should provide the reasoning behind their decision. Such translator-reviser negotiations are often mediated by the project manager (as will be discussed in Chapter 8). Once they reach a final version, the translator incorporates all the agreed revisions into the bilingual file. Only when the product is quality assured can it be released in different locales.

Multiprofessional cooperation

As should be clear by now, it takes a village to localize content. In professional environments, localization projects include all sorts of professionals: engineers, software developers, programmers, product designers, market analysts, project managers, language specialists, etc. Although translation proper is handled by translators (during one of the substeps of project execution, here called the localization or translation phase), questions related to strategic planning—including indirect translation—are addressed and decided on in earlier stages (during the pre-localization or pre-translation phase), at the level of product preparation (particularly language tiering and internationalization) and project preparation.

This means that such questions as whether to translate indirectly, how to prepare content for translation into multiple languages, what to translate indirectly and how (via what language, using machine translation or not, with subtitles directly from

94 Localization

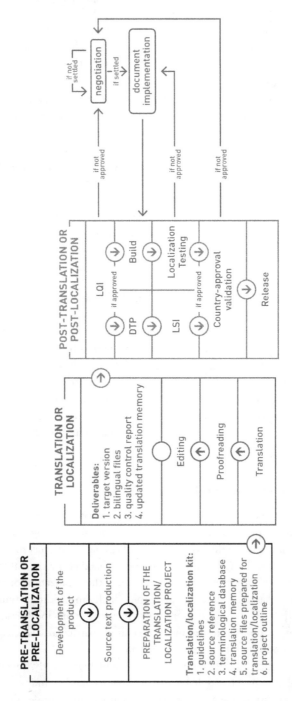

FIGURE 4.2 Localization process (from Valdez 2019)

the original voiced text or indirectly through other subtitles, with which rules for durations, text size, line breaks and reading speed, etc.) are typically not part of the translator's responsibilities. Rather, these questions are handled by professionals who do not necessarily have a background in translation, although they directly impact on the quality of the pivot version and final translations. It may therefore make sense for indirect translators to participate in decision-making processes happening upstream, all the way to the stages of product design and project preparation.

Challenges brought about by localization processes and ways to go about them

In addition to the many constraints outlined earlier in this book, localization involves other complex challenges. Below you will find several tips for key practices that may help improve the quality of the localization process. These tips draw and expand on a number of sources coming from industry and academic research (Brandall 2018; Esselink 2000; IGDA 2011–2012; Google n.d.; Jiménez-Crespo 2009; Méndez González and Calvo-Ferrer 2017; O'Hagan and Mangiron 2013). For reasons explained above, these tips often relate to not only what happens during the translation or localization phase but also to what happens at the level of pre-translation or pre-localization.

Product names

Some brand names bring about unintended connotations, even if they seem innocuous to many. If companies are not farsighted enough to avoid this unfortunate situation and act upon it early on (e.g., by renaming the product), the problem will need to be solved downstream in the localization process (by someone in the translation team) when the cost could be higher. One of the most notorious examples of how things can go wrong when translation is not considered early on relates to Mazda's "Laputa" minivan launched in 1991. The name was meant to make the client think of the island in *Gulliver's Travels*. The Japanese brand did not experience many problems on the translation front when launching the car in English language territories. Indeed, the name did not raise any red flags in English. However, the name caused issues downstream, as it was entirely inappropriate in Spanish ("la puta" means "the prostitute" in Spanish). The problem was further exacerbated by the accompanying ad, which reportedly announced that "Laputa is designed to deliver maximum utility in a minimum space while providing a smooth, comfortable ride" and "a lightweight, impact-absorbing body" (Mazda 2004).

Changing size

Digital content (such as applications and web pages) can be designed from the outset to be flexible enough to allocate space that is required to display certain graphics and texts. Such flexibility makes it possible to contract or expand different

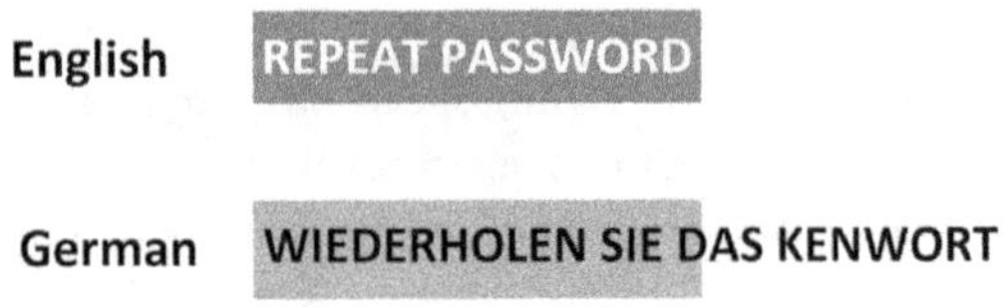

96 Localization

English   REPEAT PASSWORD

German   WIEDERHOLEN SIE DAS KENWORT

FIGURE 4.3 Language length problems for button display

areas. However, despite such flexibility of digital domains, many translators still need to work within the space limits that are built into the material they are asked to translate, as some elements impose their own limits in terms of space. Translators need to consider changes in size when text strings are to appear in dialogue boxes, menu entries, or as window titles or labels for buttons.

Translating text strings will make no sense if, in the localized version, there is not enough space to display them. The final user will simply not be able to read them because they will not fit onto the button, as illustrated in Figure 4.3.

Making decisions about the space allocated to a certain string on the basis of the pivot language might be misleading. Therefore, you may want to plan for extra space or opt for shorter words. As a rule of thumb, layouts in English should allow for twice as much text in other languages. Moreover, the fewer words and characters in English you use, the more likely it is that your text will expand in translation.

If the pre-localization team does not prepare for the text to grow beyond the pivot language version, further translators' options often become very limited. These translators will not have enough space to fit in a suitable translation and will have to keep the word untranslated (in English) or use one that makes little sense. This will negatively impact on users' experience and, in the long run, how they interact and engage with the content. It may also exacerbate the inequality between languages and cultures: we may be imposing English-centric norms on local languages instead of letting these languages explore the full range of their resources (Pym 2013).

Mind the images

As mentioned earlier in this book, images are not universal. They can thus create a challenge in localization. Ideally, images should be purely pictorial (they should not contain words at all). However, this is not always realistic. If a specific word needs to be associated with a specific image, it is important to create a "translatable" layer of text that can be overlaid on the image. This way, the translators will be able to access the localizable string with standard localization tools and translate it accordingly while leaving the image intact. If this is not done, the users will see images with pivot-language text in them.

If, for some reason, it is impossible to extract text from the image, the same image can be created in every language in which the user interface will be available.

FIGURE 4.4 Different ways of indicating the number three in Polish, Japanese and Portuguese

Alternatively, the pre-localization team can write two distinct versions of the same content: one version will make a reference to the image, the other will not. Depending on the final targeted language, these images can then be hidden or replaced.

This strategy will be useful even in the case of purely pictorial images, as they can carry different meanings in different parts of the globe. This can be illustrated with the example in Figure 4.4 where the number three is conveyed through a different gesture in European Portuguese (right), Japanese (centre) and Polish (left). If this number is to be portrayed with an image or an icon on a webpage (say, to indicate that the user is at stage three of the enrolment procedure), the image needs to be replaced depending on the locale.

Mind the colours

Colours have different meanings and suggest different connotations depending on the culture. If you are not mindful of this, you may accidentally discourage users from engaging with your product. For example, while red often signifies passion in Western cultures, in China it symbolizes luck and prosperity (this is why a bride wears red) and in South Africa it is associated with mourning. Furthermore, in some stock markets in Asia, red is used to indicate a rise in stock prices, but in the North American and European markets it indicates the opposite. It may also be that a colour itself is innocuous, but it adheres a specific meaning when combined with symbols. Therefore, it is important to guarantee that colours can be manipulated according to the market being targeted.

Strings

As mentioned, developers split sentences into several segments and batch them together using placeholders (this is known as concatenation). In such scenarios, the word order is hard coded. Splitting sentences into bits and batching these segments together presupposes certain grammar rules and sentence structures. The problem is that grammar structures differ according to the language.

Take, for instance, modifiers. In English, the modifier typically comes before the noun ("strange things"), but in many Romance languages, such as Portuguese, the order is reversed ("coisas estranhas"). If the developer fixes the structure (imposing

98 Localization

that the modified has to come before the noun), Portuguese translators cannot adjust it to their language needs by changing the word order. This is obviously a recipe for a translation disaster.

For this reason, developers should ideally create strings that are complete sentences. Using placeholders that the translator can work around will also be very helpful, as long as the developer explains what each placeholder stands for and gives the translator the flexibility to modify the word order if need be. Breaking strings into bits that are too small will also be problematic with issues related to name conventions. For instance, the distinction between a given name and a surname depicted in the string in Example 4.4.

Example 4.4

Dear [user:given_name],

Such a string is commonly used in automated emails, whereby "[user:given_name]" stands for the given name of the email recipient. When an email with this type of placeholder is sent, the system automatically replaces the placeholder with the given name of the recipient.

The problem is that the distinction between given name and surname is again very Anglocentric, and it can easily lead to poor results if translated into other languages. Table 4.1 provides a snapshot of just how different name formats can be.

Sometimes, the best solution is to create one single field/string (e.g., one that contains a full name) instead of creating a vast array of variants. This way, the final translators will not need to adhere to the conventions of the pivot culture, and they will be able to adjust them to the requirements of their own culture.

Another example associated with this potential challenge are the titles Dr, Ms, Mrs, etc. In Portuguese, there is no distinction between Ms and Mrs, but Eng. (which stands for engineer) is used in addition to Dr. This lack of direct correspondence between the English pivot and the Portuguese language is problematic

TABLE 4.1 Name conventions according to different locales

Language community	Standard name convention
English-speaking locales	Given name & surname (sometimes there is also a place for maiden/middle name)
France, Hungary, Japan, Korea, the Netherlands	Surname & given name
Portuguese-speaking locales	Given name & second name & maternal surname & paternal surname
Spanish-speaking locales	Given name & paternal surname & maternal surname

Localization **99**

FIGURE 4.5 Incorrect localization into Hebrew

when it comes to placeholders. The client must be informed that they need to delete certain titles and add others.

Mind the reading conventions

As a rule of thumb, webpage design will place the most important menus and buttons where the users are most likely to see them in the first instance. According to Nielson (2006), English language users start navigating from the top left, and they look across the page horizontally. This is why, in the case of English (and many other European languages), it makes sense to place the most noteworthy elements on the left (as an example, see Figure 4.1, where "Introduction" is placed in the top left-hand corner). However, in the case of languages that are read from right to left (Arabic, Farsi, Hebrew, Urdu, etc.), the most significant elements need to be placed on the right. The way in which the target language is read needs to be considered not merely during the translation phase but much earlier, i.e., during the production of the actual original.

The language and its writing system need to be considered early on, during the website's design, because they greatly affect the organization of the page layout. So, an app that is targeted at users from both Hungary and Israel needs to be built in such a way that the user interface can accommodate scripts that go in both directions (left to right and right to left). If a possible change in the writing system is not anticipated at the level of product preparation, the interface may not be correctly mirrored for users who read from right to left. This is illustrated in Figure 4.5, where the Hebrew localized version should read 400 million downloads (not 004). At the same time, the accompanying documentation (e.g., online help, video tutorials) needs to avoid layout-specific expressions (such as "the menu on the right") because these are likely to cause mistakes downstream. In these situations, having a pivot version with a different direction layout than the source text might help in the further translation process.

Mind the numbers

If an app or website is to be internationalized, close attention needs to be paid to conventions related to number formatting. How numbers are formatted depends on the region. For instance, in an English text, 2.999 kg is just about three kilogrammes. But, in a Spanish text, it means almost three thousand kilogrammes. If

TABLE 4.2 Examples of different postcodes

Country	Postcode (example)
Japan	163 8001
Netherlands	2311 CT
Poland	46 043
Portugal	1700-299
UK	IV11 8YP
US	85705

these numerical sequences are not properly localized, users will likely be confused. It is therefore important to remember that the symbol that separates decimals is not the same in every language. Neither is the way we group numbers. Some languages use commas (22,222,222), others decimal points (22.222.222), and there are also those that use spaces (22 222 222).

Another example we can give here is related to postcodes. Countries such as Argentina, Canada, Ireland, the Netherlands, Malta and the UK use alphanumeric postcodes (combining both letters and numbers), whereas many others use postcodes with numerical values only. This is illustrated in Table 4.2.

If a webform designed in Japan is localized without enough care, it may be able to accept US data for the American pivot locale, but it will not be able to accept Dutch data, since the webform will only accommodate numbers in the postcode field.

Other numerical sequences you need to pay careful attention to include date formats (22.02.2022 or 02.22.2022; 5 October, 5th October or October 5), time formats (15h30, 15:30 or 3:30 pm), currency values (€25, 25 €), etc. In all these instances, it is good to request access to localizable strings. This way, numbers will not be hard coded, and you will be able to decide what exactly needs to be changed for your language (order of numbers, layout, punctuation, symbol position, etc.). It is also useful to store all dates and times in an ISO format and make use of a library in order to format these dates and times for the given locale. It will also help to convert the time to different time zones.

Constant modifications to the original and pivot versions

As mentioned earlier in this chapter, the source and pivot texts can be updated or patched due to constant updates and revisions. For this reason, terminology creation and tagging should be as structured as possible. Ideally, everyone working on the project should have an idea of what the project is as a whole and where it is heading. By everyone, we mean the pre-localization team; the localization team, including those producing and revising the pivot and final translations; and the post-localization team.

Brainstorming at an initial stage is one of the possible techniques to ensure overall coherence. Sometimes, instead of working as a group, translators can break down into specialized teams and propose the brainstorming results to the group. This technique allows for discarded ideas to be kept as backups, which can be used if necessary.

Moreover, arguments in favour of or against a given terminology highlight the reasons for naming decisions (e.g., whether to translate the name of a character in a game and how). In this case, general rules or discussed exceptions should be recorded. This way, these decisions are already justified and can be a starting point for translators working into other languages.

The overall tracking of decisions for several languages would allow translators the freedom to make informed decisions on whether to follow the logic behind the source text or behind one of the pivot languages.

The challenge is to keep track of all these decisions in a multilingual process. Traditionally, we have relied on adding unique identifiers to the string. Currently, many translation management systems provide tools to automate the process.

Blindfolded translation

In localization projects, translators often work on decontextualized strings. For example, they cannot see how the actual webpage will look or where exactly their translation will be displayed. This lack of access to information about the communication act can be problematic in situations where strings include variables or ambiguous wording. A case in point are the words "contact" and "book". Without knowing the context, how can you tell whether this is meant to be translated as a noun for a label ("kontakt" and "książka" in Polish, "o contacto" and "o livro" in Portuguese, respectively) or a verb for an action button ("skontaktuj się z" and "zarezerwuj" in Polish, "entrar em contacto", and "reserve" in Portuguese). Also, translators may not know how the product works, especially if it is new and not yet released. This is particularly the case for the so-called low-diffusion languages, which are often not prioritized by developers and may therefore wait longer for the product's release than the major languages that work as pivots.

It is important to request access to context. Contextual information can be provided directly in the source files you will be working on. If a translation is being handled in a spreadsheet (e.g., an Excel file), contextual notes can be provided in an additional, dedicated column. If a translation is being handled in text-based code files (such as HTML, JSON or XML), code comments can do the trick. The translators should be given descriptions about what the buttons do so they can localize them according to their function. The product team can provide screenshots showing the actual place on a webpage, access to the UI, or draft web pages (mocks), which can also provide useful details. The pre-localization team or localization project manager should provide translators with style guides on the tone and register and the character limits to be used in the user interface for names in games. For instance, an annotation of this kind could be very helpful: "This is a UI button allowing the user to go to section 2.22. The maximum character limit is 8." Securing open channels of communication between the pre-localization team and translators is crucial. This way, the text to be translated will be displayed with notes that explain the meaning and purpose of the text. In Example 4.5 you can see how, in these strings, "more" can be used in two different ways.

Example 4.5

EN: read more   EN: see more
(displays a full description)   (displays more apps)
PT: ler tudo   PT: mostrar mais
PL: czytaj dalej   PL: pokaż więcej

A message description should indicate to the translator what will happen when the user clicks on the button containing this string. This way, the translator will be able to provide the correct translation for the word "more" in Portuguese or Polish.

Silver linings

Since the original and localized content are constantly updated in the localization industry, translation (including indirect translation) is often part of a long-term maintenance programme (Pym 2014). Potentially, this gives translators the opportunity to gain a better understanding of the product, the pivot workflow and its participants. This knowledge may be used to mitigate the risk involved in the decontextualized ecosystem of translatable strings rendered via a third language. Moreover, extensive planning and consideration of internationalization provide the opportunity to solve problems before they appear.

Further discussion

- *Pivot localization in non-commercial settings.* Consider the pros and cons of pivot localization used in disaster relief (online contact forms), collaborative learning environments (e.g., Khan Academy) and other non-commercial contexts.
- *Indirect translation vs. crowdsourcing, collaborative translation and wikifization.* How do crowdsourcing, collaborative translations and wikifization impact on pivot localization processes? What can pivot localization workflows in the industry learn from these emerging practices?

Activities

Activity 1. Work in a multiprofessional and plurilingual team where the translators are not competent in all the working languages and collaborate to produce a translation via a third common language

Below we outline situations where something went wrong in pivot localization processes. Read them carefully and think about at which (sub)stage of the process these problems should have been anticipated. You may want to check Figure 4.2 for a visual representation of a localization project lifecycle. Some tell-tale clues are provided in the Translation Studies Portal.

SITUATION 1

Look at Figure 4.6. The product with this user interface was originally developed in Japanese. It was first localized into American English and from there into Polish. In the Polish language version, the text in the dialogue window reads "Usunąć ten produkt? [Discard this product?]". The options provided in the second line are exactly the same. This means that two distinct words in English ("discard" and "cancel") are rendered as one and the same word ("usuń"). Problematically, these two buttons serve different purposes. The one on the left gets rid of the text the user is creating. The one on the right closes the dialogue window and brings the user back to the text they are working on.

SITUATION 2

A video game was originally developed for a Polish market. It was then localized for the North American locale, where it became an instant bestseller. This localized version was used as a start text for the Arabic version, but it turned out to be a commercial failure. The gamers in Arabic language territories considered some of the visual and verbal content offensive (nudity, references to pagan gods, etc.). They

FIGURE 4.6 Dialogue window in Polish

also complained about constant delays between pressing buttons and seeing action happening on screen due to poor internet connection.

SITUATION 3

An app originally developed in Chinese is localized for the North American market and from there into FIGS. Users of the FIGS versions are not happy with the online help. The instructions on how to fix issues are difficult to follow because key terms are used inconsistently across different content types (user interface, video tutorials and help documentation).

SITUATION 4

An app is simultaneously produced in Chinese and English as well as other languages. When the Brazilian version is released, it becomes clear that some parts of the help documentation have not been translated but have been left in English. The users are confused and do not fully understand how to solve certain problems.

SITUATION 5

A medical device originally developed by a Chinese company is commercialized across Europe. The instruction manual was first developed in Chinese, then localized for the North American market and from this pivot version into the Danish locale. After the device is released on the Danish market, it becomes clear that the instruction manual has been fully localized into Danish but the labels on the device itself have not. The labels with Chinese characters have been left untouched. Danish operators cannot use the device properly.

SITUATION 6

A video game is simultaneously produced in Polish and English as well as other languages. The game is inspired by a well-established Polish novel, which has been successfully translated into various European and Asian languages. When the game is released in different locales, gamers complain that the characters' names differ from the ones used in the translated novels.

SITUATION 7

A video game designed in China is first localized for the North American market. This locale is then used as a start text for a further translation into European Portuguese. In the Portuguese localized version, a key term (in Chinese: 婚 r, in English: "wedding") is translated as "boda". "Boda" is a very old-fashioned, rarely used Portuguese word. This is why, during the post-localization phase, the Portuguese language specialist disagrees with this translation solution and suggests a more modern term: "casamento". However, "casamento" is too long to fit within the allocated space on the website.

Activity 2. Use the most relevant software to translate from multiple source texts and languages

PART A. Documentation

In this activity, we will zoom in on the video game series *The Witcher* (CD Projekt Red 2007). The game was simultaneously produced in Polish and English as well as other languages. The game was also influenced by established (indirect) translations of *Wiedźmin*, a series of Polish novels by Andrzej Sapkowski. For better contextualization, you may want to watch this 30-minute documentary explaining the behind-the-scenes work of product and localization teams: www.youtube.com/watch?v=Gxg5INjNopo.

Consider the following names of three characters from this video game, in particular the names from the Polish and English language versions (see Table 4.3). Check the links to find out more about the characters. Try to find out what the Polish and English names mean.

PART B. Translation strategies

What do you think? Would the Polish name version work in your language? How about the English version? Do you think it would make sense to translate these names into your language? Why (or why not)?

PART C. Brainstorming

Brainstorm with colleagues who work into your language and/or different languages. Collectively, try to come up with several alternative solutions for the name in English (for the UK and the US locale).

While you do that, record the rationale behind each choice for the benefit of subsequent translators. This way, they will be able to make informed decisions about what to do in their language. For this, you can try using spreadsheets (e.g., Excel) or

TABLE 4.3 Character names for the video game *The Witcher*

Name in the Polish language version	Name in the English language version	More information on this character
Jaskier	Dandelion	witcher.fandom.com/wiki/Dandelion
Płotka	Roach	witcher.fandom.com/wiki/Roach
Bianca	Ves	witcher.fandom.com/wiki/Ves
Janek	Johnny	witcher.fandom.com/wiki/Johnny

a workflow management software. Some online systems offering free trials that you could consider include the following:

- Gridly: www.gridly.com
- XTRF: https://xtrf.eu/
- Projetex: www.projetex.com/

PART D. Testing

Ask a different group of colleagues to analyse the character's name from the original and the English translated versions. Ask them to consider whether they want to keep the Polish and American versions or propose a new name.

PART E. Debrief

What did the second group of colleagues do? Did they use the English version, the Polish version or invent a new one? What did they think about your solutions? Did they serve as a useful starting point or source of inspiration? What did they think about the rationale you provided for each option? Was the spreadsheet or workflow management system you used helpful? How easy was it to track the different language name versions, their back-up alternatives and the rationale behind each solution?

Activity 3. Pre-edit source material for the purpose of potentially improving further translation using appropriate pre-editing techniques

PART A. MT

Find a short text excerpt (around 150 words) in the language in which you can write most easily. Using a machine translation system, translate the source text into a target language that you know well.

PART B. Analyse output

Carefully analyse this raw translation. Identify and explain issues that you can see in the translation. If the raw translation does not present problems, try running the source text through a few different machine translation engines. Links to several machine translation engines are available on the Translation Studies Portal. The output will differ, as each system can perform better or worse depending on many factors (how it was trained, with which data, etc.).

PART C. Pre-edit

Improve the original source text to make it easier to translate with the machine translation engine that created the worst output in Part A or Part B. For pointers on how to do it, reread the section on controlled language and pre-editing (above), as well as the guidelines for translation-friendly writing from the chapter on scientific and technical translation.

PART D. Compare

Run your pre-edited text through the same machine translation engine to generate a translation into the same target language as above. The essentials of writing for translation might be of help here (see the chapter on scientific and technical translation). Analyse the output. Did your edits help fix issues that you identified in Part B? How exactly? Are some of the initial problems still there or have new problems emerged?

> **Resources**: Links to free tips on post-editing. Links to free online machine translation systems and game localization contests.
> **Activities**: Extra activities, tell-tale clues and additional resources for Activity 1.

References

Brandall, Tim. 2018. "Pseudo Localization at Netflix." *The Netflix Techblog*. August 6, https://netflixtechblog.com/pseudo-localization-netflix-12fff76fbcbe [Accessed August 2021].

CD Projekt Red. 2007. *The Witcher*. PC edition, CD project. Microsoft Windows.

Chandler, Heather. 2005. *The Game Localization Handbook*. Hingham, MA: Charles River Media.

EC (European Commission). 2018. "A New Deal for Consumers: Commission Strengthens EU Consumer Rights and Enforcement." https://ec.europa.eu/commission/presscorner/detail/en/IP_18_3041 [Accessed November 2021].

Esselink, Bert. 2000. *A Practical Guide to Localization*. Amsterdam: Benjamins.

Google. n.d. "Udacity Localization Essentials by Google." https://eu.udacity.com/course/localization-essentials--ud610 [Accessed August 2021].

Guerberof-Arenas, and Antonio Toral. 2020. "The Impact of Post-editing and Machine Translation on Creativity and Reading Experience." *Translation Spaces* 9 (2): 255–282.

IGDA Localization SIG. 2011–2012. *Game Localization Best Practices*. http://englobe.com/wp-content/uploads/2012/05/Best-Practices-for-Game-Localization-v21.pdf [Accessed August 2021].

Jiménez-Crespo, Miguel A. 2009 "The Evaluation of Pragmatic and Functionalist Aspects in Localization: Towards a Holistic Approach to Quality Assurance." *IJIAL* 1: 60–93.

Jiménez-Crespo, Miguel A. 2021. "Localization." In *The Routledge Handbook of Translation and Globalization*, edited by Esperança Bielsa and Dionysios Kapsaskis. London: Routledge.

Koponen, Maarit. 2016. "Is Machine Translation Post-Editing Worth the Effort? A Survey of Research into Post-editing and Effort."
The Journal of Specialised Translation 25: 131–148. www.jostrans.org/issue25/art_koponen.pdf.

LISA. 2003. The Localization Industry Primer. 2nd ed. www.immagic.com/eLibrary/ARCHIVES/GENERAL/LISA/L030625P.pdf.

Mangiron, Carme. 2017. "Research in Game Localisation: An Overview." *The Journal of Internationalization and Localization* 4 (2): 74–99.

Mangiron, Carme. 2018. "Game on! Burning Issues in Game Localisation." *Journal of Audiovisual Translation* 1(1): 122–138. https://doi.org/10.47476/jat.v1i1.48.

Maylath, Bruce, and Kirk St. Amant, eds. 2019. *A Guide for Technical and Professional Communicators. Translation and Localization*. London: Routledge.

Mazda. 2004. Newsroom. https://newsroom.mazda.com/en/publicity/release/2001/200104/0424e.html. [Accessed November 2010].

Méndez González, Ramón, and José Ramón Calvo-Ferrer. 2017. *Videojuegos y [para] traducción: aproximación a la práctica localizadora*. Granada: Comares.

Nielson, Jakob. 2006. *F-Shaped Pattern for Reading Web Content*. www.useit.com/alertbox/reading_pattern.html. [Accessed August 2021].

Nitzke, Jean, and Silvia Hansen-Schirra. 2021. *Short Guide to Post-Editing*. Berlin: Language Science Press.

O'Brien, Sharon. 2003. "Controlling Controlled English: An Analytical of Several Controlled Language Rule Sets." In *Proceedings of EAMT-CLAW*, 105–114. Dublin: EAMT.

O'Hagan, Minako. 2022. "Indirect Translation in Game Localization as a Method of Global Circulation of Digital Artefacts: A Socio-economic Perspective." *Target* 34.

O'Hagan, Minako, and Carmen Mangiron. 2013. *Game Localization: Translating for the Global Digital Entertainment Industry*. Amsterdam: John Benjamins.

Peng, Wenqing. 2021. "Video Game Localization as Homecoming in Total War: Three Kingdoms." *The Translator*. DOI: 10.1080/13556509.2021.1923262.

Pym, Anthony. 2011. "Website Localization." In *The Oxford Handbook of Translation Studies*, edited by Kirsten Malmkjaer and Kevin Windle, 410–424. Oxford: Oxford University Press.

Pym, Anthony. 2013. "Localization, Training, and the Threat of Fragmentation." https://usuaris.tinet.cat/apym/on-line/training/2013_localization.pdf (blog). [Accessed November 2021].

Pym, Anthony. 2014. *Exploring Translation Theories*. London: Routledge.

Romero-Fresco, Pablo. 2019. *Accessible Filmmaking: Integrating Translation and Accessibility into the Filmmaking Process*. London: Routledge.

Schäler, Reinhard. 2006. "Reverse Localization." *MultiLingual Magazine* 17 (3): 82.

Schäler, Reinhard. 2010. "Localization and Translation." In *Handbook of Translation Studies Online*, edited by Yves Gambier and Luc van Doorslaer. Amsterdam: Benjamins.

Singh, Nitish, and Arun Pereira. 2005. *The Culturally Customized Web Site: Customizing Web Sites for the Global Marketplace*. Oxford: Elsevier.

Square Enix. 2016. *Final Fantasy XV*. PlayStation 3. Square Enix.

Tobe, Mamiya. 2018. "『ファイナルファンタジーXV』ローカライズって辛えわ。"12言語同時発売"の裏にあった知られざる努力とは？ [Final Fantasy XV: Localization is Challenging: Efforts Behind Simultaneous Releases in 12 Languages]." Accessed December 12, 2020. www.famitsu.com/news/201804/03154859.html.

Valdez, Susana. 2019. *Perceived and Observed Translational Norms in Biomedical Translation in the Contemporary Portuguese Translation Market: A Quantitative and Qualitative Product- And Process-Oriented Study*. Unpublished PhD. University of Lisbon and Gent University.

Wijman, Tom. 2020. "Global Game Revenues Up an Extra $15 Billion This Year as Engagement Skyrockets." Newzoo. https://newzoo.com/insights/articles/game-engagement-during-covid-pandemic-adds-15-billion-to-global-games-market-revenue-forecast/ [Accessed November 2021].

5
LITERARY TRANSLATION

Introduction

Concerned with both popular and canonical literature, this chapter deals with the challenges involved in the different stages of producing literary translations from translated texts and for further translation (including commissioning and revising translations). It will pay particular attention to issues related to cultural awareness, copyright and ethics.

Learning outcomes

Upon successful completion of this chapter, readers will know how to:

- Assess the relevance and accuracy of intermediary versions of a source text.
- Use previous corresponding translations in other languages in a legal, ethical and constructive way.
- Take into account the potential risk of central mediating languages having a domesticating effect.

Warm-up activity

Does the image in Figure 5.1 indicate instances of indirect translation? What ethical challenges may this indirectness present to the translator responsible for the English pivot version? How about the translator of the Portuguese version?

DOI: 10.4324/9781003035220-5

FIGURE 5.1 *Zaproszenie do Moskwy* [Invitation to Moscow] by Zbigniew Stypułkowski in Polish (1951/1977), English (1951) and Portuguese (1952)

Indirect translation and cultural awareness issues

It is an acknowledged fact that the pre-existence of a translation of a literary work in a major language enhances the possibility of a translation from and into a small language, even when the second translation is meant to be direct (Heilbron 1999; Casanova 2004). A book that is a commercial success in one country may prove to be a non-starter in another, so publishers are often anxious about investing in translation and tread carefully. A success in a globally or regionally trendsetting market is known to enhance the prospect of success in other book markets (McMartin 2020). This is why literature in small languages often tends to be translated into English first or regional pivots, e.g., German in Nordic Europe (McMartin 2020). If the English translation fares well and the sales figures are good, the risk of failure in other translation markets appears smaller. English versions are then distributed as reading copies among potential translation rights buyers (e.g., commissioning editors) and success in a trendsetting market—seen as a token of prestige and thus also an important selling point—is often announced in the second translation's promotional material (blurb, publisher's website, etc.).

Since this is a common sequence of events in the book market, literary agents should be aware of the potential distorting effects of using central languages as mediating languages. Historically, the effects of French on foreign texts can be used as an example. From the seventeenth century up to the nineteenth century, foreign literary texts in translation were expected to meet the French classical taste:

> The early part of the seventeenth century was the great age of French Classicism, but translations were increasingly expected to conform to the

literary canons of the day. The free dynamic translations known as Les Belles Infidèles aimed to provide target texts which are pleasant to read, and this continued to be a dominant feature of translation into French well into the eighteenth century. Classical authors were reproduced in a form which was dictated by current French literary fashion and morality.

Salama-Carr 2006, 411

Currently, the Anglo-American market is famous for domesticating literary artefacts (Woodsworth 2000). English translations tend to minimize the foreignness of the target text and reduce the foreign cultural norms to target language cultural values, all to create the impression of naturalness (Venuti 1995) and homogenize foreign literary products (Spivak 1993). It is not uncommon to hear about texts which have undergone drastic changes in their English language versions. A contemporary example of a domesticating translation is Goldblatt's translations of Mo Yan's novels (Marín-Lacarta 2012; Cheng 2021). In a similar vein, Hadley's (2017) "concatenation effect hypothesis" claims that indirect translations tend to omit elements of the text that are identifiable with the original source culture and are also presented as something other than translations (e.g., adaptations, versions).

Marín-Lacarta shows how Mo Yan's novels have been domesticated in/for the American market through a series of editing strategies used by both the translator and the editors. These editing strategies include, on the one hand, omissions of: (i) cultural references, which would not be understood by the target reader, (ii) detailed descriptions, in order to produce a "more-to-the point" story and (iii) mental flashbacks from characters, to have a more linear narrative. On the other hand, editing comprises very few additions of explanatory in-text notes about cultural elements (Marín-Lacarta 2012, 462). These additions aim to render the text "more elegant and fluent" (Marín-Lacarta 2012, 463). Finally, editing also entails either deleting paragraphs and sentences or changing their order, thus producing a "more linear and fluent" target text that is in line with a "logical/ sequential narrative" (Marín-Lacarta 2012, 467).

However, this general approach may be changing. Indeed, in 2000, Woodsworth noted "some evidence that more recently the American tendency towards more fluent translations is [was] being offset by more inventive foreignizing texts […]" (2000, 71). This is why each translation and translator should be dealt with as a unique case. Still, Marín-Lacarta (2012, 436) argues that editing is a typical feature of literary translations in/for the Anglo-Saxon market at large and that, although not all English language translations of Chinese literary works show the same degree of domestication, the enormous success of Goldblatt's translations indicates a domestic preference for fluent translations.

In any case, when working from an English pivot or directly from the original, translators should keep this long-standing tradition of domestication in mind and be aware of the tricky situations it might create. Why might this risk of domestication be problematic for a translator commissioned to translate from the original? Chances are the commissioning editor decided to have the text translated after reading only the English version (Marín-Lacarta 2017, 144–145). According to Gorlée (2017), this is because publishers in the UK and US may not have a vast variety of language competences in-house to be able to read through submitted manuscripts in the original language. So, the editor may be unaware of the extent to which the translation differs from the original.

When a translator works from the original version, these discrepancies will quickly become clear. Against this background, the translator's dilemma tends to be which is the lesser of two evils: letting the publisher learn about the issue on their own after the translation is complete or informing the publisher about the differences before starting work on the translation, perhaps by making a list of the major discrepancies. The decision about what to do needs to be pondered carefully, as there are several opposite outcomes to the alternative actions a translator may take (Bartlett 2013; Society of Authors 2016).

If you inform the publisher at the outset and provide them with a shortlist of major discrepancies, they will likely appreciate your attention to detail and continue to trust you. At the same time, the new information may make them change their minds. They may want to alter the start text and translate from the English translation instead. You may not be the right person for the job. Chances are that the publisher will need to hire a different translator for this task, which means that you will lose your commission and contract. Alternatively, the publisher may give you the go-ahead to translate directly, regardless of the discrepancies. Or they may ask you to do a compilative translation, where you work directly from the original, but, to avoid discrepancies, you also draw on the English translation (assuming that you have the language competences for that).

If you are expected to work from English on a literary work originally written in a language you do not know, there are ethical issues to be considered (see the following section). You should also be aware of the distorting power of relay languages (discussed above) and work accordingly.

Do you necessarily need to reject indirect translation based on cultural awareness issues? In an interview given in 2017, Michael Cronin addresses the problematics of translating for translation as both an empowering tool for minor languages—which often get excluded from translation markets—and as a means of promoting the hegemonic worldview constructed by the English language:

> I think it is perfectly acceptable – it's a challenge but I think it needs to be faced – that there are many languages people have to translate out of that language into another language. If Finnish speakers are going to get access to Portuguese [works], if Lithuanian speakers are to get access to Irish Gaelic, we have to think about the notion of relay languages. My only concern about relay languages is that I would be worried that English would become the sole relay language, which means then you get distortion effects which are already getting into scholarship [i.e., scientific discourse, see Chapter 3], where the forms of the English language, its syntax, and the way in which it

constructs thoughts and ideas would become hegemonic. The English language would distort them.

Maia 2017, 18:55

Hence, relay-takers should be mindful of the potential risk of central mediating languages having a domesticating effect. As literary experts, indirect translators of literature have to begin by carefully reading the mediating texts as informative of other cultures, asking if the image of the other conveyed through the text is in line with preconceived ideas of the particular mediating culture.

Moreover, indirect translators of literature should go beyond just being aware of potential distorting effects. They should try to identify passages where the mediating text either silences the cultural other or manipulates the original so that the translation conveys an image of the source culture which is in line with previous beliefs or even prejudices (in other words, **ethnicizing** it). Indirect translators should adopt their own strategies while bearing this in mind. To do this, indirect translators should equip themselves with knowledge both about the author they are translating (including the author's references and models) and the relayer's concept of translation and method of translating.

Furthermore, when translating from a translation, it is good practice to read, compare and assess different language translations of the same source text (both direct and indirect). This process is similar to "stereoscopic reading" (Rose 1997), "using both the original language text and one (or more) translations while reading" (Rose 1997, 90) or activating intertextuality (Chan 2010). This comparative reading will hopefully uncover some problematic passages in the source text. It will also help identify more or less controversial solutions used in these translations. Such problematic areas may include syntax manipulating one's thoughts (as Cronin mentioned above) or culture-specific items such as mentions of local history, gastronomy, religion, lifestyle, etc. These passages may require extra attention from the relay-taker. They may also require detailed detective work. It may be that the relay-taker will prefer to eclectically combine different mediating texts.

A real-life example may help at this point. Maria João Lourenço (1956–) is a well-reputed literary translator and the official translator of Murakami's works into European Portuguese, all done via English. In 2017, she was interviewed by Marta Pacheco Pinto about her (successful) experience as an indirect translator. The main tips for indirect literary translators that can be extracted from this interview (Pinto 2017) are summarized below:

> (a) Get to know and assess the work done by your (possible) relayers. Maria João Lourenço displays a thorough knowledge of the different English language translators of Murakami's works: Alfred Birnbaum, Jay Rubin and Philip Gabriel, and, most importantly, their translations and the translation philosophy that underlies their work. For instance, Lourenço states

that Birnbaum reproduces a more idiomatic Murakami, whereas Rubin and Gabriel favour the rhythm of the prose. The take-away message is that an indirect translator of literature should not only be well versed in literature but also a very well-trained reader of literary translations.

(b) Build a parallel corpus of translations of your source text. When asked about her method for recreating the cultural differences present in Murakami's works, Lourenço reveals that, before receiving the English language translation, she has already bought and compared other translations of the source text in languages she can read (in her case: German, Italian and Spanish). Sometimes, she reads the Brazilian-Portuguese translation of the same book in advance. However, Lourenço does not clarify whether she merely consults these mediating texts or reads them carefully. Translators using mediating texts, especially those texts which are written in cognate languages, should be aware of the danger of being too influenced by a mediating text. They risk following too literally the lexical selection and sentence structure of one particular translation. Please bear in mind that all translations are protected by copyright. If you make a translation from a new mediating text, you should inform both your publisher and the relayer (Pool 2013; Society of Authors 2016; Bartlett 2013).

(c) Research, research, research. Maria João Lourenço reads all the English language authors that influence Murakami's works. In other words, besides constructing parallel interlingual corpora that comprise different translations of Murakami's originals (which, as explained above, are a useful tool for indirect translation), Maria João Lourenço also builds parallel intralingual corpora (Floros 2004). In particular, she collects English language originals that influence Murakami's writing. Moreover, she has a thorough knowledge of Murakami's concerns about the social problems in present-day Japan. Last but not least, she employs translation theory to justify her own translation strategies.

(d) Discuss and team up with relayers, other translators, the author and others. Maria João Lourenço states that she often corresponds with Anna Zielinska-Elliott (Murakami's translator into Polish) and sends questions to Murakami's assistant.

Ethical challenges

Let's now consider the ethical challenges posed by the situation discussed above. Your editor invites you to translate via a third language (say, English) a literary work that was originally written in a language you do not know. In this situation, it may be advisable to begin by thinking clearly whether or not you would be willing to accept the challenge. On the one hand, you may feel you lack the linguistic and cultural knowledge that seems relevant for this particular translation. On the other hand, you may feel pressured by the still prevailing stigma or taboo connected to translating a literary text from another version.

Unlike with many other professions (e.g., medical doctors), there is no universal code of ethics for translators. However, some attempts to create such a code have been made. For the purpose of this chapter, the most relevant efforts seem to include the following:

- "Recommendation on the Legal Protection of Translators and Translations and the Practical Means to Improve the Status of Translators" (UNESCO 1976).
- "Translator's Charter" (FIT [The International Federation of Translators] 1963/1994). FIT is an international association, and many different national associations of translators draw heavily and expand on this code when proposing their local or field-specific code of ethics.
- "ISO 17100/2015: Translation Services. Requirements for Translation Services" (ISO 2015).
- "Code des usages" [Code of Use] and "Guide de la traduction littéraire" [Guide for Literary Translation] (ATLF [Association des Traducteurs Littéraires de France] and SNE [Syndicat National de l'Édition] 2012 and ATLF and SNE 2013 respectively).

Of these five very different documents—a recommendation for translators and translation, a charter for translators, a quality standard for translation services, a guide for literary translation and a code of use—only two, UNESCO 1976 and ATLF 2013, deal with the ethical challenges of resorting to indirect translation. The UNESCO recommendation may seem very discouraging, brief and, to some extent, not very helpful: "As a general rule, a translation should be made from the original work, recourse being had to **retranslation** [meaning, indirect translation] only where absolutely necessary" (UNESCO 1976).

Often, the national associations of professional translators include some ethical principles in their own codes of professional conduct. In some countries, there are no professional associations and likely no written codes of ethical conduct. In other countries, various translators' professional bodies and thus various sets of ethical codes co-exist. These are often multi-authored living documents that evolve over time. They are seen as a validating sign of professionalization and are used for teaching purposes or as a tool for certification or monitoring performance.

Our survey of ethical principles that guide a translator's performance in various fields (not only literary) shows no standardization across professional associations worldwide. However, many share similar values. These include:

- Representing the original closely and accurately.
- Showing no bias towards various stakeholders involved in the translation process.
- Informing interested parties about conflicts of interest.

- Avoiding accepting tasks for which the translator is not trained or qualified, or tasks that can damage the image of the translation profession or the translator themselves.
- Aiming for excellence (through self-learning, life-long education, etc.).
- Striving for compensation for our translations and striving for professional and social recognition.
- Giving due credit and financial compensation to the work of fellow translators.
- Supporting and sharing experience and knowledge with colleagues.
- Seeking working conditions and professional relationships that ensure quality.
- Informing translation buyers about any unresolved issues in due time.
- Prioritizing working from the original and into the translator's own mother tongue.

Considering the last recommendation, an indirect translator may feel hopeless in their task of translating, via a third language, a literary piece written in a language they have not mastered (as is the case with Maria João Lourenço and Japanese).

To deal with this challenge, it may be helpful to consider the seven norms that make up the "European Code of Ethics for Literary Translators", developed by the CEATL (Conseil Européen des Associations de Traducteurs Littéraires).

To begin with, this code of ethics stipulates that a translator should have an excellent command of the language from which they will translate and of the target language. This suggests that, according to the CEATL, other language skills are helpful but not essential. Hence, it is not unethical to translate a literary text from a translation into a language that the translator has mastered, even if the original language is unknown to the translator.

Second, according to CEATL, indirect translation of literary texts is an acknowledged possibility, provided that the use of mediating texts is constructive. Following this code of ethics, when translating a literary text from a translation, one must respect both the copyright (point 6) and the ethical obligation of acknowledging the work made by fellow colleagues (point 4):

> When it is not possible to translate from the original and the translator is obliged to translate from a translation, the translator must obtain the permission of the author and cite the name of the translator whose work is being used.
>
> *Cited in Hatim and Munday 2004, 305*

This is much in line with one of the common points extracted from different codes of practice for translators worldwide: giving due recognition, as well as due compensation, to the work of fellow translators.

Literary translators may have to take a stand vis-à-vis the publishing house regarding their translations' paratextual presentation so that paratexts give visibility to not only one translator but two. This seems particularly noteworthy, considering that literary translators are often mentioned only in tiny letters on the copyright page. Relayers are frequently silenced and dehumanized by mentions such as "translated from the English".

Furthermore, the relationship between target text (author) and mediating text (relayer) should be enriching all around. Using the CEATL's code of ethics once more, point 7 states:

> The translator undertakes not to do anything that may be damaging to the profession, either by agreeing to conditions that jeopardise the quality of the work or by deliberately harming a colleague.
>
> *Cited in Hatim and Munday 2004, 305*

In this context, the common practice of publicizing direct retranslations as a correction to previous indirect translations made by fellow translators should be frowned upon.

This is not to say that being constructive means being loyal or faithful to the mediating text. If a translation constructs, shapes and "brings back to life" a source text (Lefevere 1985; Brodzki 2007), an indirect translation should do all of that twice over. As mentioned previously, translators working into hypercentral cultures tend to comply with the norm to domesticate the cultural content of foreign works. An indirect translator should be aware of this tendency and, bearing this in mind, may choose to either follow this trend or go against it.

Legal challenges

National laws differ a lot. Many countries follow a similar general approach to copyright, but there may be national differences both in terms of the scope and time of copyright protection. Therefore, translators need to have a good understanding of their own copyrights, as well as the copyrights of other agents involved in the translation project.

Who retains the copyright?

In principle, translations have their own copyright just as the originals do. The 1976 UNESCO Recommendation reads (point 3):

> Member States should accord to translators, in respect of their translations, the protection accorded to authors under the provisions of the international copyright conventions to which they are party and/or under their national laws, but without prejudice to the rights of the authors of the original works translated.

This recommendation draws on the "Berne Convention for the Protection of Literary and Artistic Works" adopted in 1888 and amended in 1979. The amended recommendation stipulates that

> translations, adaptations, arrangements of music and other alterations of a literary or artistic work shall be protected as original works without prejudice to the copyright in the original work.

Likewise, FIT's "Translator's Charter" reads (1963/1994, point 18):

> the exclusive right to authorize the publication, presentation, broadcasting, *retranslation* [including, indirect translation], adaptation, modification or other rendering of his/her translation, and, in general, the right to use his/her translation in any form shall remain with the translator. [Emphasis and explanations in square brackets added]

As should be clear by now, the translation copyright does not replace the copyright of the original version. Often, they work independently. The translation may be included in the copyright but the original may not (Society of Authors 2016; Bartlett 2013). This means that, if a translation is used as a stepping stone for a further translation, the translator or the publisher of this translation may need to be compensated for this use. Who should be compensated for this use (the translator or, instead, the publisher) will often depend on what is stipulated in the legal agreement for the first translation. Sometimes, the contract specifies that agents who handle the translators' or publishers' copyright should receive the compensation.

The Society of Author's "Guidance to Relay Translations" states:

> If you assign copyright to your publisher, you thereby give up all ownership and control over your translation (unless the contract specifically says otherwise, which would be unusual), and will have no say over relay translations. If you retained copyright, the probability is that you will have granted the publishers the exclusive right to publish the translation (and, often, to do other specified things e.g., license the use of quotations and possibly dramatisations).
> *Society of Authors 2016, 1*

As is clear from this quotation, translation contracts do not typically mention relay rights, at least not explicitly. If the contract does not mention indirect translation but instead stipulates that the publisher retains the general copyright, this usually means that the translator will not be in a legal position to decide about issues related to the relay. This is often the case in Anglo-Saxon countries.

In turn, if the contract does not mention indirect translation but specifies that the translator retains the general copyright, this usually means that the translator controls the relay translation rights (not the publisher or the agent who handles copyrights on the publisher's behalf). This is likely to be the case in continental Europe, where, thanks to the way that intellectual property is handled, translators are more likely to be recognized as creators. This also seems to be the case in China, where the copyright law, namely articles 34 and 36, stipulate that, when publishing or exploiting a work created by adaptation, translation, etc., permission should be obtained and copyright fees should be paid to "both the owner of the copyright in the work created by adaptation, translation, annotation, arrangement or compilation and the owner of the copyright in the pre-existing work" (Asianlii n.d.).

However, it should be stressed that translators' rights are a fast-evolving topic. The American Authors Guild Foundation published on its website "The Authors Guild Literary Translation Model Contract and Commentary", in which the issue of the relay translation of literary works is addressed. The aim of the translation model contract is to assist translators in negotiating contracts with publishers. This is why, in addition to the model itself, a commentary has been added after each section with relevant information for the translator to use in their negotiation.

The first section of this document ("1. Grant of Rights", subheading c) reads:

> All rights subsisting in material created by the Translator that are not explicitly granted in this agreement are reserved with the Translator, including the *right to license translations from the Translation into third languages*, and the right to create derivative works based on or using elements of the Translation.
>
> *Authors Guild n.d., Section 1, emphasis added*

In the commentary, the following information has been added:

> If the author or rightsholder of the work has granted translation rights only into English, then permission is required from them to translate the work into French, even if the French translation is being created from the English translation. But because relay translations also implicate the rights of the translator, the translator's permission is needed as well. It is in your interest to reserve for yourself the right to license relay translations from your work, so that you can work directly with an interested translator from a third language; if the publisher retains this right, you should request a percentage of any licensing fees.
>
> *Authors Guild n.d., Section 1*

Interestingly, in this context, derivative works mean products made from a translation, although translations themselves have long been deemed not original but derivative works. To put it differently, translation is gaining more and more recognition as a creative work, which, in turn, requires a revision of relayers' rights.

Another central effort in this direction is the CREATOR campaign by the UK's Translators Association, part of the Society of Authors, which also put forward a model for a fairer publisher-translator contract. More importantly, in 2016, it published a "Guidance on Relay Translation" (already quoted above), which suggests that

Copyright is infringed if the skill and labour which goes into creating a work (in this case the translated version) is relied on to a substantial degree by someone else. So [...] if a new translator were to rely substantially on the English translation as the basis for their third-language translation, they would need permission; failing which the relay translation would be an infringement of the copyright in the English translation.

Society of Authors 2016, 1

Forms of compensation

The way in which the copyright owner is compensated depends on the contract. Copyright holders can receive fees as an outright payment. Such a fee may be calculated based on the wordcount of the translation from which the second translator will be working, but the complexity of the text and the pivot translator's status on the literary market can also play a role. Alternatively, fees can be paid progressively, in batches, and calculated on the basis of the revenue obtained from sales of the relayed translation. The latter method may be more common when the first translator has experience of translating the work of a popular foreign author on a regular basis (Society of Authors 2016). Relay fees tend to be low, especially from the standpoint of the relayer, who may be used to rates that are standard in bigger markets (American, English, French, etc.) and high-income countries (Society of Authors 2016). A relayer's fees can be particularly low when they are deducted from the relay-taker's commission (i.e., the second translator) and not the publisher's (Society of Authors 2016) or when the indirect translation is meant to be sold in a smaller market or low-income country. For instance, if translations based on your English language version are to be sold in Sweden and Nigeria, you may expect a higher relay fee from the Swedish edition.

When it comes to recognition as the creator of the mediating text, you can negotiate for your name to be displayed on the resulting translation. A mention on the front cover may be too far-fetched, although, with time, this may become a more likely possibility, perhaps as a result of initiatives such as "Name the Translator" (www2.societyofauthors.org/translators-on-the-cover). For now, however, an explicit reference somewhere in the prelims may be more within reach (e.g., on the copyright page, typically in tiny type under the first translator's name and maybe also in the translator's foreword, if it exists). It may be wise to ask for proofs of the prelims. This way, the translator can check that everything is in order before the final translation is printed.

Approval of the second translation may be useful where there is a strong suspicion that the second translator may make unauthorized modifications of ethically, culturally, ideologically or politically sensitive content. If the first translator does not understand the language of the second translation, a summary of major changes may be provided in the language of the first translation. If the alterations are substantial, they can be specified in the accompanying material (preface, footnote or appendices).

However, all these forms of compensation are taken from an ideal scenario. The cruel reality is that, more often than not, permission to reuse a translation is not sought, and indirect translations are published without the knowledge and/or acknowledgement of the first translator. This often happens not because of a deliberate action but rather out of ignorance, as participants in the translation process are often unaware of translators' rights (Society of Authors 2016, 1).

Although not knowing the law is no excuse for piracy, the Society of Authors is very cautious in guiding translators on how to deal with copyright infringement situations. In case you find out your translation has been further translated without your permission, the first step, according to the Society of Authors, would be to approach the indirect translator in a friendly way. The second step would be to ask for a penalty fee, provided that you have gathered enough evidence to show

> that passages in the new translation clearly derived from content which appears in your translation but not in the original work. You would also need to show that the use of your material was "substantial" (something not defined in law but which is a matter of quality as much as of quantity).
>
> *Society of Authors 2016, 2*

The third step, should you feel that your entire creative work has been used for further translation, would be to ask not only for copyright fees but also financial compensation for moral damage. What is more, translators may embark on a court battle to have the derivative work withdrawn from the market. However, before they go to court, they should be very well informed about copyright legislation in the country where the indirect translation was issued.

How to prevent a breach of relay rights

It seems that, when it comes to relay rights, prevention is better than cure. Here are some suggestions for how to minimize the risk of having your rights infringed:

- You can request that the contract include a clause specifying that you hold the rights to the relay. If the publisher insists that they keep the general relay rights, you can always propose adding a clause specifying that translations based on your translation need to explicitly mention your name as the creator of the first translation and the publisher will pay you a percentage of the revenue from selling the relay rights.
- You can reach out to the person handling the original author's copyright issues, as well as the publisher's copyright issues. Ask them to forward on to you (or your legal representative) all requests for relay rights they may receive.
- You can announce that you have relay rights on your website and social media.

Once again, the Authors Guild Literary Translation Model Contract can be of assistance here. In section "4. Grant of Rights", the model suggests that the licencing for relay translations pertains to subheading "c. subsidiary rights". In the commentary, translators are advised to ask for 25% of the publisher's net receipts for most derivative works created from the English language translation. However, if your translation is used for a further translation, the Authors Guild Literary Translation Model Contract encourages relayers to ask for higher fees:

> If the publisher is licensing your translation to create another translation (a "relay translation"), then you should get a higher share of the publisher's net receipts, at least 35–40%. In trying to assess a value range for subsidiary rights licensing fees, a good rule of thumb is to ask yourself whether the new work could exist without your translation.

If you are the translator who is working from a translation and it is the publisher who requested that you use a specific language version, it is highly recommended that you double check with the legal department that permission to reuse has been properly granted. Again, it may be that the publisher is simply unaware that, in some situations, it is the translator, not the publisher, who controls these rights (Society of Authors 2016, 2).

If the decision to base your translation on a pre-existing translation is yours, it may be wise to first run it by your publisher and explain your reasons. If your publisher gives you the thumbs up, you may also consider consulting the original author. They may be worried about the use of a pivot version. In such situations, you may need to persuade them by explaining why translating via a third option is preferable. Remember that, in such a scenario, the fees to be paid to the first translator or their publisher may be subtracted from your fees, and it may be up to you to do all the leg work needed to obtain the relevant copyrights. You may also want to double check with your publisher that they will announce the indirect nature of your translation somewhere in the text. This may not only be a legal obligation but also a practice that may help prevent situations where your translation is judged only with reference to the original text.

As with any other translation, you will be expected to provide an accurate translation. It may be a good idea to reach out to the first translator, informing them about your plans to translate his or her work. Many translators enjoy discussing their work with fellow professionals and are happy to provide clarifications (Society of Authors, 2016). It would be good practice to acknowledge this additional support somewhere (in a preface, your social media, etc.). Such a dialogue is often enriching to both translators and may lead to further cooperation.

Further discussion

- *Indirect literary translation as a must.* When is the indirect translation of literature an absolute necessity? Try providing examples from your language contexts, both historical and present day.

- *Indirect translation and plagiarism.* What are the ethical and legal challenges surrounding indirect translation and plagiarism? For some food for thought, read the article on the copyright dispute surrounding the French translation of a Polish novel that was turned into a Netflix show (Archyw 2021).
- *The translator's style in indirect translation.* To what extent can we talk about a translator's style in indirect translation? Which style will prevail, the relayer's or the end translator's? Can we talk about a translator's style when multiple agents are involved?

Activities

Activity 1. Assessing the relevance and accuracy of intermediary versions of a source text

Read the short story "I Go to the Convenience Store" by Kim Ae-ran, published in the literary journal *Koreana* (issue 2017 "Winter"; the journal's archive is available online at www.koreana.or.kr/koreana/an/arn/selectArList.do?mi=1068; mirror pages can be found at web.archive.org/web/20200722211034/https://koreana.or.kr/user/0008/nd52347.do?View&boardNo=00001317&zineInfoNo=0008&pubYear=2017&pubMonth=WINTER&pubLang=English). The short story is available in ten languages. All versions are direct translations from Korean.

Part A. Locating culturally marked elements

Select a version in a language you know best and consider the following ideas:

- If there had not been any references to Seoul and Korea, could you say this story is not located in your cultural context? If yes, what tell-tale elements can you find?
- Does it show that the story was not originally written in the language you are reading it in? If yes, which elements indicate the foreign origins of this text?
- Can a text that includes foreign elements avoid sounding foreign?

Part B. Translating culturally marked elements

For each of the tell-tale elements you marked in Part A, propose an alternative solution and include them in the translated text. Let your proposal rest for a day or two and then compare it with the original translation.

- Do both texts tell the same story? What differences can you find? Which text sounds more natural in your language? Can both texts be considered a window to a different culture?

- If your translation were to be used as a pivot for further translation, what would be the "gains and losses" as compared to the original translation? Which version would provide a better starting point for a translator whose final translation is to be included in an anthology showcasing the specificity of Korean culture?

Activity 2 Using previous corresponding translations in an ethical and constructive way

Activity 2.1 Creative process

Paratexts are where translators have traditionally shared their insights into the translation process. Currently, social media (blogs, Twitter, etc.) also offer this possibility. Find and read a text where a translator discusses their work (such as translator's notes, introduction, interviews, memoirs or even your own log!). Consider the creative process explained in the text. Now, consider Kussmaul's reflections on translation and creativity:

- "I shall restrict myself to non-routine processes, because they are the ones which usually create problems and require creativity" (1995, 54).
- "Shifting as a basic translating activity thus, among other things, seems to be closely related with creative behaviour" (1995, 45).

What do you think: would you regard the translation of literary works as a creative process or as one composed only (or mainly) of routine processes without any **shifting** involved?

Activity 2.2 Intellectual property

Read and reflect on the general definition of intellectual property available on the World Trade Organization's website (www.wto.org/english/tratop_e/trips_e/intel1_e.htm): "Intellectual property rights are the rights given to persons over the creations of their minds." To what extent do you consider literary translations as (1) creations (2) of the mind? To what extent do you consider translation as a (1) non-creation (2) that does not depend on one's intellectual performance?

According (once again) to the World Trade Organization's website, copyright is granted first and foremost to "authors of literary and artistic works". "Performers (e.g., actors, singers and musicians), producers of phonograms (sound recordings) and broadcasting organizations" are also said to be protected but only by "neighbouring rights".

Try to find definitions of translation in mainstream translation studies overviews, handbooks, glossaries, dictionaries and/or encyclopaedias. Read these definitions carefully to see if you can find references to authorship, performance, recording and/or broadcasting.

Literary translation 125

Now re-read these definitions to see if you can find references to related concepts, such as agency, performativity, reproduction and transmission. Please reflect on the results of this brief analysis and decide how literary translation should be classified as an object of copyright. Should it be protected through the "rights of authors of literary and artistic works"? Or maybe through "neighbouring rights"? Or perhaps through both or none of the above? Explain your rationale behind each option.

Activity 2.3 Copyright

In this activity, we will move on to the specific case of copyright in the literary market in your country.

Find two or three examples of indirect literary translations in your language. Now look for translations of other literary products that result from **rewriting**—such as literary criticism, historiographies, anthologies, adaptations, etc. (see Lefevere 1985, 232–233). Check to what extent the authors of these rewritings are entitled to copyright protection in the literary market you selected. For example, who would be entitled to copyright protection in the case of, say, an anthology of feminist literature from the 1990s that includes original and translated texts already published in other outlets? Would it be the person who put the anthology together? The authors of the originals? The translators? All or none of the above?

Now zoom in on the indirect literary translations you selected and check to what extent the work of the first rewriter (i.e., the first translator) is credited in the paratext. Is there a reference to their name? To the title of their work? Or perhaps only to the mediating language? What does this tell us about the status of translators among other rewriters (literary critics, anthologists, etc.)? Do you think that they receive royalties for the subsequent use of their translations?

Take a moment to reflect on this and then consider the following questions: how would you feel if someone translated your rewritings (e.g., a book review or a translation you authored) and did not credit you with it? To what extent would they be breaking the law? To what extent would their behaviour be ethical? (For the latter question, you may make a parallel with music: at first, sampling was uncredited and unremunerated, but, in order to reuse a music sample, you now need to get permission from the copyright owner, such as the songwriter and recording company.)

Activity 2.4 Support translation

PART A. Consider and reflect

Imagine that you have been asked to translate Charles Dickens' masterpiece *A Christmas Carol*, which is freely available in English, French, Finnish, Dutch and German on Project Gutenberg's website (www.gutenberg.org/), since it is a literary text in the public domain. Besides these versions, translations in other languages are also widely available. Now imagine two possible scenarios:

126 Literary translation

> Scenario 1. You are translating the text into one of the above-mentioned languages (so you are doing a retranslation).
> Scenario 2. Your translation will be the first translation of this text in your language, but there are corresponding translations in other languages that you can read.

For each scenario, write down the pros and cons of using a previous corresponding translation(s) in addition to the source text while translating the text. Try to justify these pros and cons with your observations, readings, knowledge of the field or experience in it. If you want, you can copy this table and use it as a starting point to better structure your thoughts.

	Pros	Justification	Cons	Justification
Scenario 1				
Scenario 2				

PART B. Translate and confirm

Translate a fragment of Dickens' text to see to what extent this hands-on experience confirms your expectations regarding the advantages and disadvantages of using previous translations.

a. First, select four excerpts of similar length from *A Christmas Carol*—for instance, the first five lines of Chapters 1, 2, 3 and 4. Decide on the language of your source text (we assume it will be English, but you can use a different language version), then select one translation published in a language you can read. It may be a translation already published in your target language, a translation published in one of your working languages or even a language in which you have only reading competence.
b. Now focus on excerpt 1. Read it carefully in the source language you selected, then translate it directly from the source text without consulting previous translations. (You may, of course, use other translation tools, such as dictionaries and glossaries.) Note down the time you spend on this task.
c. Read excerpt 2 carefully. Before translating it, read the previous translation you chose. Now put the translation back and translate from the source text. Note down the time you spend on this task.
d. Read excerpt 3 from your source text carefully. Translate the selected excerpt from the source text with the previous translation alongside. Note down the time you spend on this task.
e. Translate excerpt 4 directly from the source text (without reading it carefully beforehand). Revise your translation by comparing it to the source text and the previous translation. Note down the time you spend on this task.

f. Let your four translations sit for a day or two and then re-read them. How constructive was reading the source text beforehand in tasks (b), (c) and (d)? Do you think it contributed to a better, more complex and eclectic understanding of the source than in task (e)?
g. Now try to check which of the tasks was the most time efficient. To do so, divide the number of minutes by the number of translated words for each task. Was your decision-making process quicker when you resorted to previous translations? Or did consulting these translations turn out to be a waste of time?
h. Compare your translations with the previous translations that supported your work. Check how similar and how different they are. Now reflect on your translation process to decide how far you agree with the following statements:
    - The use of the previous translation (as seen in task (f)) helped me to deepen my understanding of the source text.
    - The use of the previous translation hindered my work because it constrained my creativity. Even when I liked a solution used in the previous translation, I felt the need to contradict it so that my version would read differently.
    - My target text displays instances of contamination. I can recognize translation passages that are not my own but the previous translator's and that may amount to plagiarism.
i. Finally, compare the conclusions drawn in tasks (f), (g) and (h) with the list of pros and cons you wrote down in Part A. Have your views changed? What new elements were brought to light during these tasks? In your future work as a literary translator, will you consider resorting to pre-existing versions of a source text? Explain why (or why not).

Activity 3. Take into account the potential risk of central mediating languages having a domesticating effect

Part A. Translating for further translation

First, select a literary text originally written in your own language. This can be an excerpt from a novel, a short story, a poem, a folk song, etc. The excerpt should contain various references to items that are specific to your native culture. These references can relate to material objects (food, clothing, transport, articles for everyday use, etc.—for example, *machete, sari, gravad lax*) and also immaterial phenomena (ways of life and customs, family relations, religious and education concepts, institutions, taboos, etc.—for instance, *desenrascanço, stryj, ubuntu, Waldeinsamkeit, boarding school*).

Now, translate this text for further translation according to three different scenarios. The scenarios are part of a literary festival organized to promote the cultural heritage of your country. They are all authentic examples of dilemmas that literary translators frequently face in this context.

- In Scenario 1, you will translate knowing what the final language will be. You will be in touch with the subsequent translator throughout the whole translation process (including the production of both the mediating and ultimate target texts).
- In Scenario 2, you will know the final language, but you will not have access to the subsequent translator until they have finished writing the ultimate target text.
- In Scenario 3, you will not have any information on the final languages, nor will you be in touch with the subsequent translator until they have finished their translation.

Before working on each scenario, consider the setting, both physical and social: it should make sense to you in your political, geographical, linguistic, social and economic context. Then, fill in the table with the following considerations. How different will the challenges be in each scenario? Which scenario do you think will be the most difficult for a translator translating further and why? Which do you think will be the most difficult for a subsequent translator and why? Will it make more sense for the mediating text to domesticate or foreignize the source text? If you want, you can copy this table and use it as a starting point to better structure your thoughts.

	Main challenges for you	*Main challenges for the subsequent translator*	*Domesticate or foreignize?*
Scenario 1			
Scenario 2			
Scenario 3			

Part B. Scenario 1

As mentioned, in this scenario you will translate for translation with a specific target language in mind. You will also have access to the translator who will be translating your text. To do this activity, you should find a partner who speaks at least one language you do not know. (For example, you probably know someone who does not know the language of the text you have chosen—say, Polish—and who can translate it into a language you do not know—say, Korean—via a third language that you share—say, English.) Ask this person into which language they will be translating your text.

Think about how you will translate in order to make your partner's work easier (you can check this chapter for tips). Now, translate this text into your common language.

When you are done with your translation, set up a meeting with the subsequent translator. Brief them about the source text and your translation and make yourself available to clear up any doubts during their translation process. Keep a record of the questions asked by the subsequent translator. Can you see any patterns? Maybe there are solutions you could have adopted to make further translation simpler or more accurate? How many of these translation solutions are connected to the specificity of the ultimate target language?

Once your partner has finished their translation, request feedback on how clear and useful your translation was. Feedback on your translation brief and additional material could also be useful. Ask what else you could have done or done differently. Discuss how this translation process was different to translating from the original. Think of other questions you would like to have answered and ask them.

Take a moment to reflect on this feedback before moving on to the next scenario.

Part C. Scenario 2

In this scenario, you will also translate for translation with a specific target language in mind, but, this time, you will not have access to the subsequent translator as they do their translation.

As in the previous scenario, the task will work best if you find a partner with a different language combination to provide feedback at the end. You can ask someone who does not know the language of the text you have chosen (say, Polish) to translate it into a language you do not know (say, Portuguese) via a third language that you share (say, English). The text you will translate is exactly the same as in Scenario 1, but a different ultimate target language is recommended.

Once you know the language that your partner will be translating into, think about how you can make their work easier. Remember that, this time, you will not be able to exchange views with the subsequent translator. Take a moment to reflect on what you will need to change in your translation and/or the accompanying material.

When you are done, send your translation and other documents to your partner. When your partner has completed their translation, ask for feedback. As in Scenario 1, try to find out how clear and useful your translation and additional material were. Ask what else you could have done or done differently. What was the most difficult for your partner in this task? Did they need to consult preexisting translations? Were they helpful? In your partner's opinion, in what respect was this translation process different to translating from the original? In what respect was it the same? Think of other questions you would like to have answered and ask them. Again, take a moment to reflect on this feedback before moving on to the next scenario.

Part D. Scenario 3

In this scenario, you will translate for translation *without* a specific language in mind and *without* having access to the subsequent translator as they do their translation.

Bearing this in mind, take a moment to reflect on how you can make the subsequent translator's work easier. The feedback from previous scenarios may provide some clues. Once you have given it some thought, revisit your translation and the accompanying material and introduce the necessary changes.

Now your translation is ready to be translated further. Find a friend to help you out, someone who does not know the language of the ultimate source text and who can translate your translation into a third language. It does not really matter whether you understand this language or not.

As in the previous scenarios, ask for feedback when your partner has completed their translation. Try to check how clear and useful your translation and additional material were. Ask what else you could have done or done differently. What was the most difficult for your partner in this task? Did they need to consult pre-existing translations? Were they helpful? In your partner's opinion, in what respect was this translation process different to translating from the original? In what respect was it the same? Think of other questions you would like to have answered and ask them.

Part E. Follow-up questions

Now that you have completed all three scenarios, think about what you have learned and focus on the following questions.

a. *Your translation:*
   - How did your translating procedures compare?
   - What was the biggest challenge for you in each of the scenarios?
   - What was the easiest part in each of them?
   - Order the scenarios from the most difficult to the easiest from your standpoint as a translator translating for further translation. Explain your reasoning.
   - How did knowing what the final language will be influence your translation process?
b. *Subsequent translators:*
   - How different were the challenges they reported?
   - Who reported the greatest difficulties?
c. *Translating for translation:*
   - Is this new to you or do you do this regularly?
   - Have you thought about it before? Have your views changed? If so, how?
   - Do you see the benefits of using these reflections in all your work as a translator? If not, why?
   - Would you say that translating for further translation is very different from doing a "regular" translation? Explain your reasons.
   - Can you see universal strategies for translating for translation (for example, explicitation, domestication, etc.)?

> **Resources**: List of code of ethics of international translation associations. Tips on how to retrieve missing links.
> **Activities**: Extra activities and adaptations for group work and multilingual classrooms.

References

Archyw. 2021. "Cieszynian is Suing Netflix. The Dispute over the Witcher." *Archyworldys*. July 29, 2021. www.archyworldys.com/cieszynian-is-suing-netflix-the-dispute-over-the-witcher/ [Accessed November 16, 2021].

Asianlii, Asian Legal Information Institute Database. n.d. "Copyright Law of People's Republic of China." www.asianlii.org/cn/legis/cen/laws/cloproc372/ [Accessed November 16, 2021].

ATLF and SNE. 2012. "Code des usages pour la traduction d'une œuvre de littérature générale" https://centrenationaldulivre.fr/sites/default/files/2020-02/code_des_usages_de_traduction_2012_0.pdf [Accessed February 24, 2022].

ATLF and SNE. 2013. "Guide de la traduction littéraire." https://livre.ciclic.fr/sites/default/files/fichiers/atlf_guide_traduction_0.pdf [Accessed February 24, 2022].

Authors Guild. n.d. "Literary Translation Model Contract". www.authorsguild.org/member-services/literary-translation-model-contract/ [Accessed December 1, 2021].

Bartlett, Don. 2013. "Relay Translation." *In Other Words: The Journal for Literary Translators* 42: 60–61.

Brodzki, Bella. 2007. *Can These Bones Live? Translation, Survival, and Cultural Memory*. Stanford: Stanford University Press.

Casanova, Pascale. 2004. *World Republic of Letters*, translated by Malcom B. Debevoise. Harvard: Harvard University Press.

CEATL, European Council of Associations of Literary Translators. n.d. "European Code of Ethics for Literary Translators." *Tradulex*. Accessed August 1, 2021. www.tradulex.com/Regles/ethics_CEATL.htm.

Chan, Leo Tak-Hung. 2010. *Readers, Reading and Reception of Translated Fiction in Chinese*. Manchester: St. Jerome Publishing.

Cheng, Guanyu. 2021. "A tradução indireta de literatura chinesa contemporânea para português europeu: o caso de Mo Yan." PhD thesis. Universidade Católica Portuguesa.

Floros, Georgios. 2004. "Parallel Texts in Translating and Interpreting." *Translation Studies in the New Millennium* 2: 33–41.

FIT, International Federation of Translators. 1963/1994. "Translator's Charter." www.fit-ift.org/translators-charter/ [Accessed August 1, 2021].

Gorlée, Dinda L. 2017. "Bending Back and Breaking." *Symplokē* 15 (½): 341–352. doi:10.1353/sym.0.002.

Hadley, James. 2017. "Indirect Translation and Discursive Identity: Proposing the Concatenation Effect Hypothesis." *Translation Studies* 10 (2): 183–197. doi:10.1080/14781700.2016.1273794.

Hatim, Basil, and Jeremy Munday. 2004. *Translation: An Advanced Resource Book*. London/New York: Routledge.

Heilbron, Johan. 1999. "Towards a Sociology of Translation: Book Translation as a Cultural World-System." *Acoustics, Speech, and Signal Processing Newsletter, IEEE* 2(4): 429–444. doi:10.1177/13684319922224590.

ISO, International Organization for Standardization. 2015. "ISO 17100/2015 Translation Services. Requirements for Translation Services." www.iso.org/standard/59149.html.

Kussmaul, Paul. 1995. *Training the Translator*. Amsterdam/Philadelphia: John Benjamins.

Lefevere, André. 1985. "Why Waste Our Time on Rewrites? The Trouble with Interpretation and the Role of Rewriting in an Alternative Paradigm." In *The Manipulation of Literature: Studies in Literary Translation*, edited by Theo Hermans, 215–243. London: Croom Helm.

Maia, Rita Bueno. 2017. "Interview with Michael Cronin", Lisbon Consortium, July 1, 2017. Video, 21:09. www.youtube.com/watch?v=WMos8Nc_l3A.

Marín-Lacarta, Maialen. 2012. *Mediación, recepción y marginalidad: las traducciones de literatura china moderna y contemporánea en España*. PhD thesis. INALCO.

Marín-Lacarta, Maialen. 2017. "Indirectness in Literary Translation: Methodological Possibilities." *Translation Studies* 10(2): 133–149. doi:10.1080/14781700.2017.1286255.

McMartin, Jack. 2020. "Dutch Literature in Translation: A Global View." *Dutch Crossing*, 44 (2): 145–164. doi: 10.1080/03096564.2020.1747006.

Pinto, Marta. 2017. "Entrevista com Maria João Lourenço." *Cadernos de Tradução*, 37(1): 274–296. doi: 10.5007/2175-7968.2017v37n1p274.

Pool, Kate. 2013. "Relay Translation: Some Guidelines." In *Other Words: The Journal for Literary Translators* 42: 62–66.

Rose, Mary Gaddis. 1997. *Translation and Literary Criticism: Translation as Analysis*. Manchester: St. Jerome Publishing.

Salama-Carr, Myriam. 2006. "French Tradition." In *Routledge Encyclopedia of Translation Studies*, edited by Mona Baker, 409–417. London: Routledge.

Society of Authors. 2016. *Guidance on Relay in Translation*. www2.societyofauthors.org/wp-content/uploads/2020/05/Guidance-on-Relay-Translations.pdf [Accessed November 16, 2021].

Spivak, Gayatri C. 1993. "The Politics of Translation." In *Outside in the Teaching Machine*, 179–200. London/New York: Routledge.

Stypułkowski, Zbigniew. 1951. *Invitation to Moscow*. London: Thames & Hudson.

Stypułkowski, Zbigniew 1952. *Convite de Moscovo [Invitation to Moscow]*, translated into Portuguese by Carlos Gomes da Costa. Lisbon: Parceria António Maria Pereira.

Stypułkowski, Zbigniew. 1951/1977. *Zaproszenie do Moskwy [Invitation to Moscow]*. Londyn: Odnowa.

UNESCO, United Nations Educational Scientific and Cultural. 1976. "Recommendation on the Legal Protection of Translators and Translations and the Practical Means to improve the Status of Translators." *Unesco*. http://portal.unesco.org/en/ev.php-URL_ID=13089&URL_DO=DO_TOPIC&URL_SECTION=201.html [Accessed August 1, 2021].

Venuti, Lawrence. 1995. *The Translator's Invisibility: A History of Translation*. London/New York: Routledge.

Woodsworth, Judith. 2000. "6. Translation in North America." In *The Oxford Guide to Literature in English Translation*, edited by Peter France, 81–88. Oxford: Oxford University Press.

6
AUDIOVISUAL TRANSLATION

Introduction

In this chapter we deal with translating for and from a translation in the context of audiovisual translation (AVT), focusing mainly on subtitling for hearing viewers. While the chapter touches on issues related to the use of pivoting approaches in the marketing of audiovisual content and the handling of different forms of multilingualism in these multimodal products, emphasis is placed on creating and translating a pivot version to make foreign content accessible to viewers of a third language. Particular attention is therefore given to the technical and linguistic challenges associated with pivot language templates.

Learning outcomes

Upon successful completion of this chapter, readers will be able to:

- Translate for further translation, i.e., produce a translator-friendly text that can be conveniently used as a pivot text (e.g., a pivot template) for subsequent translations into a third language.
- Translate general and domain-specific material in one or several fields from an already translated text (e.g., a pivot template) in one or several source languages into your target language(s), producing a "fit-for-purpose" translation.

Warm-up activity

Look at the English language template created for a Portuguese language film (Figure 6.1). What challenges would you face if you were to translate these English language pivot subtitles into a different language?

DOI: 10.4324/9781003035220-6

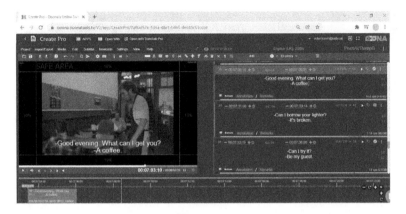

FIGURE 6.1 Screenshot of an English language template in OOONA

Indirect translation in the history of audiovisual translation

The writing of the history of AVT is still a work in progress, and the history of pivot AVT is still practically unexplored. However, it seems fair to assume that, historically speaking, pivoting approaches were not uncommon. They are likely to go right back to the translation of **intertitles** in silent films, considering how international the market for this industry was. For instance, right from the outset, subtitling was a truly collaborative, back-and-forth process, with various subtitlers working from literal translations provided by other translators (O'Sullivan and Cornu 2019).

Another historical example of pivot translations can be traced back to the arrival of the "talkies", when the film industry began to be dominated by Hollywood. Global distribution was heavily impacted by major American companies (e.g., Universal Pictures, Paramount Pictures, Warner Bros), which often controlled local distribution circuits worldwide either directly or through mergers with local companies. To boost their exports, local TV broadcast companies, particularly from countries with less known languages, tended to strategically translate into English the scripts or synopses of programmes they wanted to market internationally (Gambier 2003). From these English versions, the material was translated into myriad other languages.

Another case in point is the film translation process in various republics of the former Soviet Union, where subtitles were translated on the basis of re-edited post-production scripts with Russian dubbing (Gambier 2003). By doing it this way, the recourse to the Russian language version often constituted a form of censorship.

These examples illustrate that historical instances of indirectness can be found in more than just the way dialogues were subtitled or dubbed. They show that, for a long time, indirect translation has been part and parcel of the process to decide which local audiovisual production should be picked for international distribution and reach other language audiences.

Indirect translation in AVT today

Today, pivot AVT is a widespread practice. Examples can often be found in both long-standing, traditional modes (such as **subtitling**, **dubbing** or **voice-over**) and relatively recent ones, including non-professional AVT translation (e.g., **fansubbing** or **fandubbing**) and audiovisual access services (such as subtitling for **D/deaf and hard-of-hearing people** [SDH], **surtitling** for the theatre, conferences, **live subtitling** and **respeaking**, **audio description** and **audio subtitling**). All the dialogue in an audiovisual production can be rendered via a third language. This was, for instance, the case for the Korean language film *Parasite* (Bong 2019), which was translated into Portuguese via English. Alternatively, in the so-called polyglot films, where plurilingualism appears as a mode of narrative and aesthetic expression (Zabalbeascoa 2019), only some lines can be translated indirectly. A case in point is the film *It's a Free World…* (Loach 2007) about migrant communities in the UK. The film is mostly in English, but some characters speak other languages, including Polish. When the film was released in Spain, the Polish dialogue was dubbed into Spanish via English.

Pivot AVT is clearly not restricted to films and series but can also be found in Instagram snippets, educational and corporate videos, commercials, trailers, news broadcasts, political speeches, interviews, webtoons and myriad other genres. **Multimodal texts** accompanied by translations made indirectly can be accessed in a variety of platforms, devices and settings. For example, a Hindi language melodrama can be translated into Catalan live during an international film festival from Spanish-language subtitles. For accessibility reasons, an English translation of a dialogue script originally written in Icelandic—with **mise en scene** and stage directions—can be used as a co-text to produce an audio description script for a streaming platform in, say, Polish. And an anime programme in Japanese can be fandubbed into Spanish via English.

In this chapter, we focus solely on subtitles made from a pivot template in a professional ecosystem. Therefore, we do not cover the use of third language mediation in non-professional or amateur environments (e.g., fansubbing), in other audiovisual modes (e.g., dubbing, voice-over) or in audiovisual access services (e.g., audio description). One reason for this focus has to do with the space limitations of this textbook. Different modes of AVT operate under different constraints and give prominence to different components of a multimodal text (spoken or written language, aural or visual information). Suggesting efficient pivot approaches for all these circumstances would be impossible here. The second reason is the amount of dedicated research. While industry and academic research on professional pivot template files has recently increased and started to yield valuable pedagogical implications that we incorporate here, studies on indirectness in non-professional environments, other AVT modes and accessibility are lagging far behind.

Pivot language templates in professional subtitling

When it comes to subtitling, how is the industry dealing with the increased number of other-language productions? They design workflows based on centralized subtitle creation. Thanks to such centrally managed processes, studios are able to "keep track of and archive their assets, such as subtitle files, and hold the copyright to reuse them as necessary for adaptation or reformats to other media, e.g., for broadcast, **video on demand** (VOD), airline releases, etc." (Georgakopoulou 2012, 81). One of the main pillars of this centralization is a template file (also known in the industry as a **template**, master file, master (sub)titles, genesis file, or transfile), i.e., "a subtitle file consisting of the **spotted subtitles** of a film done in the SL [source language], usually English, with specific settings in terms of words per minute and number of characters in a row, which is then translated into as many languages as necessary" (Georgakopoulou 2003, 220).

The origins of templates can be traced back to **dialogue lists** (sometimes called a screenplay, script, dialogue transcript, combined continuity, etc.) (Díaz-Cintas 2001), which, traditionally, have largely been used only in the translation of motion pictures to be screened in theatres (Díaz-Cintas and Remael 2020, 42). As an older relative of a template file, a good dialogue list contains a verbatim transcription of all dialogue exchanges heard in the audio. Importantly, although not all dialogue lists are this complete (Díaz-Cintas and Remael 2020, 39), a good dialogue list might also contain annotations with extra information that explains any instances of challenging idiomatic expressions or expressions that could be interpreted in more than one way (e.g., wordplay). You can find an example of a dialogue list in the Translation Studies Portal.

All these elements are also expected to be included in templates used in today's industry. However, in contrast to a dialogue list (which traditionally took the form of a text file), a template is a subtitle file with time codes and dialogue divided into chunks (Oziemblewska and Szarkowska 2020). For an example, see Figure 6.2.

Dialogue lists did not disappear with the introduction of templates. More recently, some media service distributors (such as Netflix) started to operate with more complete dialogue lists for pivot templates, which also indicate frame-accurate timing and transcribe any visible on-screen text, either originated from the principal photography (e.g., labels, signs) or also burned-in text added during the post-production process (such as episode titles, text messages, creatively designed verbal graphics) (Díaz-Cintas and Remael 2020).

The introduction of template files was prompted by the boom of the DVD industry in the 1990s and particularly by studios' desire to combat piracy and shorten the time span between theatrical and DVD releases (Georgakopoulou 2012). Since DVDs commonly include multiple subtitle streams, different language versions of subtitles needed to be created in a very short window of time. From an operational standpoint, the introduction of template files resulted in splitting the subtitling into two separate activities: **spotting** (a more technical task) and translation (a linguistic and cultural task). This new agile ecosystem brought clear benefits

Audiovisual translation 137

FIGURE 6.2 Screenshot of an English language template in OOONA (with annotations)

to language service providers, as it helped to achieve faster turnaround times. It also helped to streamline workflows, avoid the duplication of work, minimize costs, facilitate the quality control of translated texts, and enlarge the pool of potential translators (Georgakopoulou 2019).

However, this atomization of the profession was decried by many professional subtitlers, who often see templates as a threat to their professional status and translations. This is clear from a testimonial provided by an anonymous subtitler surveyed by Oziemblewska and Szarkowska (2020, 7):

> Widespread template use has led to the massive growth of a class of "template translators" with little, improper or no spotting training and necessary years of specialist experience, who can by no means be called subtitlers […]. This strongly erodes the image and understanding of the profession, drastically reduces final product quality and risks the disappearance over a surprisingly short period of time of best practices built over decades through the reduction of both the role and the numbers of top professionals, who can already be seen as an endangered species in certain segments and areas of global AVT markets under current conditions.

What is more, this division of labour is said to have a negative impact on subtitlers' working conditions and income. Rates have decreased, since subtitlers are now often paid only for translation and not spotting (Oziemblewska and Szarkowska 2020).

In the early days, templates were usually produced in English to accompany original English language productions. However, the development of streaming media platforms in the late 2000s and the increase of non-English language productions on these platforms (Rodríguez 2017) disrupted this trend. In these environments, English language templates are also created for audiovisual programmes that were originally produced in other languages. This English language template is then used as a pivot for subtitles in other languages. Such multilingual subtitling projects often include one project manager, several translators and several revisors (for more details, see Chapter 8). As indicated in Figure 6.3, revision should ideally be applied not only to the final subtitles (TT1, TT2, TT3, etc.) but also to the pivot template (PT) to avoid mistakes downstream. This way, subsequent translators will be able to work on a revised version of the pivot template (PTr). When submitting their pivot-based translation, translators (Translator 1, 2, 3) may also need to submit a report specifying and justifying additional changes that need to be made in the revised pivot template before it is sent to translators working into other languages (Translators 4, 5).

Although English language templates are the typical centrepiece of centralized subtitling workflows, sometimes templates in languages other than English may be used. For instance, a template in Swedish can be used to subtitle an audiovisual programme from English into Portuguese. According to Nikolic (2015), this resort to non-English language pivots typically aims to make use of the predefined timing of the already spotted subtitles and has little to do with the language of the subtitles.

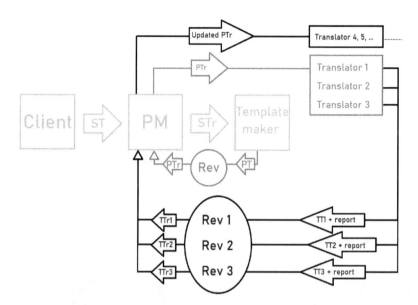

FIGURE 6.3 Production of pivot template and final subtitles into multiple languages: a sample workflow

Therefore, such pivot templates are used to help with spotting but not necessarily translation.

Despite frequent criticism, (pivot) template files became a structural piece of vendors' workflows for both video on demand (VOD) distributors and DVD/Blu-ray publishers. They are here to stay, in one form or other. Their use is likely to intensify due to two important developments that are already on the horizon. The first is the streaming giants' nascent plans to increase their non-English programming (Rodríguez 2017), even to an extent where English may not be the main language of their audiovisual productions. The other influencing factor is the currently draft EU directive which requires that, in order to be able to operate in the European Union, one third of the content on all VOD platforms will need to be of local (EU) origin (Roxborough 2018). This will only be achieved with a hike in original, home-grown productions and local acquisitions of content, which is likely to be produced in myriad languages and which will then need to be translated into a panoply of other languages to capture audiences around the world.

Main challenges brought about by pivot templates

Structural differences between the original, pivot and final languages

Languages differ immensely, even within one language group (e.g., Romance languages, Slavic languages). They may express meaning with different grammatical categories, and they may not share the same grammatical categories. As mentioned earlier, today, English seems to be the most common pivot language in the subtitling ecosystem. This is problematic because English does not necessarily have the same linguistic aspects that the original language (heard in the audio) and the final target language might have. Some illustrative examples are outlined below.

Lexis: In some languages, one English word may be translated in many different ways. For instance, when it comes to family relations, many languages make the maternal versus paternal distinction, whereas English does not. For instance, the English "uncle" translates into Polish as "wuj" or "stryj" depending on whether we are talking about the mother's brother or the father's brother. Swedish makes a similar distinction when it comes to grandparents: "grandmother" translates as "mormor" or "farmor" depending on whether she is the maternal or paternal grandmother. Other languages operate with even more fine-grained distinctions. This is the case with Tamil, where a family member's relative age and family bond (blood vs. in-law) is equally important. Here, "uncle" can be rendered in three ways: "பெரியப்ப (periyappa)" (father's elder brother"), "சிதப்ப (citappa)" (father's younger brother), and "அத்திம்பேர் (attimpēr)" (father's brother-in-law). The connections between family members could be important for understanding the storyline. If the English template contains no additional clues, the final subtitler may be forced to make an uneducated guess, particularly if they cannot understand the source language.

Homographs: Homographs are words that have the same spelling but differ in origin, meaning, and sometimes even pronunciation. They can thus often lead to ambiguity. Take, for instance, this brief example. The Polish adverbs "inteligentnie" and "elegancko" could both be translated into English as "smart" when describing how someone looks. Depending on the context, in British English, "smart" can mean either "intelligent" or "well dressed, elegant". When translating this English rendition into other languages, it may not be obvious whether it needs to be translated in the sense of "intelligent" or "elegant". Seeing the visuals is not always a given. Even if we can see the person being described on screen, without the necessary details a final subtitler may wonder if the description is meant to be ironic or factual. If the third language also contains a similar homograph, the problem can be solved, at least partially. But what if the target language has no such homograph and the subtitler needs to disambiguate?

Case: Many languages clearly distinguish between second person singular and plural (e.g., Russian: ты/вы; Italian: tu/voi). Therefore, the fact that the English pronoun "you" can refer to one person or several people is problematic, particularly when the addressee (or addressees) is (or are) off screen. Likewise, in some languages (e.g., Polish, Spanish), adjectives have different forms to specify number, gender, and the case of the noun they modify. English adjectives have no such inflections. Therefore, a standalone adjective in English can be difficult to handle when translating into highly inflected languages. The following scenario is a case in point. In a Portuguese language TV show, one of the characters points to someone who remains off screen, exclaiming "Que lindo!" (masculine singular). The English template filters this into a one-word one-liner: "Beautiful!" (unmarked). With no visual clues and no hints in the template, the Polish subtitler may simply need to guess whether the flattering exclamation refers to one woman (in which case a suitable translation could be "Piękna!"), several women ("Piękne!"), one man ("Piękny!"), several men ("Piękni!"), a baby (again, "Piękne!"), or perhaps the situation as a whole (in which case an adverb "Pięknie" would be in order). With so many options to choose from, the chances of a successful rendition are quite slim.

<u>Gender</u>: Imagine the following scenario. In a Polish language series, we see a student complaining about his "nauczycielka"—a female teacher. In the English pivot template, "nauczycielka" is translated as "teacher". Then comes a Portuguese translator who is working from the English pivot and does not understand Polish. In Portuguese there is no unmarked form for "teacher". It needs to be either feminine or masculine. Since the said teacher does not appear on screen and the pivot template fails to disambiguate, the Portuguese translator is now faced with a dilemma. They randomly opt for the masculine form "professor". In the next episode, we realize that the teacher is a woman. Since the previous episode has already been aired, the problematic subtitle cannot be amended and the viewers' experience is suboptimal.

<u>Formality</u>: Many languages share markers for formality that English simply does not have. How, exactly, can this cause problems in pivot subtitling? A real-life example is given by DuPlessis (2020):

> In a Korean series, our translator team had everyone at a workplace be formal. Since none of us spoke Korean, we didn't know how formal they were in the audio. Imagine our surprise when we found out in episode 8 that two of the coworkers were married to each other! There had never been a hint of this. In fact, some of their colleagues did not even know this and they were getting divorced, so we made up the explanation that they were indeed formal at the workplace because they were estranged and didn't want everybody to know about their relationship.

As should be clear from these short outlines, the linguistic aspects that the English language lacks are not only lexical but also deeply structural. Other areas that can lead to ambiguity for the final subtitler are tenses, causatives and diminutives (e.g., in Polish, a person called Hanna can be called a range of diminutive forms depending on the degree of formality and fondness: Hania, Hanka, Hanusia, Haneczka, Handzia, Hanula, Hanulka, Hanunia, and many others). In the English language, the array of possibilities is much smaller.

Of course, this is not to say that languages other than English would necessarily be better pivots. Yes, English is limited as a pivot language, but any pivot language would be. For instance, a template in Spanish that includes the possessive "su" wouldn't be as specific as the "his/her" in English. In turn, we do not use articles in Polish, and this formal lack could create problems if Polish were to act as the pivot.

Condensations

Frequently, the dialogue and other verbal elements in the source language are compressed in the English template to ensure that the subtitles do not exceed the agreed maximums (character per second and character per line values) and respect the shot changes (Costa 2020). Although often inevitable, such condensations are highly problematic in pivot subtitling: important details can be lost because you are interpreting someone else's interpretation. Take, for example, a situation where a simple Italian line "Buongiorno, signora. Come stai?" is condensed into "Hello, how are you?". Information about the time of day, the level of formality and the gender of the addressee is lost and, from the perspective of a pivot subtitler unfamiliar with Italian, sometimes irrecoverably.

Missing cultural background

Irrespective of language issues, a subtitler who lacks a full understanding of the source language will very likely also have limited knowledge of the culture depicted in the audiovisual product. Thus, they will often not be in a position to understand real-world **cultural references** or **intertextual references**. They will also have a hard time assessing the relevance of these references. The way the characters are dressed, their gestures, accents and locations may all be culture-specific and meaningful for the plot or an appreciation of the atmosphere. If the template maker does not explain them and fails to signal their importance, the meaning of these cultural nuances will remain obscure to the pivot subtitler and, as a result, also to other-language audiences.

Imagine a situation where a Portuguese film has been translated into German via English. In one scene, we see a Portuguese teenager humming the tune of José Afonso's "Grândola, Vila Morena". For Portuguese viewers, this tune could be a telltale clue to the teenager's pro-communist inclinations. However, these inclinations will not be clear to viewers who do not have a basic knowledge of Portuguese culture because the melody is not easily recognizable worldwide. If the English pivot template does not explain the song's hidden meaning, the German subtitler will not be aware of its importance for the speaker's characterization. As a result, they may fail to convey the teenager's pro-communist attitude to the German audience. If such information were clear, the German subtitler could hint at this attitude with the use of suggestive vocabulary, such as the way he addresses his companions. For example, a hypothetical line "Vamos curtir a noite" [Let's enjoy the night] could be translated as "Lassen Sie uns den Abend genießen, Genossen!" [Let's enjoy the night, comrades]), using a compensation technique.

Domestication

Some pivot templates abound in domesticating strategies. Instead of preserving the foreignness of the verbal components through a loan, a literal translation or a calque, they localize these foreign elements by resorting to omission, transposition or lexical recreation (Díaz-Cintas and Remael 2020, 207).

Notable examples of such domesticating strategies can be found in the English subtitles of the aforementioned Korean language film *Parasite* (Bong 2019). When confronted with a reference to Kakao Talk—a messaging app widely used in South Korea—Darcy Paquet, the translator responsible for the English subtitles, decided to replace it with WhatsApp, an application more familiar to American and European viewers (Chang 2021). The same happens with a reference to Seoul University, which is rendered as Oxford. These strategies are likely to appear in all language versions that use Paquet's translation as a pivot template (Oziemblewska and Szarkowska 2020).

Many of the localizing approaches to culture-specific elements will probably pass unnoticed to viewers who are unfamiliar with the language and culture depicted in the video. However, the domestication will raise red flags for viewers if the culture-specific elements mentioned in the original dialogue relate to the image on screen (e.g., when there is a clear interaction between speech and gesture). A hypothetical example of such a situation is a pivot translation of a scene from a Polish movie, where, in the first scene, a character points to the open palm of his hand using his index finger, saying: "Prędzej kaktus mi na dłoni wyrośnie" (literally: a cactus will sooner grow on my palm). In the next scene, we see a full-grown cactus and the characters' flabbergasted reaction. The dialogue, the accompanying gesture and the cactus seen on screen are all linked. For this link to be maintained in the remaining language versions, the rendition in the English template must be literal. If the template creator replaces this culture-bound saying with an analogue English saying that underlines how improbable something is—say, "Pigs might fly"—the subtitlers working from the pivot will not have access to all the meaning-making devices that are conveyed in the original audiovisual product. As a result, the subtitles may not make sense vis-à-vis the image on screen.

Mistranslations in the English pivot

Common complaints about pivot templates relate to language and translation mistakes. These problems can be illustrated with two quotes from anonymous subtitlers surveyed by Valdez et al. (forthcoming):

> I've sometimes had to work with English templates for Japanese or Korean audio that didn't make much sense (e.g., poor grammar).
>
> A veces tengo la sensación, por el contexto, de que algunos segmentos no están bien traducidos, pero no tengo forma de comprobar lo que dice el original para entender mejor la situación. [Sometimes I get the feeling from

the context that some segments are not well translated, but I have no way of checking what the original says to better understand the situation.]

These shortcomings may be partly due to the profile of template makers. To cut costs, many language service providers outsource parts of their subtitling production business—including template creation—to "low-cost territories with multilingual capabilities" (Georgakopoulou 2018, 520), for example India, Malaysia, or the Philippines. This, in turn, suggests that many template makers are not native speakers of the language of the audio. Nor are they trained AVT translators. As a result, they may not be able to understand all the detailed nuances of the audio. They may also lack a thorough understanding of the subtitling workflow and the challenges that may arise when translating from a template. In a nutshell, the template they create may not be as helpful for further translators as it should be.

Additional reasons include highly inadequate rates and remuneration. As aptly put by one of the anonymous respondents in another survey (Oziemblewka and Szarkowska 2020): "How can we expect to have good templates if they pay peanuts and expect the poor bastards to work at frantic rates? They're not machines, we're not machines!".

Unhelpful annotations

Template files often include annotation fields where template makers can disambiguate problematic meanings or compensate for anything that is lost in translation. However, as shown in Oziemblewska and Szarkowska (2020), very often annotation fields are left empty or provide redundant, dispersive information. As aptly summarized by one of the anonymous subtitlers they quote: "[there are] hardly ever any annotations or explanations (and when they actually give them, it's useless stuff)" (Oziemblewska and Szarkowska 2020). As recognized by an anonymous template creator cited in Valdez et al (forthcoming):

> The biggest challenge is trying to be helpful to other languages with [...] annotations, asking oneself what could be useful information for anyone [who is] not able to understand the source language. But that requires vast linguistic knowledge, such as the importance of formality, gender sentence structure of languages you don't speak.

Locked templates

Some companies are now using unlocked templates, thereby allowing their pivot subtitlers to tweak the times and the spotting, especially in cloud-based environments (Díaz-Cintas and Remael 2020, 43). However, many companies prefer locked templates (Oziemblewska and Szarkowska 2020), i.e., templates that contain the fixed in and out timecodes of the subtitles to avoid subtitle display rates that exceed the agreed maximum and ensure the observance of a minimum gap between chained subtitles. As a result, the speed of the subtitles (number of characters per second) will be defined by the pivot language. All this seriously constrains the subtitlers' options: they cannot delete a subtitle they deem problematic, nor can they merge two subtitles or split one subtitle into two. They also cannot opt to segment the dialogue in a manner that is more in line with the norms of their target language. When obliged to adhere to the fixed cueing, subtitlers often end up rendering the content of the already pruned subtitles (see above) rather than the speech heard in the soundtrack. It may therefore be that even if a subtitler happens to have some understanding of the language of the original audio, they may find it impossible to triangulate from both the original audio and the pivot template (i.e., do an eclectic translation) because of the restrictions imposed by the locked template.

Mismatch between the original audio and the template

At times, actors' lines are added during the shooting of the film and therefore do not figure in the source text that the translator receives from the commissioner (the English translation of the pre-production script). An extreme case of a mismatch between what is heard in the original and what is written in the template has been reported in Valdez et al (forthcoming):

> In one case, I had a project with Japanese audio [and an] English template to be translated into Turkish and the [Japanese] to [English] translator hadn't realised that the Japanese audio didn't belong to that video. Nothing made sense, but people thought that it was because of the cultural differences.

Templates created for other purposes

Sometimes a pivot version is not created for pivot subtitling purposes but instead for different types of subtitling (typically SDH) or even different modes of audiovisual translation, such as dubbing or voice-over (Vermeulen 2012). Such situations are most likely to occur in countries where the traditional mode of audiovisual translation is dubbing (e.g., Spain, Italy, China) or voice-over (Poland, Russia).

This reuse of translated versions is problematic because different types of subtitling, and different AVT modalities, operate under distinct constraints (for instance, dubbers need to worry about lip-synching, whereas subtitlers do not). They follow a wide range of guidelines and capture different elements of the audiovisual product (aural-verbal, aural-nonverbal, visual-verbal, visual-nonverbal). This means that a template not generated specifically for pivot subtitling can miss information that is key for a pivot subtitler.

By way of illustration, one may work from an English subtitle file that was created for SDH. In SDH, subtitlers convert verbal audio (dialogues heard in the soundtrack, lyrics, narration, voice-over) into a written text, incorporating information on the relevant paralinguistic information that the characters' utterances may convey (speech impediments, accents, irony). All this is key for a person with a hearing disability, and it might indeed be helpful for a pivot subtitler. However, what is not helpful for a pivot subtitler is the remaining types of information that a good SDH file typically conveys: an indication of who says what (a hearing pivot subtitler can typically figure this out) and labels describing non-verbal audio elements (a telephone ringing, applause, background noises). While, for a person with a hearing disability, this information is crucial for a full appreciation of the atmosphere or an understanding of the plot, for a pivot subtitler most information of this type is superfluous.

Silver linings

As is clear from the above list of challenges, creating and translating from a pivot template is hard. But there are also some advantages. For instance, some subtitlers surveyed by Oziemblewska and Szarkowska (2020) argue that translating from a template implies less work, and thus lower rates are justified: "It essentially takes away the more technical part of the work. So, if we don't do spotting, why should we get paid for it? After all, someone else did this." Others see translating from a pivot template as an opportunity to research, learn and broaden horizons (Costa 2020, 10). There are also those who think that pivot templates afford subtitlers an opportunity to translate more films, giving them greater freedom since the "target audience most probably does not understand the source language either" (anonymous quote from Oziemblewska and Szarkowska 2020). Added to this is the fact that, in high-standard pivot templates, much of the heavy-lifting has already been done for the subtitler (e.g., the detective work to clarify culture-specific references) (Valdez et al. forthcoming). Finally, working from unlocked templates is sometimes seen as rewarding:

> I don't feel that the process of timing is taken away from me, since even when working with perfect templates, I still have to "play" with the timing in order to accommodate my target language, so it is still part of the process. Creating subtitles from scratch is quite time-consuming and frustrating at times, so being able to focus mostly on the translation is much more satisfying.
>
> *Anonymous subtitler quoted in Oziemblewska and Szarkowska 2020*

All things considered, are you ready to give pivot subtitling a try?

Tips on how to create a fit-for-purpose pivot template

Below you will find several recommendations for key practices that are likely to improve the quality of pivot templates. These recommendations draw and expand on a number of sources coming from the AVT industry and academic research (Artegiani and Kapsaskis 2014; Casas-Tost and Bustins 2021; Costa 2020; Cemerin 2014; DuPlessis 2020; Georgakopoulou 2019; Netflix 2020; Oziemblewska and Szarkowska 2020; Valdez et al. forthcoming; Zilberdik 2004).

Mind the reading speed and the readability (but only if necessary)

Try to understand the workflow in which you are working. Ask the project manager if your template will be used for pivoting only or if it will also be used as the subtitles offered to the viewer. If the former, you can expect more leeway when it comes to reading speed. The final subtitler will be able to condense the text as they consider appropriate. If the latter, adjust to meet the speed, but make sure any context or meaning that is lost in the edited text is recovered in the annotations (see below). In this latter case, it may be worth renegotiating your rate. You will need to do much more leg work (e.g., include information which would otherwise be redundant) and, to a certain degree, you are killing two birds with one stone (your subtitles will both serve the viewers and be used as a source for further translators, thus generating further income). Although this is often not the case, time spent on writing helpful, informative annotations should be well remunerated!

It is also good to know if the final subtitler will be working from an unlocked version of your pivot template. Will they be able to adjust your time cues and change the dialogue segmentation to match the specific requirements of their target language? Your project manager should be able to clarify this for you. If the pivot template is locked and the final subtitler has to make do with the timing and segmentation you set in your template file, avoid subtitles with less than one second or with more than six seconds. Although these may not be the minimum and maximum thresholds established for your particular subtitling project (indeed, some companies allow subtitle durations of between 0.75 seconds and 7 seconds), these seem to be the most common limitations elsewhere. Try to avoid unnecessary one-word subtitles. These are particularly difficult to handle if the final subtitler can't delete, merge or split the subtitles to suit the needs of their target language. Moreover, avoid unnecessary compression, i.e., situations where subtitle timing unnecessarily reduces the space allowed, for instance by creating a single subtitle instead of two (Wexler 2021, 12). Most languages are more space consuming than English. For example, a word in German may often have more characters than its English equivalent. German subtitles may thus need more space to convey the meaning contained in your English translation. Since there are more characters, German viewers may also need more time to read the German language subtitle. By avoiding unnecessary compression in your pivot template, you may gain more time for subsequent subtitles into other languages.

Always mind the rhythm

Be extra careful about the rhythm of the dialogues. Do your best to keep the sentence length and structure exactly as per the original audio. The timing of your subtitles should closely match the timing of the utterances. Ideally, your subtitles should appear in the exact moment when the character starts speaking. Likewise, they should disappear when there is a break in the dialogue. For the subtitler who is unfamiliar with the language of the audio, such tell-tale clues are gold.

If possible, go literal

Most subtitlers prefer uncondensed (fully transcribed) templates (Oziemblewska and Szarkowska 2020, 11). They prefer to have access to the entire dialogue and not merely to its condensed version. This access puts them in a better position to make the right translation choices instead of blindly relying on a template creator's interpretation of spoken utterances. In the case of pivot templates, having access to elements that are typically eliminated from condensed versions of the original dialogue (phatic words, repetitions, hesitations, false starts, etc.) is key because such elements provide important tell-tale clues about the level of formality, class, tone, intent, etc.

The back translation of a template should match the original audio, while also being linguistically correct and fluent. This means that, compared to a translation aimed directly at the viewer, you can translate more literally when creating a pivot language template. Here, a good trick for creating a fit-for-purpose pivot template is to see your template not as a subtitle file but rather as a literal transcription of the dialogue that will be condensed by the subtitler at a later stage. If your client requires you to condense, do your best to provide a verbatim translation in the annotation.

Avoid domesticating

A good pivot template is not overly localized. Do not convert measurements, currencies, dates or times unless your client specifies otherwise. Leave them all as per the source audio and add an annotation explaining possible references. This will help the translators to work as closely as possible with the source audio instead of following only the pivot translation. The same applies to culture-specific references, names, locations, nationalities, titles, etc. Instead of localizing, explain their meaning and relevance in annotations, particularly if they refer to something that the viewer can see on screen. If you feel that humour, word play, puns etc. are lost in your verbatim translation, you can always compensate for it in the annotations by providing an explanation.

Make plenty of use of the annotation field

In the case of pivot templates, correct time codes and fully transcribed dialogues are very important for the quality of the final subtitles. However, precise annotations are sometimes the most important device in a template maker's toolkit, and one that can make all the difference between a high-quality pivot template and a mediocre one. If in doubt, opt for overexplaining in the annotations and ask for expert advice if needed. If you are sure that a certain element in the audio will create problems to subtitlers working into a specific language, it may be better to overwhelm them with relevant, precise information than leave them in the dark about key elements. Better safe than sorry!

To set up pivot subtitlers for success, make sure that your pivot template contains relevant annotations with informative explanations, not just links to a Wikipedia entry or an online dictionary (we are told that these are surprisingly common in certain workflows). According to Netflix (2020), elements that can often be made ambiguous or get completely lost when creating an English pivot language template, and thus require explanatory, disambiguating annotations, include:

- Grammatical and terminological specificities that the pivot language might not have such as level of formality, gender, class, tenses, causatives, diminutives.
- Linguistic registers (formal, informal, neutral, slang).
- Cultural references and intertextual references: for example, quotations from previous works or song lyrics should be clearly marked and, if possible, the author's name should be provided. If, for some reason, English domesticating or more creative strategies were used and the resulting text is quite distant from the original, annotations should include a note on the literal meaning contained in the original audio.
- Jokes, puns and wordplays.
- Cultural nuances relating to ethnicity, religion, ideological stance, gender.
- Any changes between definite or indefinite articles that need to be reflected in the final target language.
- Negation and affirmation: for example, does a reply of "no" signify agreement or disagreement with what another character has just said? At the same time, avoid disambiguating deliberate ambiguities.
- Mood: is a character stating a fact (as in the indicative) or are they expressing wishes, possibilities (subjunctive). It is often good to indicate linguistic modality in order to provide context.
- Tone and intent: sarcastic, disapproving, compassionate, etc.
- Specialized terminology (e.g., medical, corporate, legal).
- Quirky expressions or words: here it is important to clarify whether they are actually in use or made up for the specific video you are translating.
- On screen text (especially if plot relevant): location and date identifiers (e.g., Warszawa, Grudzień 1989 [Warsaw, December 1989]), newscast banners, speaker identifications (e.g., Jan Kowalski, Minister Spraw Zagranicznych [Jan Kowalski, Minister of Foreign Affairs], text in a book captured by the camera.
- Visual cues (e.g., movement and gestures, especially when they are not accompanied by words).
- Explain the levels of offensiveness of the original language (particularly if these have been attenuated in the English pivot translation).
- Specify what pronouns refer to (e.g., it, this, these).
- Relationships between characters (family, age, etc.): in Spanish "primo" can mean cousin (e.g., the son of your dad's brother). But in certain contexts, it can also be used to refer to any other man that you treat in an informal way, which can be translated as "dude". This is why an annotation should disambiguate the intended meaning in the verbatim subtitle.

- Spatial location and distance: for example, the Portuguese "cá" and "aqui" are both equivalent to the English word "here". However, there is a subtle difference in the intended meaning: "aqui" is often more specific than "cá". Take this example: "A minha mãe está cá" [My mother is here]. This can suggest that your mother is in the same country or town as you are. In contrast, if you use "aqui" ("A minha mãe está aqui"), you may be implying that your mother is physically much closer (in the same building, room or right next to you). This is why your translated dialogue should say "here" but your annotations may need to provide more details about the mother's whereabouts (does "here" mean by my side, next door, in Portugal, etc.).
- Gender of character's names: some names can be recognized as male/female but others cannot. For instance, in Hebrew, the name Adi is not gender specific. Likewise, the Italian male name Andrea would be taken as a female name in Czech, German, Hungarian and Spanish. Lack of specification in the annotations regarding name identifiers can be problematic, particularly when dialogues refer to secondary characters or those who do not appear on screen.

It might sound as though including explanatory annotations about all this will result in a template that other subtitlers will find too long, patronizing and often too basic. Perhaps it will. However, we need to remember that the ultimate aim of annotations is to compensate for what may have been lost in your translation and to be useful to as many subtitlers as possible, all over the world and from different cultural backgrounds. What seems obvious for a European subtitler subtitling a European programme may not be obvious for a subtitler working into an Asian or African language.

Of course, we are not suggesting that your annotations should be filled with redundant information about aspects that can be deduced from the image or from the verbatim dialogues. Neither are we suggesting that you include information that can easily be found in any dictionary, encyclopaedia and the like. Anecdotal annotations explaining that Vietnam is a country in Asia lead nowhere and should be avoided. Rather, we simply want to encourage template makers to think carefully about what key information has been lost in their translation and cannot be recovered from the image or the transcribed dialogues. If you feel that certain types of information are easily found elsewhere (the exact location of Vietnam) or not strictly necessary for the type of audiovisual product you are dealing with (e.g., the foreign accent of a scientist in a documentary), then consider leaving them out.

Instead of:

Pruszków, a city in east-central Poland (https://en.wikipedia.org/wiki/Pruszków)

Try:

Pruszków is a Polish city notorious for organized criminal activities.

Be ready to translate out of your mother tongue

Template makers should have a thorough understanding of all stages of the subtitling workflow, including translation. Ideally, they should also have a flair for languages. Only this way will they be able to anticipate and minimize challenges that further subtitlers are likely to face. To a large extent, templates are meant to inform other subtitlers about how the original source language works. It should also help them understand the specificities of the ultimate source culture. This is why a thorough understanding of the language of the audio is key to creating a successful pivot template, as is knowledge of the culture where the source language is spoken. It is perhaps even more important than a native command of the English language when creating a template in English. In other words, when creating a pivot language template, it may be more important to be able to explain the meaning of a culture-specific element contained in the audio than translate it into an idiomatic English expression. This implies that templates produced by native speakers of the language of the audio, and not the pivot language, could be in a better position to fully comprehend the meaning and implications of the content (Oziemblewska and Szarkowska 2020). In such situations, a proofreading pass by a native English speaker may be helpful to ensure fluency of the translation. It therefore follows that, to create a useful pivot template, you need to be prepared to leave your comfort zone and learn how to translate out of your mother tongue into English.

Tips on how to translate from a pivot template

Not understanding the language of the audio can be truly frustrating. In such a situation, it is a real blessing if you can work from a pivot template that ticks all the boxes mentioned earlier in this chapter. But what if this is not the case and the pivot template is a heavily condensed, localized version, with sparse annotations and/or inaccurate timing? Well, it is tough, but there are still measures that a final subtitler can take to improve the quality of the final subtitles.

Know how to use automatic transcription tools

One possibility is to use automatic transcription software to convert the audio stream of the audiovisual product into a written format. With the help of automatic speech recognition technology, this tool transcribes and times the original dialogue. Then, the tool can generate an automated translation of the timed transcription. The subtitler can use this raw machine translation output for **gisting**, i.e., for personal use in order to comprehend the general idea of the meaning of the dialogue originally spoken in another language. Obviously, this text translation will not be of the same quality that a human translator could provide. However, it may well enhance your understanding of the original utterances, thus compensating for information that is missing from the pivot template. It is good to experiment with different software, as they cover different languages and rely on different machine translation engines.

Yes, finding the right software and becoming familiar with it is time-consuming—some languages are not supported and the quality of machine translation output varies—but it can definitely pay off. In the end, an automatic transcription tool, combined with machine translation, generates an additional source text that you can then juxtapose with the pivot template for a more complete understanding. To a certain extent, it provides you with a comparable mini corpus of translation strategies and indicates how the same idea can be portrayed in different languages.

Another possibility is to look for the original dialogue list and run it through a machine translation system to generate a support document. There are now a number of online portals archiving and providing free access to original screenplays (although most recent titles might not be included). Of course, such support translations need to be used with care. First, the machine translation will not always be accurate. Second, the original dialogue list may, at times, be at odds with the audio because they tend to be created in the pre-production stage (e.g., they do not account for the actor's last-minute improvisations captured on screen).

Have expert advice at your fingertips

Machine translation and dictionaries can be helpful, but only to a certain degree. After all, unlike humans, machine engines and dictionaries do not have real-life knowledge. Sometimes you will need to consult a language expert. Considering that deadlines for subtitlers tend to be tight, and that finding a competent language expert takes time, it is good to start building your network early on, well before you get commissioned. Liaising with language teachers and colleagues from professional translation associations is a good way to start. Even if you do not intend to translate from a pivot template, such contacts will come in handy. The reason for this is that, even in an American or British production, you can find various instances and forms of multilingualism (as per the example with *It's a Free World…* mentioned earlier in this chapter). If a particular language is missing from your language network and you need urgent advice, you can try using various online forums where translators help each other out in moments of doubt.

Consider specializing in pivot subtitling

Practice makes perfect, or at least better. You may not understand Korean, but, after translating several episodes of a Korean show through an English pivot, you will become familiar with some aspects of the Korean culture and language (for example, you will come to understand that the Korean word "오빠 (oppa)" can be used to refer to an older brother, a friend who is one year older, a boyfriend, etc.). And if you are lucky enough to work from an informative, high-standard pivot template, your learning curve may be quite steep. So, if you keep an open mind and are ready to learn with practice, in time you may find a sweet spot in the industry.

The rationale is that, instead of contracting an inexperienced subtitler who has the necessary language competences, some companies may find it more beneficial to commission a subtitler with scarce knowledge of the ultimate source language but with long-standing experience in translating a given genre through a pivot language.

Some subtitlers believe that subtitlers whose working language is not too distant from the language of the original audio are in a better position to pivot subtitle than those whose native language is more distant (Oziemblewska and Szarkowska 2020). Although research to test this hypothesis has not yet been conducted, it may be a possibility that professional translators want to keep in mind. Of course, other factors, such as familiarity with the subject, mastery of the register used, etc. may also play an important role here.

Do not be afraid of editing the spotting

If you are working with a template that does not block your timing edits, do not shy away from editing the spotting to adjust it to your language needs. Remember that some clients do not understand the subtitling process and the need to adjust the in and out cues. They often think that unlocked templates are error prone because they provide too much leeway to subtitlers. It may be worth explaining to your clients why it is in their best interest that you work with a flexible pivot template. After all, languages and guidelines differ a lot and a template is meant to be your guide, not a straitjacket. The decision to work with a locked template or not is almost never for the subtitler to make, but you can always inform the client (or the project manager) that an unlocked template is more desirable.

Moreover, some clients may want to track the amendments that you make to the unlocked pivot template. They can even ask you to report on all the changes you make throughout the process. This can be considered a good practice, especially if these changes are then used to improve the quality of the pivot template before it is sent to other subtitlers. The downside is that the time and effort spent on such tracking and reporting may impinge on your turnaround time. Therefore, time spent on timing improvements and reporting should be additionally remunerated (Oziemblewska and Szarkowska 2020). If the pivot template doesn't follow the guidelines you are expected to follow (e.g., it was created specifically for the deaf and hard of hearing and has a slower reading speed) or if the pre-set timing is largely inaccurate and you need to do the spotting practically from scratch, you can charge more (even a non-template rate). This extra time spent on reporting mistakes in the pivot template and timing improvements should affect your rate, just like the density of the dialogue and the linguistic and subtitling complexity: dialogue-heavy content, slang, specialist terminology, dialects, intertextual references, a faster pace of dialogue, etc.—they all imply an extra level of complexity and more work. Therefore, fixed rates per runtime minute and for subtitling from a template are hardly beneficial for subtitlers. Rates should be flexible to reflect the project's volume, type, level of expertise and effort required.

Communicate with various stakeholders at every stage of the process

If any changes occur in the original audio, they need to be reflected in the pivot template and in all the target languages consecutively. It is also important that you can provide feedback on the quality of the pivot template so that it can be properly revised and improved for future reference. Equally relevant is easy, timely access to the template's creators, whom you can consult when in doubt. Ensuring high quality translation is the shared responsibility of the project manager, template creator, subtitler and reviser. Therefore, trust and open lines of communication between these workflow participants are key. Regrettably, the reality is far from ideal and consulting a template maker can often be impossible. Template makers are rarely credited (so the subtitler will not know who they are and some companies are not eager to share contact information). To mitigate this problem, some companies include a technical verification in their workflows. If your template is locked but you feel the need to readjust, you can leave notes on your file (e.g., "merge this subtitle with the next one" or "adjust out time to reduce reading speed"). These suggested modifications will then be incorporated during the technical check.

Further discussion

- *Pivot translations in other AVT modes.* How do the challenges discussed in this chapter compare to the challenges of pivot workflows in other modes of AVT? For some food for thought, check the resources sections in the portal.
- *Indirect translation and directionality.* Consider the pros and cons of workflows where the pivot works out of his or her "mother tongue" and/or "native language". Are these pros and cons equally important in all translation domains (e.g., literary translation, technical translation, interpreting)?
- *Indirect translation and access to peripheral languages in the global media ecology.* Consider how English pivot templates relate to the imbalance of languages (and cultures) in streaming media environments. For some food for thought on this issue, you may want to read Valdez et al. (forthcoming).

Activities

Activity 1. Translate general and domain-specific material from an already translated text in one or several source languages into their target language(s), producing a "fit-for-purpose" translation

On the Translation Studies Portal you will find four pivot templates containing subtitles in English. You will also find links to the website where you can find the corresponding video in European Portuguese. Please use this password to download the video: AbdulJabbar. With the help of the proposed pivot templates, practice subtitling this short video into your own language (if you know Portuguese, you may want to check the portal for an adaptation of this activity).

PART A. Subtitling via a template

You are asked to translate the movie *1111*, by M.F. Costa e Silva, into your working language. As in many workflows, the times of the pivot templates cannot be changed. Please note that

- Template A contains compressed dialogues and was not created with a further translation in mind (the subtitles are for hearing viewers).
- Template B contains a verbatim transcription. As such, it contains violations of some of the parameters.
- Template C contains compressed dialogues and annotations.
- Template D contains subtitles created specifically for D/deaf and hard-of-hearing people (SDH).

You will find these templates, and details on how to open them, in the portal.
In your translation, please follow the parameters indicated below.

Max. display rate: 17 cps (Latin alphabet letters), 9 cps (double-byte characters)
Max number of lines: 2
Max. number of characters per line: 42 cpl (Latin alphabet letters), 16 cpl (double-byte characters)
Min. gap between subtitles: 2 frames
Max. duration of subtitles: 6 seconds
Min. duration of subtitles: 1 second

PART B. Reflection

When you are done, reflect on the following:

- Did you enjoy translating from a language you do not know?
- What are the main challenges you have faced when subtitling using the English template? Would you add any other challenges to the list provided in this chapter?
- Look back at the subtitlers' testimonials provided in this chapter. To what extent do you agree with what they say?
- Were the English subtitles useful? How? Do you consider one set of subtitles to be better than another? Why?

PART C. Optional follow-up

As an optional follow-up to this activity, you may try subtitling this video again, but this time you will be able to change the times of the pivot templates. When you are done, revisit your answers to the questions above. Have your answers changed now that you have more flexibility in terms of timing?

Activity 2. Translate for further translation, i.e., produce a translator-friendly text (a pivot template) that can be conveniently used as a pivot text for subsequent translations into a third language

In this activity you are asked to put yourself in the shoes of a pivot template maker.

Pick a scene from a film or TV show that was originally produced in your mother tongue (or the language in which you feel most fluent). Find English language subtitles for this scene. Subscription video on demand (SVoD) platforms, such as Netflix, Amazon Prime Video or HBO, are possibly the best place to find non-English productions with professional English subtitles. Our suggestions for some languages are provided in the companion website. Note that, in all likelihood, these will be either subtitles for SDH or for hearing viewers. They will not have been created for the sake of pivot subtitling.

Watch the selected scene carefully, paying careful attention to the way the English subtitles convey the meaning contained in the original (the verbal and non-verbal audibles, and the verbal and non-verbal visuals).

Imagine that these subtitles are meant to serve as a pivot for translation into further languages.

Reflect on the following:

- Do the subtitles follow the recommendations outlined in the section "Tips on how to create a fit-for-purpose template"? Would you say that the subtitles provide full access to the meaning of the original to someone with no knowledge of the source language and culture? To what extent will they be helpful to further subtitlers who are unfamiliar with your language and culture? Which elements seem redundant?
- How exactly would you translate this scene? What would your subtitles look like and what would you write in the annotation fields? Draw up a list of different aspects (level of formality, gender, cultural references) that may need explanation in the annotation box.

Resources: Template samples. Video. Links to databases for audiovisual material. Link to online lecture on pivot dubbing.

Activities: Instructions for selecting audiovisual excerpts. Extra activities. Adaptation of Activity 1.

References

Artegiani, Irene, and Dyonisios Kapsaskis. 2014. "Template Files: Asset or Anathema? A Qualitative Analysis of the Subtitles of 'The Sopranos'." *Perspectives* 22(3): 419–436. https://doi.org/10.1080/0907676X.2013.833642.

Bong, Joon-ho, dir. 2019. *Parasite.* CJ Entertainment.

Casas-Tost, Helena, and Sandra Bustins. 2021. "The Role of Pivot Translations in Asian Film Festivals in Catalonia: Johnny Ma's Old Stone as a Case Study." *Journal of Audiovisual Translation* 4 (1): 96–113. https://doi.org/10.47476/jat.v4i1.2021.85.

Cemerin, Verdana. 2014. "Lost in Translation or Not? The Use of Relay Among Croatian Subtitlers." In *Translation Studies and Translation Practice: Proceedings of the 2nd International TRANSLATA Conference, 2014,* edited by Lew N. Zybatow, Andy Stauder and Michael Ustaszewski, 245–253. Frankfurt: Peter Land.

Chang, Elena. 2021. "Translating into Hollywood: A Case Study of the Oscar Winning 'Parasite'." *Deep Focus* 9 (Winter): 10–12. www.ata-divisions.org/AVD/wp-content/uploads/2021/01/Deep-Focus-Issue-9.pdf.

Costa, Daniela. 2020. "Getting out of your Comfort Zone: Translating Subtitles from Foreign Audio and an English Template?" *Deep Focus* 6 (Spring): 7–10. www.ata-divisions.org/AVD/wp-content/uploads/2020/09/Deep-Focus-Issue-6.pdf.

Díaz-Cintas, Jorge. 2001. "Striving for Quality in Subtitling: The Role of a Good Dialogue List." In *(Multi) Media Translation,* edited by Yves Gambier and Henri Gottlieb, 199–211. Amsterdam and New York: John Benjamins.

Díaz-Cintas, Jorge, and Aline Remael. 2020. *Subtitling: Concepts and Practices.* London: Routledge.

DuPlessis, Dietlinde. 2020. "Pivot Languages in Subtitling." *Deep Focus* 6 (Spring): 10–13. www.ata-divisions.org/AVD/wp-content/uploads/2020/09/Deep-Focus-Issue-6.pdf.

Gambier, Yves. 2003. "Working with Relay: An Old Story and a New Challenge." In *Speaking in Tongues: Language across Contexts and Users,* edited by Luis Pérez González, 47–66. València: Universitat de València.

Georgakopoulou, Panayota. 2003. *Redundancy Levels in Subtitling. DVD Subtitling: A Compromise of Trends.* Unpublished PhD Thesis. University of Surrey.

Georgakopoulou, Panayota. 2012. "Challenges for the Audiovisual Industry in the Digital Age: The Ever-changing Needs of Subtitling Production." *Journal of Specialised Translation* 17: 78–103. https://jostrans.org/issue17/art_georgakopoulou.php.

Georgakopoulou, Panayota. 2018. "Technologization of Audiovisual Translation." In *The Routledge Handbook of Audiovisual Translation,* edited by Luis Pérez-González, 516–539. London: Routledge.

Georgakopoulou, Panayota. 2019. "Template Files: The Holy Grail of Subtitling." *JAT, Journal of Audiovisual Translation* 2 (2): 137–160. https://doi.org/10.47476/jat.v2i2.84.

Loach, Ken, dir. 2007. *It's a Free World…* Filmcoopi Zürich et al. 1 hr. 31 min. UK.

Netflix. 2020. "Pivot Language Template Guidelines." https://partnerhelp.netflixstudios.com/hc/en-us/articles/219375728-Timed-Text-Style-Guide-Subtitle-Templates#h_01EXJ1B1VSKZP6HAM6SW1F480V. [Accessed February 2021].

Nikolic, Kristijan. 2015. "The Pros and Cons of Using Templates in Subtitling." In *Audiovisual Translation in a Global context. Mapping an Ever-changing Landscape,* edited by Rocío Baños Piñero and Jorge Díaz-Cintas, 112–117. London: Palgrave Macmillan.

O'Sullivan, Carol, and Jean-François Cornu. 2019. "History of Audiovisual Translation." In *Routledge Handbook of Audiovisual Translation* edited by Luis Pérez González, 15–30. London: Routledge.

Oziemblewska, Magdalena, and Agnieszka Szarkowska. 2020. "The Quality of Templates in Subtitling. A Survey on Current Market Practices and Changing Subtitler Competences." *Perspectives*: 1–22. https://doi.org/10.1080/0907676X.2020.1791919.

Rodríguez, Ashley. 2017. "Netflix Says English Won't Be its Primary Viewing Language for Much Longer." *Quartz*, March 30, 2017. https://qz.com/946017/netflix-nflx-says-english-wont-be-its-primary-viewing-language-for-much-longer-unveiling-a-new-hermes-translator-test/. [Accessed February 2021].

Roxborough, Scott. 2018. "Netflix Quota in Europe may Lead to TV Buying Spree." *The Hollywood Reporter*, November 10, 2018. www.hollywoodreporter.com/tv/tv-news/netflix-content-quota-europe-may-lead-tv-buying-spree-1150805/ [Accessed February 2021].

Valdez, Susana, Hanna Pieta, Ester Torres-Simón, and Rita Menezes. Forthcoming. "Pivot Language Templates: What Do They Tell Us About Language Hierarchies in Streaming Service Platforms." *Target*.

Vermeulen, Anna. 2012. "The Impact of Pivot Translation on the Quality of Subtitling." *International Journal of Translation* 23 (2): 119–134.

Wexler, Deborah. 2021. "Top-ten Principles of Subtitle Timing" *Deep Focus* 9 (Fall): 11–14. www.ata-divisions.org/AVD/wp-content/uploads/2021/11/Deep-Focus-Issue-12.pdf.

Zabalbeascoa, Patrick. 2019. "That' Just What We Need, A Fourth Language: A Multilingual Humour in Film and Television Translation." In *Multilingulism in Films*, edited by Ralf Junkerjürgen and Gala Rebane, 15–34. Berlin: Peter Lang.

Zilberdik, Nan Jackques. 2004. "Relay Translation in Subtitling." *Perspectives* 12 (1): 31–55. https://doi.org/10.1080/0907676X.2004.9961489.

7
NEWS TRANSLATION

Introduction

In this chapter we discuss the details of written news translation. We dwell on the challenges involved in translating for and from a translation that arise from the complex multiple-source, multiple-author and multiple-language situations characteristic of the journalistic environments where news translation occurs. The aim is to help you gain a better understanding of the important role of indirect translation in the global circulation of information and teach you how to produce a translator-friendly text for the news. You will also learn how to select and combine different sources and how to efficiently and ethically adapt an already translated story that includes quoted discourses.

Learning outcomes

Upon successful completion of this chapter, you will know how to:

- Produce a translator-friendly text that can be conveniently used as a pivot text for subsequent translations into a third language.
- Assess the relevance and accuracy of the intermediary versions of a source text.
- Summarize, rephrase, restructure, and adapt rapidly and accurately using already translated written and/or spoken communication, keeping the most relevant features.

THE NATIONAL NEWSPAPER
ALL WORLD. ALL NEWS. ALL HERE.

LOCAL | INTERNATIONAL | FINANCE | SPORTS | ENTERTAINMENT | OPINION

Editions:
North America
Australia
Hong Kong
Europe
En español

FIGURE 7.1 (Mock) international newspaper with several locales

---

Warm-up activity

Look at the international newspaper published in different language versions (Figure 7.1). Which challenges will the journalists/translators face when reporting on world news in a national newspaper? How do you think these national rewritings of world news are retranslated and republished into the other language editions of this newspaper?

Indirect translation in the history of news translation

Valdeón (2022) sketches a brief history of indirectness in news production from the early modern period to the Covid-19 pandemic. Between the fourteenth and late seventeenth centuries, major European cities communicated their news through newsletters and pamphlets. These were produced by polyglots who rewrote in one target language (say, Italian) news coming from different source contexts and languages. These polyglots then sent their news reports to selected correspondents. When the reports reached the main European cities, they underwent further translation processes.

The late seventeenth century saw the rise of the first corantos (the precursors to newspapers). Dutch coranteers had a network of informants who supplied news from different contexts to be translated. This news sometimes consisted of oral stories. These Dutch language translations would be further translated whenever they reached other parts of the continent. In this context, four series of events helped expand news circulation and production, thus increasing the need for news translation. First, wars in Europe, such as the Thirty Years' War, boosted demand for a more rapid circulation of news. Second, due to colonial expansion, readers in the metropolises wanted to read news from distant territories in which indigenous and various European languages and pidgins coexisted. Third, the creation of postal services and other advances in transportation and communication strongly impacted news circulation. Last but not least, rulers quickly understood the importance of (controlling) news dissemination. Hence, with the development of news circulation and production emerged the need for gatekeeping processes, such as cutting and omitting passages of the source text in further translations.

For their part, Bielsa and Bassnett (2009) situate the birth of global news in the mid-nineteenth century, when two interconnected events occurred: the invention and expansion of the telegraph, and the creation of the first global agencies. Bureau Havas, the predecessor of AFP (Agence France-Presse), was founded in 1832 with the aim of translating foreign newspapers into French. These already translated texts would be further translated into other languages. Julius Reuter, one of Havas' employees, founded his own news agency, which followed his former employer's model. This was how Reuters was created in London in 1851. Moreover, in France and in Great Britain, the first newspapers were born and consumed both locally and across Europe and North America. These were *La Presse* (1836), *Le Petit Journal* (1863), *The Daily Telegraph* (1861) and *The Daily Mail* (1891). The internationalization of these newspapers was possible thanks to (a) the telegraphic networks, which made it possible to translate news from distant lands (these translations were then incorporated into the above-mentioned French and English); and (b) the centrality of French and English as global languages.

Bielsa and Bassnett also suggest that dominant-language mediation in the creation of global news shaped journalistic style as we know it today:

> The news agencies not only developed a global infrastructure for news production and distribution […], they also made it their task to extend their values of impartiality and objectivity and discursive practices based on factual description worldwide.
>
> *2009, 43*

This argument brings international news style and international scientific discourse closer together. This is because both fields of practice have been shaped by English language domination (see Chapter 3). Following a similar line of thought, van Doorslaer (2010, 181) argues that, in the case of newsrooms in Belgium, the use of global news agencies, such as the AFP and the American Associated Press (AP), seems to correlate with the growing presence and importance of international news related to France and the United States in Belgian news. It should be borne in mind that contexts with lower financial resources tend to rely more heavily on the work of global news agencies (Bielsa and Bassnett 2009, 36). At the same time, the international press relies on global agencies to collect news from the periphery. Sousa (2020), in turn, shows that, even inside one country, peripheral regions (e.g., the Azores islands as opposed to continental Portugal) tend to depend more on news agencies for news writing. All in all, in a globalized news network held by two major contexts and languages, some countries, regions and languages may find themselves even more sidelined and silenced.

Indirect translation in news translation today

Translation agencies

In news translation chains, one could be tempted to identify first and foremost international news agencies as relayers and journalists as relay-takers. However, this separation is purely theoretical and the reality is much more complex, as new translations are multidirectional (van Rooyen 2019). On the one hand, in news agencies we can distinguish between agencies that provide news (dispatches), media subscribers, and agencies that also publish for end consumers (for example, Reuters). On the other hand, besides rewriting translation dispatches, there are many other translation processes that contribute to the making of international news.

For example, when analysing the UK media coverage of former French President François Hollande's speech on the dismantling of the Calais refugee camp, Bennett (2021) hypothesizes on the many instances of translation that have occurred between two languages—French and English. Between the delivery of the spoken speech (the source text) and the publication of the pages of different British newspapers (target texts) covering this event, more than ten different texts have been produced. These intermediary texts resulted from recording, transcribing, summarizing, selecting, translating, etc. As described by Bennett:

> Many foreign journalists will have been present when the French president gave his press conference on 29th October, and, in some cases *the speech* [0] will have been *recorded* [1] by them, before being *transcribed* [2] and *translated* [3]; in fact *segments* [4] of the recording were reproduced on various British television channels, though normally with an *English summary in voiceover* [5]. In others, journalists will have made use of the French government website (France Diplomatie) where *excerpts of the speech* [6] appeared already *in English* [7], two days later. But in most cases, *the story* [8 (newspapers will have probably received more than one story)] will arrive at the editorial office via news agencies or other media organizations, after which it will be *reformulated* [9] in accordance with the orientation and style of the newspaper in question. Indeed it is very common for the same piece of news to be transmitted in a chain from one newspaper to another, successively *repackaged* [10, etc.] to suit the expectations of the different target publics.
>
> Bennett 2021, 370–371, numbers and italics added for emphasis

Not all the texts we have numbered above were published. For example, [6] and [7] refer to an English translation of a selection of passages from the original speech and the selection of passages in French were not made public. Still, British journalists had at their disposal different sources of information and different mediating texts based on one source text. This is why, in this case, news agencies were not the only relayers.

Furthermore, according to Bielsa and Bassnett (2009), by the 2000s, news agencies were losing their role as first-hand news suppliers. First, the development of satellite technology and the appearance of channels of continuous information, such as CNN (Cable News Network), started to blur the thus far binary distinction between "information wholesalers (the news agencies) and retailers (media organizations addressed to the public), by also selling their news to other media" (Bielsa and Bassnett 2009, 53). Another case in point is BBC Monitoring, supported by the BBC (British Broadcasting Company). Among other services, BBC Monitoring provides reports that consist of "[a]ccurate and nuanced translations of international media reporting including important speeches and statements" (https://monitoring.bbc.co.uk/ouroffer). These reports are then retranslated to different languages, contexts and media. In the same article quoted above, Bennett (2021, 371) makes the following aside about the Portuguese context: "It is notable, for example, that the Portuguese newspaper *O Público*, cites the BBC and not French sources in its coverage of Hollande's speech from Douela-Fontaine on 29th October." There are multiple reasons for this preference, including the prestige of English language sources and reporting, as well as the fact that a new generation of translators have a better command of English than French.

Second, social media is now revolutionizing news reporting and supply. The chain of information is now being subverted: it is the general public who sometimes publishes the first news piece on social media, which is then reedited by news agencies. Moreover, the fact that, nowadays, social media translate foreign-language posts to match the language of the user creates yet another layer of indirectness in news production. Facebook and Twitter succeeded in getting their content translated into different target languages by means of similar crowdsourcing projects. Facebook also offers "the option of having UGC (newsfeed items, primarily) translated automatically and in real-time based on a user's language preferences" (Desjardins 2017, 23).

All in all, all these recent changes have pushed news agencies to communicate with the general public via their websites and social media platforms, thus further blurring the distinction between agencies who provide news only for media subscribers or also for end consumers.

Our survey of the French AFP's, the English Reuters' and the American AP's style manuals seems to confirm a change in these agencies' aims and positioning within the news communication chain. This change, in turn, leads to some overlapping procedures related to translation in both news agencies and newspapers. In our survey, we analysed the agencies' manuals, looking for statements that deal with the acknowledgment of translation in news writing and in the crediting of sources. We compared the results of this analysis with what we know about translation in news outlets from previous studies (discussed below). This allowed us to discern the following differences and similarities.

As shown in Table 7.1, AFP and Reuters, on the one hand, and AP, on the other, seem to disagree when it comes to crediting source texts and translations. However, as mentioned, also this distinction is purely theoretical. Style guides merely suggest what a model situation should be. There are also hidden translation

164 News translation

TABLE 7.1 Translating for and from and crediting translation in news agencies and newspapers

News stories by news agencies	News stories by newspapers
≠ Primarily written for editing and/or translation but also end consumers (Reuters).	≠ Written to be read by end consumers.
= Target texts should be read easily.	= Target texts should be read easily.
≠ Copyright is respected and plagiarism is avoided (AFP, AP), which sometimes entails making a clear distinction between translations and non-translations (Reuters).	≠ Texts include both translated sections and original writing (not explicitly marked as such).
= "The AP often has the right to use material from its members and subscribers; as with material from other news media, we credit it. Unless we are clearly retransmitting in full a story by a member outlet, we do not transmit stories in their original form; we rewrite them, so that the approach, content, structure and length meet our requirements and reflect the broader audience we serve." (AP)	= Source texts are rewritten and are not always credited.

phenomena in the writing of news dispatches that take place inside agencies' bureaus from AFP and Reuters or even before. In news gathering by a reporter, oral statements may be interpreted into a foreign language. Bureaus collaborate with foreign correspondents who write in the language of the agency (which is then translated for other newswires), local journalists who write news reports in the local language, and translators. These professionals work in teams and share translation solutions. So, when style guides suggest that news dispatches should credit translations and translators, this seems to hold true in cases where an official communication or a foreign news report is directly and entirely translated from one source language into a target language and then retranslated for different media, as the AP style guide indicates. Consequently, when giving guidelines for the sign-off of stories, Reuters' *Handbook of Journalism* distinguishes between, on the one hand, crediting the writing and, on the other, crediting the translating, although the former presupposes instances of the latter:

> WRITING BY - used on stories where the **bylined** reporter on the spot can report but not write, for whatever operational reason. Note that the contact details in this case should also be for the writer. Reason: the reporter in this case is very probably not easy to reach. This field may also be used where a journalist has written a story *that draws substantially on a series of stories from another Reuters service, possibly even adding some local reporting, rather than*

producing a straight translation of a story. (Writing by Olaf Brandt; Editing by June Sink) ((olaf.brandt@reuters.com; +1 646 897 1335; Reuters Messaging: olaf.brandt.reuters.com@reuters.net))

Reuters 2008, 88, emphasis added

However, for the sake of training, international news agencies' guidelines propose techniques to translate for further translation. On the other hand, the comparison outlined in Table 7.1 has the merit of shedding light on copyright obligations in news writing. It thus echoes the question already asked by Hernández Guerrero (2009, 120–121, cited in Valdeón 2022): are copyrights being respected or not.

Newspapers

Present-day news are highly hybrid texts: they are multi-authored and multi-sourced (Valdeón, 2022). An illustrative example is the Spanish newspaper *El País*, which, as well as its Spanish local and online edition, also publishes editions for Spanish-speaking America, Brazil, Catalonia, Mexico and one English version for international readers. Many of the articles contained in these editions are indirect translations: a Spanish language journalist writes a piece quoting or using, say, a French language source in translation. Afterwards, this Spanish language article with embedded bits of translations will be translated almost literally into Catalan, English and Portuguese.

What is more, news translations are compilative because journalists/translators gather and (re)write multiple source texts (van Rooyen 2019). Instances where journalists/translators directly translate entire news articles, dispatches or press releases are rare (Davier 2022). This is why "in journalistic translation research […] it may make more sense to work with units of translation that are smaller than a text" (Davier 2022).

Furthermore, news translations can be intralingual, interlingual, intersemiotic, or a combination of all three types of translation:

> An internet based English telex message from a source in India that is rewritten for tomorrow's edition of *The Independent*, is an example of an intralingual translation. An Italian news article in *La Repubblica* that is adapted for an item on the news of German public TV station ZDF, is an example of an intersemiotic translation.

van Doorslaer 2010, 182

It goes without saying that when *The Independent*'s article is translated into German, or when a German TV piece is broadcast in Poland with Polish subtitles, these translation products become indirect. Likewise, we can talk about intra and interlingual indirect translation when official communications (e.g., from health authorities) are first paraphrased into lay language for the benefit of local viewers, then this intralingual paraphrase is picked up by international media and rendered into other languages (Valdeón 2007, 102).

Moreover, news translation is often based on non-existent originals (Davier 2022). This is because journalists frequently base their stories on ephemeral, raw material (such as oral interviews or press releases) that never reach the general public and disappear soon after the newspaper story is published. Hence, sometimes the only way to reconstruct an "original" is through the reading of multiple newspaper articles where this original is rewritten in different languages.

As should be clear from the above, indirect translation pervades news production yet remains largely invisible, although exceptions may be found—for example, in Francophone Canada (Gagnon 2012). Since, from a lay person's perspective, translation is often understood as a rather literal (or at least faithful) rendering of one text produced in one source language into a new language, journalists who engage in translating activities do not acknowledge their target texts as translations, be they direct or indirect. News production consists of narrating what happened and was observed elsewhere, assembling sources of information, combining them, rewriting, adapting to readers' expectations and interests, cutting down on what is deemed not new, irrelevant or offensive, while providing supplementary information and complying with generic rules and the ideological stance of the newspaper.

Indirect translation and fact-checking

In news translation, different texts participate in the making of one target text that may afterwards be used as a start text for a further translation. For this reason, the line between source and target texts is extremely blurred, to the extent that it becomes irrelevant. In fact, to grasp a fuller understanding of the distinct instances of indirectness in news production, it seems productive to use a broader definition of indirect translation (as outlined in the Introduction). This broader definition allows us to consider back translation, **eclectic** and compilative translation as subsets of indirect translation, and all these practices are extremely common in news translation (see Ringmar 2007 and Ivaska 2021 for terminological differences between eclectic and compilative translation).

A good illustration of back translation in the news can be found in Valdeón (2007 110), who analyses BBC Mundo's and CNN en Español's coverage of the 2004 terrorist attacks in Madrid. The reports by these media organizations were translated from English and not originally from Spanish. Since Spanish was the language of the initial claims about the attack quoted in the text, the translation chain was Spanish>English>Spanish.

Back translating quotes without acknowledging the source is ethically problematic. Some sensitive words can entail political and ideological stances. A case in point is the translation of "terrorist(a)" as "separatist(a)", as discussed in Valdeón (2007). The Spanish government first blamed the Basque terrorist group ETA for the attacks in Madrid: "the Basque terrorist group that has campaigned for the independence of the Basque country from France and Spain over the last fifty years"

(Valdeón 2007, 100). In their coverage of the initial official statements, BBC and CNN reporters translated the Spanish language statements into English. Valdeón (2007) notes that, whenever the Spanish authorities referred to ETA as "terroristas", journalists/translators changed it to "separatists", thus shifting the emphasis away from the violence of the attacks towards the group's political aspirations. These translations were then back translated into Spanish literally and posted in BBC Mundo and CNN en español, thus creating a dissonance with the views being presented in the Spanish language news. Valdeón (2007) considers this to be a case of "negative mediation".

Back translation has two other applications in news translations, both of which relate to the reconstruction of truth. First, as mentioned, the initial source text is often missing in news translations. This is the case for news that draws on oral speech:

> A source text in a language A quoting a language B will reproduce the source words in translation in language A. Then, the whole article may be translated into language B. However, the translators are not likely to use the original words in language B. Instead, they translate language A into B. In other words, the text is rendered back into the original language via language A. This process is probably more frequent than we may think.
>
> *Valdeón 2022*

Valdeón (2022) classifies the above practice as **circular indirect translation** (see Figure 7.2).

Significantly, Toury (2012, 53) associates back translation with **pseudotranslations** (a non-translated text disguised and/or received as a translation) and, more broadly, with literary forgery. In the era of fake news, pseudotranslation (either partial or complete) can be used to forge news. At the same time, back translation can be used to distinguish fake news from real news. This is because back translation allows us

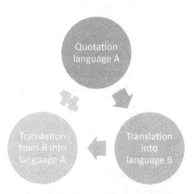

FIGURE 7.2 Circular indirect translation / back translation

to check whether a piece of news results from circular indirect translation or from pseudotranslation.

Take, for instance, *Snopes* (www.snopes.com), a website that uncovers invented stories where we can find Jordan Liles article about a quotation that many websites, memes and weblogs wrongly attribute to Anne Frank's diary. The quotation reads: "Dead people receive more flowers than the living ones because regret is stronger than gratitude." Liles' article results from successful fact-checking. The journalist looked for mentions of this quotation on Newspapers.com and Googlebooks.com, only to find that it was a fabricated pseudotranslation by a Tumblr user in 2013. Liles reveals that he looked for this quotation (or parts thereof) in "Frank's own writing", using the English language translation by Susan Massotty. We could, of course, argue that this fact-checking research would have been more thorough if Liles had back translated the relevant excerpt. In particular, he could have back translated the quotation into Dutch and checked Anne Frank's original writing. Nevertheless, back translation does not reconstruct the original wording, as we show in this chapter in line with Pym (2014, 22) and others. Hence, considering the limitations of this method, back translation could have been used together with eclectic/compilative translation (see below).

Liles used other methods to consult the original to which he did not have access due to the language barrier: eclectic and compilative translation. From the list of references provided in his article, we can infer that Liles consulted more than one translation of Frank's diary. The fact that a given quotation is missing from one translation does not raise a red flag. One translator may have omitted the passage for whatever reason. However, the possibility that different translations of the same source text would omit the same passage seems more remote. In other words, the fact that a quote (or its reformulation) is missing from all English language translations may be a tell-tale clue that this passage does not belong to the Dutch original. However, since this method also has limitations, combining it with back translation might have been more productive.

Both compilative and eclectic translations are part and parcel of news translation. The fact that compilative translation is central to news writing is evident from Elliot's (1995, 108) statement, according to which news writing (understood as journalistic research) is about assembling reliable sources, so as "to compile true pieces of information from which to develop the story". When it comes to eclectic translation, it seems safe to suggest that the sooner trainee translators/journalists become aware that news writing entails a good deal of translation, and that translation is manipulation (i.e., using someone else's words and work, taking it out of its natural context and rewriting it according to a new context and a new function), the sooner these trainees will understand that eclecticism in source text gathering is beneficial in news production.

Although not all news translations deal with conflict, Baker's (2006) concept of reframing usefully supports the point we are making above. According to Baker, the concept of framework deals with belief systems that shape expectations. These expectations, in turn, shape the way we perceive and interact with the "Other".

Baker argues that, on the one hand, "translators and interpreters are responsible for the texts and utterances they produce. Consciously or otherwise, they translate texts and utterances that participate in creating, negotiating and contesting social reality" (Baker 2006, 105). On the other hand, "the same set of events can be framed in different ways to promote competing narratives with important implications for different parts to the conflict; this often results in frame ambiguity" (Baker 2006, 197). In order to illustrate this ambiguity and its consequences, Baker discusses two different translation solutions for the Arab word "wilaya" (which means both "nation" and "electoral region") in a tape Osama Bin Laden aired in 2004. Whereas Al Jazeera translated "wilaya" as "nation", Memri TV translated it as "electoral state". The latter thus implied that Bin Laden interfered with US elections, threatening the security not only of the US as a whole but of every state that voted in a particular manner.

For all the reasons outlined above, journalists-to-be should equip themselves with knowledge of the different editorial and ideological lines of the newspapers and news agencies providing the source texts. Besides, journalists/translators should aim to compile sources that provide different framings of one story, although they may not always have the time to do this. This way, they will gain a more holistic reading of the story, which will put them in a better position to reframe the story according to the new readers' expectations.

Challenges in news translation (and some ways to go about them)

KISSER: Keep It Short, Simple and Easy to Relay

In news agencies, translations are typically produced at a fast pace. In fact, in her interviews with journalist translators working for AFP and Agence Télégraphique Suisse (ATS, the Swiss national news agency), Davier (2017, 132) discovered that translating fast was seen as a priority in this professional ecosystem. So much so that publishing a news dispatch rapidly was deemed more important than publishing it with no typos. One cannot but wonder if these statements relate to the journalists' reluctance to translate from already translated sources. According to Davier, some interviewees translated frequently from translations, although they considered that translating indirectly may "blur" the source message (Davier 2017, 162).

To be fast, journalists/translators begin by reading the source text, using bilingual dictionaries to translate technical words. Some said they used machine translation (e.g., Google Translate) for **gisting**. Others resort to specialized terminology databases. There are also those who use archived dispatches as models for the writing of new ones (Davier 2017, 165).

Regarding translation strategies, the interviewees tend to use literal translation only to deal with quotations. The most common translation strategy for handling the narrative element of a news story was adaptation. Adapting, in the case of professionals working for AFP and ATS, encompassed two interrelated textual transformations: summarizing and *regionalizing*. For Davier, regionalizing is a synonym of localization (see Chapter 4), and it is described by professionals in the following manner:

> According to the editors, regionalizing information is more than just explaining it to a specific audience. In agencies, regionalization (or "localization" in translational terms) is also selecting the information that will be transferred from one culture to another. When passing from one language-culture to another, news dispatches get not only reframed, but also summarized. In this context, journalists refuse to speak of translation. But can we deny that this is a process of intercultural transmission?
>
> Davier 2017, 158, our translation

Considering summarizing, we should bear in mind that the word limit is very strict in the case of news dispatches (600 words at best and typically much less). To respect the word count limits, journalists/translators rewrite and condense the source text or selected parts thereof. The criteria that govern both the selection of material to translate and the rearrangement of the narrative are connected to localization. The journalists/translators need to convince the readers of the newsworthiness of a story and hierarchize the information accordingly. In this context, regionalizing/recontextualizing may involve adding new information, particularly if the source text contains culture-specific elements from the original context.

As for the implied readers, Davier's interviewees translate primarily for the benefit of other journalists/translators. Therefore, they are very much aware that their translations will be subject to another round of editing and translating (Davier 2017, 155). At the same time, the interviewees acknowledge that end consumers may eventually read the news dispatches. This is said to be the case with less resourceful newspapers, who tend to rely heavily on material supplied by news agencies (58).

The style manual for Reuters gives important tips on how to tackle the challenges of writing news dispatches for translation. The Reuters' *Handbook* recommends that a news story should be written "quickly, clearly and simply […] in a language that is easy to translate" (Reuters 2008, 56 cited in Bielsa and Bassnett 2009, 70). To find guidelines on how to produce a translator-friendly news story, one has to go through the alphabetical entries of "The Reuters General Style Guide", "Sports Style Guide" and "Specialised Guidance". The challenges, and ways to overcome them, are summarized in Table 7.2. Please note that the text in Table 7.2 is taken directly from the Reuters' Handbook. The information placed in brackets contains our suggestions. These suggestions are not direct quotations but draw on solutions that the Reuters' *Handbook* makes with respect to similar challenges.

As is clear from Table 7.2, the challenges of writing for translation deal mostly with language variation, comprising dialects, registers and technical jargon. Other challenges involve sentence length, ambiguous formulations and cognate words

News translation 171

TABLE 7.2 Reuters' guidelines for producing translator-friendly news stories

Challenge	Justification	Solution	Plan B
Quotes in colloquial or parochial language (p.372)	Not easily translated or understood in other countries.	Avoid it (or paraphrase in standard English).	Explain what they mean, e.g., He said: Clinton is behind the eight ball (in a difficult situation).
Slang (in quotes) (p.404)	Not readily understood outside the English-speaking world or your own country, creates problems for translators.	Avoid it or give a paraphrased version.	Explain it in brackets, e.g., He's in the cat-bird seat (in a favoured position).
Regional words (p.124)	Non-English language services and clients will find difficult to understand and translate.	Watch out (i.e., try to avoid it, translating it to non-regional English).	(Explain it in brackets.)
Some + figure (p.405)	Some is more likely to confuse translators.	Write "about 500" people rather than "some 500 people".	
False friends (p. 139)	For example, in France the normal form of bankruptcy is "faillite", the term "banqueroute" refers to fraudulent bankruptcy. The danger if they are confused is obvious.	Be as precise as possible in reporting what a company or court says, especially if a translation is involved.	
Sports metaphors (408)	They are often particular to a single sport or culture and are difficult to translate.	Think twice (i.e., try to avoid it, use it only when necessary).	(Explain in brackets.)
Complex constructions (399)	A sentence with more than one subordinate clause can be hard to follow and difficult to translate.	Sentences should generally be short but, to avoid a staccato effect, vary their length.	

between source language and target language. When these challenges cannot be avoided, giving explanatory notes may well simplify the work of subsequent translations.

All in all, according to Reuters, a translator-friendly news dispatch is written in standard language, using short sentences and precise terminology (neither ambiguous nor metaphorical).

Compare parallel source texts

Due to the specificity of news translation and the fact that most journalists/translators do not acknowledge their work as translating, the concept of **transediting** (Stetting 1989) has been used in translation studies to tackle translation in the news (Schäffner 2012). This concept highlights the interventionist and domesticating ways in which journalists rewrite their source texts. Chesterman, in turn, summarizes the concept of transediting by stressing that journalists/translators often proofread their source texts: "This is a term suggested by Stetting (1989) to designate the sometimes radical re-editing that translators have to do on badly written original texts" (Chesterman 1997, 112). In fact, although translators do not describe their work as translation, recent sociological research in news translation showed that desks assess the quality and relevance of mediating texts, including the accuracy of the translation, before they translate a news piece into further languages (see Chapter 8).

To better understand the translation processes deployed when covering speeches by Pope John Paul II at the United Nations, Sousa (2020) interviewed journalists working for two Portuguese newspapers, *Diário de Notícias* and *Jornal de Notícias*. The managing editor of the first newspaper explained that, after receiving a news dispatch from AFP or Reuters about the Pope's speech, journalists first verified in which language this speech was given. If it were, say, in Spanish, the journalist would look for a Spanish language source to avoid translating from a translation. However, the managing editor also adds: "Of course, if the speech was in Russian, we would not be able to do this [i.e., to avoid indirect translation]; journalists have to stick to a language they know" (Ferreira 2019, 10, cited in Sousa 2020, 99, our translation). A similar scenario, according to this same managing editor, would take place if Pope Francis went to Brazil and a Portuguese language speech was therefore available. In this case, the journalists would not translate from Reuters or AFP.

The managing director of the second newspaper reveals that, if she had to write about the Pope's speech, she would start by looking for a Portuguese language version, mainly on official websites (presumably, the Vatican's). Then, she would assess the quality of this Portuguese language version. For this, she would compare it with other translations, such as (in her case) the French version. If the Pope gave the speech in a language she does not know, she would try to reconstruct the speech by reading different translations. She also adds that

> When I want a certain sentence, I look it up in a French newspaper, a British newspaper and a Spanish one. This way I can figure out what that sentence is when I do not understand the original language, which is the case with Italian for me.
>
> *Carneiro 2019, 20, cited in Sousa 2020, 110, our translation*

The managing directors of both newspapers argue that this textual comparison is a working technique typically used to address yet another challenge in news production, namely quotations (see below). They also stress that, in news writing, a common go-to solution would be to read information in different languages, then use this information to write a news piece from scratch.

Be extra careful with quotations

In their introduction to the volume *Politics, Media and Translation*, Schäffner and Bassnett (2010) analyse a quote from a news article published in October 2006 in the newspaper *The European Voice*:

> Former German chancellor Gerhard Schröder gives an interview to *Le Figaro* […]. Asked by the French paper if […] Schröder answers: "Absolument". Oh wait, perhaps he doesn't really speak French. "It's not just in the energy sector, where it's obvious", he says, presumably in German.
>
> *Schäffner and Bassnett 2010, 1, ellipses in the original*

According to Schäffner and Bassnett (2010), this is a good illustration of two ways in which translation shapes news writing. On the one hand, the ellipses signal that *Le Figaro* did not publish the entire interview with Schröder, only sections of it. On the other hand, the explicit reference to the language of the utterance indicates that the interview was first translated from German into French, although the German chancellor was quoted in direct speech: first in French and then in English. For Schäffner and Bassnett (2010, 2), this example "illustrates that in the production of both the French and the English text, translation and interpreting had been involved, even if they are hidden in the final published texts".

Quotations seem to be particularly challenging in news translation because they contain elements that make translation more visible. They tend to be seen as source texts that require accurate translation (Reuters 2008, AFP 2016, AP n.d.).

When conducting her two ethnographic projects, first with AFP and ATS, Davier (2022) found only one example of back translation that could be labelled as a circular indirect translation, i.e. A>B>A. Quite significantly, this example involved quotations:

> I uncovered only one example of back translation in both projects I conducted, and this example is not substantiated with textual excerpts: it was only broached in a discussion with one of the editors-in-chief of the Swiss news agency, ATS while she was giving a tour of the trilingual newsroom (French-German-Italian). She described a situation in which a francophone journalist covered a press conference in German (text1 L1) and translated a few quotations into French (text2 L2) in her news dispatch, which was sent to the wire for other media outlets and reused as a mediating source text within ATS for a French-to-German translation. The original quotations in German were erased, continuing to exist in French only, and were translated

into German (text2 L1) with the mediation of the mediating language, French. Given the absence of lexical overlap between language systems, it is highly likely that the ultimate target text differs from the ultimate source text language 1.

Davier 2022

The last sentence of the above extract sheds light on the pitfalls of using back translation in direct quotes. The direct quotations published in German newspapers contained words that differed from the ones used in the original German utterance. In other words, German language media declared that a particular individual had said such and such, but those words had not been spoken by that particular individual.

International news agencies provide specific guidelines on how to quote, edit and translate sources (AFP; AP; Reuters 2008). AFP (2016, 9) and AP (n.p.) give similar instructions:

- Do not alter a quotation.
- Do not take a quotation out of context.
- If the speaker misspoke, quote verbatim; if a verbatim quote exposes the speaker to ridicule, paraphrase.
- Do not edit or correct quotations.

Regarding the last point, elsewhere in the guidelines we can find a recommendation that goes in the opposite direction: "[when speakers use a different dialect], as in interviews with people not speaking their native language, it is especially important that their ideas be accurately conveyed" (AP n.d., n.p.).

Moreover, AP provides instructions on how to tackle the intralingual and interlingual translation of quotes:

- Nonstandard spellings may be used to recreate dialects (but never derogatorily).
- Quotes in another language should be translated faithfully.
- The quote's original language may be noted, if appropriate.

Reuters (2008), in turn, provides some tips on the general strategy to be used when translating quotes:

- Translations should be idiomatic, not literal (deemed pedantic).
- They should convey the tone of the original quote.

More importantly, Reuters (2008) warns against the back translation of quotes:

> Beware of translating quotes in newspaper pickups back into the original language of the source. If a French politician gives an interview to an American newspaper, it is almost certain that the translation back into French will be

wrong and in some cases the quote could be very different. In such cases, the fewer quotes and the more reported speech, the better.

Reuters 2008, 4

Prepare for changes in context, textual genre and allocated space

Why do journalists not label their work as translation? Partly because news translation is a highly creative and transformative act. According to Hernández Guerrero (2006, 129), whenever a news story is translated and published in a new location, it undergoes a series of transformations so that the target text complies with the new spatial and temporal framework, new audience and (possibly) new function. What is more, the target reader determines to a large extent how texts are translated.

All news stories are recontextualized every time they are translated across languages, territories and media outlets. According to Schäffner and Bassnett (2010), these recontextualization strategies include:

- Selection (of material to translate, according to readers' interests).
- Addition (information may need to be backgrounded for new readers).
- Deletion (for one group of readers a piece of information may be new, for others it may be well known and redundant).
- Rearrangement (journalists decide how to best structure the content).
- Substitution (e.g., change of genre).
- Reformulation (rewriting to comply, for example, with the editorial and/or ideological line of a newspaper).

The way we translate news depends on the textual genre and the needs of the new communication framework. According to Hernández Guerrero (2006), news genres can be informative, interpretative or argumentative. The generic rules for these three text types differ with language and local tradition, but some core features remain largely the same. Translating informative texts typically involves more creative strategies. According to Hernández Guerrero (2006, 135) "in the case of informative genres, the originals are used as the basis for creating a new text in Spanish that must function as news for a different audience, and be integrated into the new textual conventions" (our translation). In turn, interpretative source texts (e.g., journalistic chronicles) and argumentative source texts (e.g., opinion articles) are often treated with more respect (e.g., translated without drastic changes). (But see "Possible solutions on Activity 1.3" on the portal for examples that may contradict this.)

Let's focus on one particular genre—namely, informative news. Here, Spanish generic conventions differ from the French conventions. Spanish news headlines tend to be more direct, explicit, and written as a normal sentence. They give away some information contained in the main text. Conversely, French headlines are less direct, leave information implicit and, because they are elliptical, they may be accompanied by footnotes (Hernández Guerrero 2006, 127–129).

Hence, translators should be very much aware of the generic norms that prevail in news writing in their sociocultural context. They should also be able to recognize differences between local genre conventions and other news writing traditions. Ideally, a journalist/translator should develop something akin to a comparative grammar (as per the French-Spanish juxtaposition outlined above), which could inform some translation strategies. When translating from a translation, journalists/translators should be mindful of the fact that multilingual newspapers often provide literal translations of news written according to English language rules.

With each new publication, a text may change its section. If a news report originally published in the Business section is now meant to be part of the Sports section, new recontextualization and/or framing will be in order. This may include eliminating some passages and adding new, sports-related information. In this case, it may be a good idea to compile source texts that were published in different newspaper sections, since it can provide relevant information adapted by other journalists/translators.

With the shift from one section to another, the space allocated to a particular story may change too (Hernández Guerrero 2006, 129). If the new location for a news story is smaller, journalists/translators will need to condense the story and probably select some parts of it, while eliding others. If the new location is bigger, journalists/translators will need to expand, adding new material to the source text. In this case, it may be worth compiling source texts published in different outlets. Such a compilation can provide relevant supplementary information added by fellow journalists/translators.

Be responsible and aware of ideological manipulation

The three authors quoted above (Bassnett, Schaffer and Hernández Guerrero) stress that news texts are highly referential in that they contain in themselves features of their spatio-temporal framework. Schaffer and Bassnett (2010, 5) clarify that recontextualization occurs whenever someone else's discourse is taken from its first context. For example, a discourse changes when it enters into an ongoing dialogue in the new context.

In her previously mentioned analysis, Bennett (2021) found that the British press systematically translated the legal term "mineur" (minor) as "children" in the context of dismantling the Calais refugee camp. "Children" is the accurate legal equivalent for minor and, at first glance, it even seems to be a more empathic way of addressing refugee minors than "mineurs". However, according to Bennett, this translation solution is an example of a tendentious or even ironic translation. Due to this translation solution (translating "mineur" as "children"), Hollande's appeal for Britain to receive child refugees was read in light of the coetaneous controversy about a "possible abuse of British hospitality by migrants that are not properly 'children'" (Bennett 2021, 368).

The translation of sensitive terms such as these raises questions about ethical and social responsibility in news translation. Bennett considers that those who translate for end consumers should be aware that their translation choices have a great impact in society in general. To return to the example above, translating "mineurs" as "children" might have pushed British people to an unwelcoming attitude vis-à-vis refugee minors.

In the same vein, Bennett suggests that journalists/translators working in news agencies have a smaller degree of agency, because they are not writing for end readers. According to Bennett, this in turn means that journalists/translators working as relayers are not as responsible for the consequences of their translation choices, because:

> The translator working for BBC Monitoring or some other news agency producing English versions of political declarations for dissemination around the globe knows from the outset that his/her translational options will not be reproduced faithfully, but will be freely interpreted and reformulated in the successive "recontextualizations" that occur downstream.

This may well be true for Bennett's case study (a French language discourse translated into English). However, English language versions of discourses written in more peripheral languages may come to acquire a more binding status. In this case, relayers, such as journalists/translators working in news agencies, may have a higher degree of agency but also of responsibility.

Recontextualization strategies, such as omission or selection, can lead to a negative public reaction. In early 2020, the controversy surrounding the selection of translators for the work of the young poet Amanda Gorman was partially provoked by successive indirect translations of an AFP dispatch (used and credited by France 24 (AFP 2021a) and *Le Journal de Montréal* (AFP 2021b), among others) and an article in *The Guardian* (Flood 2021). Dutch activist Janice Deul's text addressing the choice of Marieke Lucas Rijneveld as translator as a "missed opportunity" was manipulated in such a way that she was accused of exerting censorship on white translators. The crude criticism and even insults targeted at Janice Deul seem to call for a revision of the agency and social responsibility of relayers in news translation. More information on the Gorman controversy may be found on the portal. See Activity 1.2.

Further discussion

- *Agency in news translation.* Do you think relayers and relay-takers in news translations have different degrees of agency? How do you think the performance of both may impact society?
- *Spread of fake news.* How do you think indirect translation relates to fake news? To what extent does indirect translation contribute to the spread of fake news? To what extent can it help counter this practice?

Activities

Activity 1 Produce a translator-friendly text that can be conveniently used as a pivot text for subsequent translations into a third language

Activity 1.1 Analyse published news

PART A. Local news

Find a piece of local news or social media news that could become newsworthy worldwide. What would be the characteristics of that news? You can find some examples of local news that reaches global audiences in BBC Monitoring or News from Elsewhere.

PART B. Text analysis

Look at the checklist. Does the news piece include the following?

- KISSER
- Parallel sources
- Quotations
- Changes

PART C. Global reach

What would be the difficulties if you wanted to present this piece of news in a different country? What would need to be added or deleted? Could you translate it as is? What type of adaptations would it need?

Activity 1.2 Controversies

PART A. Documentation

Look for media coverage in your main working language of the Gorman/Rijneveld controversy. How were Janice Deul's arguments presented? What quotations were retrieved by different media outlets? Can you trace back the sources (e.g., do articles credit a news agency or newspaper?) Consider possible recontextualization strategies that may be used in this new language. For example, the substitution of some words when translating "unapologetically Black".

PART B. News writing

Try to write a 600-word story in which you report on: Rijneveld's dismissal from the translation; Janice Deul's (2021a) contribution to it (using Haidee Kotze's translation (Deul 2021b) in case you do not know Dutch); and the translation of *The Hill*

We Climb in your working language. Please remember to properly (re)contextualize all the information (your readers should be informed about all agents in the story). You may want to follow the inverted pyramid method, which consists of "ordering the elements of the story in declining order of importance" (Reuters 2008, 26).

PART C. Agency

Read Haidee Kotze's "English translation: Janice Deul's opinion piece about Gorman/Rijneveld". Consider the manipulation strategies that, according to Kotze, took place before the original Dutch text was published. Reflect on how this impacts the journalist's agency.

PART D. Analysis

Analyse the text you produced in Part B in terms of recontextualization strategies and reflect on possible manipulations of Janice Deul's arguments in your text. Think about the impact of your translation choices to both readers and journalists (who may rewrite your text).

PART E. Back translation

Compare Kotze's English language translation with the source text and consider the instances of back translation that have taken place. If you do not know Dutch, you can concentrate on the English language passages that are present in the Dutch original. Can you classify these back translations as circular indirect translations or are they different? How can these impact the reading and further translation of Deul's article?

Activity 2 Assess the relevance and accuracy of the intermediary versions of a source text

Activity 2.1 Global news agencies

Imagine that a religious leader makes a speech during an official visit to your home country. In the speech, the following subjects are touched upon: famine in French-speaking Africa; Covid-19 in India; and violence in North America. Now imagine that you are expected to write a piece on this speech, using (among other sources) the press releases by the international agencies: AFP, AP and Reuters.

- What differences would you expect to find between these three press releases?
- What other sources would you look for (if any)?
- Would you use all three press releases?
- Which of the three subjects mentioned above would be of interest to your home readers? Why?

Activity 2.2 Local news agencies

Use this Wikipedia entry ("List of News Agencies: https://en.wikipedia.org/wiki/List_of_news_agencies) to find translation agencies in your country and/or language. Then, check if these agencies have a style manual for journalists. These may be available online or only in print version. Should the style guide only be available in book form, try to find it through a local library. Then, consider the following questions:

- How is translation for and from a translation tackled in this manual?
- What guidelines can you find for editing news?
- How about guidelines for writing?
- How can these relate to translating for and from a translation?
- How can these relate to the subsets of indirect translation called back translation and eclectic/compilative translation?

Activity 2.3 Newspapers in your country

PART A. Ideological stances

Look at the newspapers in your country. What are their ideological stances? How do their agenda differ? Which papers would you consider tabloid or serious? How can these ideological stances impact on their translations? How can this knowledge affect the way you use their translations?

PART B. News sources

Select a recent news story published in three of the newspapers discussed in PART A. Read it critically. Then check the newspapers' websites and try to ascertain their main sources. Do they rely more on international or local agencies? Which parts or features of the target text suggest the use of a particular source text?

Activity 2.4 Quotations

Read the article "No, Anne Frank Did Not Say 'Dead People Receive More Flowers'" (Liles 2021).

Translate the pseudo-quotation by Anne Frank into your working languages and look for mentions of it on Google, Google Images and Google Books.

Try to back translate this quotation into Dutch. If you do not know Dutch, try using a machine translation system. Look for mentions of the pseudo-quotation on Google, Google Images and Google Books. What do your findings tell us about the use of pseudotranslations in the news? What do they tell us about the relationship between pseudotranslation and fake news? How important was the language of this pseudotranslation (English) for the dissemination of this piece of fake news?

News translation 181

After doing the previous research, how would you go about translating a news item with the quotation wrongly attributed to Anne Frank (namely, "Dead people receive more flowers than the living ones because regret is stronger than gratitude")?

Activity 3 Summarize, rephrase, restructure, adapt rapidly and accurately using already translated written and/or spoken communication, keeping the most relevant features

Activity 3.1 Textual adaptations

PART A. Preparing a text for further translation

Go to "Oddly Enough Headlines" (www.reuters.com/news/archive/oddlyEnough News). Select a piece of news that you find particularly funny. Justify your choice. Prepare this piece of news for further translation into one of your working languages. Consider the following:

- What challenges do you face during this preparation?
- What strategies can you use to be more time efficient?
- Have you considered following the strategy described by the news agencies mentioned above?

PART B. Parallel texts

Select a newspaper of your choice. It can be in any language. This newspaper will be the location for your news story. Decide where in the newspaper your translated news item will appear (in which section). Read two or three articles published in the same section. Try to describe the most important textual features of these parallel texts.

PART C. International adaptations

Search the web for other media that has recontextualized your chosen news story in your working languages. What adaptations did they make?

PART D. Functional translation

Translate the news story for these three publishing platforms:

- The Twitter account of the newspaper (the tweet with your translation should have no more than 280 characters (including spaces)).
- The printed version of the same newspaper (the news article should have no more than 1,000 words).

- The newspaper's website (the news article should have no more than 1,000 words; please bear in mind that, here, you can use hyperlinks redirecting your readers to related content).

Activity 3.2 Opinion pieces

Read the article "FactFind: What exactly was said in the French PM's letter about UK fishing row?" (www.thejournal.ie/factfind-castex-letter-uk-france-fishing-row-brexit-5589055-Nov2021/).

Write an opinion piece (i.e., a news article of the argumentative type) on this controversy. In your article, be sure to:

- Summarize all the key issues.
- Express your opinion about what happened. For example, is the journalist/translator Alex Wickam responsible for this controversy? Could it have been avoided? How exactly?
- Explain how this controversy relates to the notion of indirect translation (including back translation and compilative/eclectic translation).
- Show that this controversy spanned beyond France and the UK.

When you are done, think about to what extent you resorted to indirect translation (including back translation and compilative/eclectic translation) when writing your opinion piece.

> **Resources**: Tools to diagnose and enhance your readability. Full-length quotations on translating for translation in news agencies' guidelines.
> **Activities**: Solutions to Activity 1.3 and some extra activities.

References

AFP. 2016. *Editorial Standards and Best Practices*. June 22, 2016. www.afp.com/sites/default/files/22_juin_2016_charte_deontologique_.pdf [Accessed November 2021].

AFP. 2021a. "Amanda Gorman's White Dutch Translator Quits Over 'Uproar'." *France 24*, March 2, 2021, www.france24.com/en/live-news/20210302-amanda-gorman-s-white-dutch-translator-quits-over-uproar [Accessed November 2021].

AFP. 2021b. "Pay Bas: La traductrice blanche d'Amanda Gorman démissionne après un 'tollé'." *Le Journal de Montréal*, March 3, 2021, www.journaldemontreal.com/2021/03/03/pays-bas-la-traductrice-blanche-damanda-gorman-demissionne-apres-un--tolle [Accessed November 2021].

AP (The Associated Press). n.d. *News Values and Principles*. www.ap.org/about/news-values-and-principles [Accessed November 2021].

Baker, Mona. 2006. *Translation and Conflict: A Narrative Account*. London and New York: Routledge.

Bennett, Karen. 2021. "Agency and Social Responsibility in the Translation of the Migrant Crisis." In *Translating Asymmetry – Rewriting Power*, edited by Ovidi Carbonell i Cortés and Esther Monzó-Nebot, 361–377. Amsterdam: John Benjamins.

Bielsa, Esperança, and Susan Bassnett. 2009. *Translation in Global News*. New York: Routledge.

Chesterman, Andrew. 1997. *Memes of Translation. The Spread of Ideas in Translation Theory*. Amsterdam and Philadelphia: John Benjamins.

Davier, Lucile. 2017. *Les enjeux de la traduction dans les agences de presse*. Lille: Presses universitaires du Septentrion.

Davier, Lucile. 2022. "Translational Phenomena in the News: Indirect Translation as the Rule." *Target 34*.

Desjardins, René. 2017. *Translation and Social Media: In Theory, in Training and in Professional Practice*. London: Palgrave.

Deul, Janice. 2021a. "Opinie: Een Witte Vertaler Voor Poëzie van Amanda Gorman: Onbegrijpelijk." *De Volkkrant*, February 25, 2021, www.volkskrant.nl/columns-opinie/opinie-een-witte-vertaler-voor-poezie-van-amanda-gorman-onbegrijpelijk~bf128ae4/?referrer=https%3A%2F%2Fwww.monabaker.org%2F [Accessed November 2021].

Deul, Janice. 2021b. "OPINION: A White Translator for the Poetry of Amanda Gorman: Incomprehensible", translated by Haidee Kotze. In: Kotze, Haidee, "English Translation: Janice Deul's Opinion Piece about Gorman/Rijneveld." Haidee Kotze (*Medium* blog), March 18, 2021. https://haidee-kotze.medium.com/english-translation-janice-deuls-opinion-piece-about-gorman-rijneveld-8165a8ef4767 [Accessed November 2021].

Elliot, Deni. 1995. "Journalistic research." *Accountability in Research* 2 (4): 103–114.

Flood, Alison. 2021. "'Shocked by the Uproar': Amanda Gorman's White Translator Quits." *The Guardian*, March 1, 2021. www.theguardian.com/books/2021/mar/01/amanda-gorman-white-translator-quits-marieke-lucas-rijneveld [Accessed November 2021].

Gagnon, Chantal. 2012. "La visibilité de la traduction au Canada en journalisme politique: mythe ou réalité?" *Meta: Journal des Traducteurs* 57 (4): 943–959.

Hernández Guerrero, María José. 2006. "Técnicas específicas de la traducción periodística." *Quaderns: Revista de Traducció* 13: 125–139.

Hernández Guerrero, María José. 2009. *Traducción y periodismo*. Bern: Peter Lang.

Ivaska, Laura. 2021. "The Genesis of a Compilative Translation and its De Facto Source Text." In *Genetic Translation Studies: Conflict and Collaboration in Liminal Spaces*, edited by Ariadne Nunes, Joana Moura and Marta Pacheco Pinto, 72–88. London: Bloomsbury.

Liles, Jordan. 2021. "No, Anne Frank Did Not Say 'Dead People Receive More Flowers'", *Snopes*, October 16, 2021. www.snopes.com/fact-check/anne-frank-flowers-quote/ [Accessed November 2021].

Pym, Anthony. 2014. *Exploring Translation Theories*. 2nd edition. London and New York: Routledge.

Reuters. 2008. *Handbook of Journalism*. E-book. www.trust.org/contentAsset/raw-data/652966ab-c90b-4252-b4a5-db8ed1d438ce/file [Accessed November 2021].

Ringmar, Martin. 2007. "Roundabout Routes: Some Remarks on Indirect Translations." In *Selected Papers of CETRA Research Seminar in Translation Studies 2006*, edited by Francis Mus. www.arts.kuleuven.be/cetra/papers/files/ringmar.pdf. [Accessed November 2021].

Schäffner, Christina. 2012. "Rethinking Transediting." *Meta* 57 (4): 866–883. https://doi.org/10.7202/1021222ar.

Schäffner, Christina, and Susan Bassnett. 2010. "Introduction: Politics, Media and Translation: Exploring Synergies." In *Political Discourse, Media and Translation*, edited by Christina Schäffner and Susan Bassnett, 1–31. Newcastle-upon-Tyne: Cambridge Scholars.

Sousa, Márcia Teresa Borges de. 2020. *Como se reescreve um Papa? A tradução no campo jornalístico dos discursos pontifícios proferidos na assembleia geral da ONU*. PhD Thesis. Universidade Católica Portuguesa.

Stetting, Karen. 1989. "Transediting – A New Term for Coping with the Grey Area Between Editing and Translating." In *Proceedings from the Fourth Nordic Conference for English Studies*, edited by Graham Caie, Kirsten Haastrup, Arnt Lykke Jakobsen et al. 371–382. Copenhagen: University of Copenhagen.

Toury, Gideon. 2012. *Descriptive Translation Studies - And Beyond*. Amsterdam and Philadelphia: John Benjamins.

Valdeón, Roberto. 2007. "Ideological Independence or Negative Mediation: BBC Mundo and CNN en Español's (translated) Reporting of Madrid's Terrorist Attacks." In *Translating and Interpreting Conflict*, edited by Myriam Salama-Carr, 99–118. Amsterdam: Rodopi.

Valdeón, Roberto. 2022. "On the Role of Indirect Translation in the History of News Production." *Target 34 (2)*.

van Doorslaer, Luc. 2010. "Journalism and Translation." In *Handbook of Translation Studies* vol. I, edited by Yves Gambier and Luc van Doorslaer, 180–184. Amsterdam: John Benjamins.

van Rooyen, Marlie. 2019. *Tracing the Translation of Community Radio News in South Africa: An Actor Network Approach*. PhD Thesis. KU Leuven.

8
PROJECT MANAGEMENT

Introduction

This chapter moves away from translation domains and looks at indirect translation through the lens of project management. It will cover key points like time management, revision, project coherence and after-life. It aims to connect the missing dots in previous chapters and provide a different approach to indirect translation.

Learning outcomes

Upon successful completion of this chapter, readers will know how to:

- Take account of and adapt the organizational and physical ergonomics of specific working environments where translation is carried out from multiples sources and languages either individually or in plurilingual teams, where translators are not competent in all the working languages and collaborate to produce a translation with recourse to a third common language.
- Be aware of and comply with the current market demands and conditions for translating for and from a translation in different fields.
- Organize, budget and manage translation projects that make use of previous translations (the intellectual property of previous translators) and/or produce texts to be used for further translations.
- Critically approach the use of mediating languages in online translation memories.

186 Project management

> **Warm-up activity**
>
> Put yourself in the shoes of the project manager in the situation illustrated in Figure 8.1. What challenges might you face when managing this multi-source translation? Can indirect translation help you identify strategies for reporting the "truth" about this event?

What does a PM do?

A project manager (PM) is the person who manages specific aspects of a translation project and is responsible for the process (ISO 2015, 4). A PM is the central point of contact for language specialists and clients, especially in large scale projects. Specifically, project management will include, among other things, "disseminating information, issuing instructions related to the assignment, and managing the translation project to all parties involved" (ISO 2015, 8). Other tasks might vary slightly depending on the field, but, all in all, PMs are responsible for calculating timescales and costs and organizing the work in a sensible manner for everyone involved. They are also responsible for quality management, a process present throughout the project. Let's keep in mind that quality management consists of quality control—which focuses on fulfilling quality requirements—and quality assurance—which focuses on providing confidence that the quality requirements have been fulfilled (see Drugan 2013 and Chapter 3).

Therefore, they need to excel at locating the appropriate translator, conveying the client's needs and supervising a timely quality delivery. Moreover, given that

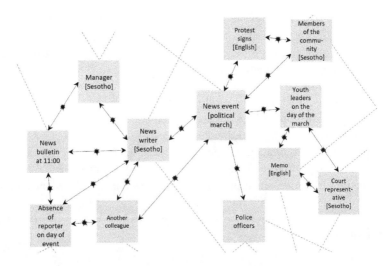

FIGURE 8.1 Multilingual exchanges during the production of a news translation for a local radio station in South Africa (adapted from van Rooyen 2019)

"the quality of the output is directly related to the quality of the client's input" (as accurately claimed by Olohan and Davitti 2017, 398), PMs must also work with clients to identify their potential needs and educate them on improving their input. That is, "[p]reparation by the TSP shall cover administrative, technical, and linguistic aspects according to the project specifications of each translation project" (ISO 2015, 8).

Drugan (2013, 77–80) divides the tasks involved in the translation process into three stages: pre-translation, translation and post-translation. In the pre-translation stage, we could claim that PMs are responsible for pricing, planning, human resource management, source files and resource preparation. In the translation stage, they would monitor the feedback cycle. In the post-translation stage, they are in charge of the quality control process, the translation quality assurance [TQA] process, the project management process and the project review.

Esselink (2000, 429) defines the following tasks for a localization PM: creating quotes and proposals, project setup, resourcing, scheduling, finances, quality management and communication. For Dunne and Dunne (2011), project management can be mapped into five processes: initiation, planning, execution, monitoring and signing-off. Chan (2015, 63) sets more specific responsibilities for the PM: planning, executing and closing projects; managing the cost, time and scope of the project; setting achievable objectives; and building the project requirements. See Table 8.1 for a comparison of terminology and responsibilities.

While there are differences in how authors approach and classify the different responsibilities held by project managers, there is agreement on how PMs must monitor time, budget, human resources and quality pre-production, during

TABLE 8.1 Authors' divisions of PM tasks

Esselink 2000	Dunne & Dunne 2011	Drugan 2013		Chan 2015
Creating quotes and proposals	Initiation	Pre- translation stage	Pricing	Planning projects
Project setup	Planning		Planning and human resources	Managing costs
Resourcing			Preparation of source files and other resources	
Scheduling	Execution	Translation stage	Monitoring feedback cycles	Managing time and scope
Quality management	Monitoring	Post- translation stage	QC process	Building project requirements
Finances*	Signing-off		TQA process	Closing projects
			Project management processes	
Communication*			Project review	

production and post-production. This is also highlighted in the standard ISO 17100/2015, which states that the translation service provider, and the PM as their person in charge, "shall ensure compliance with the client-TSP agreement from the moment it is confirmed to the agreed end of the project" (ISO 2015, 9).

Facing multilingualism and diversity

Multilingual projects will often include several translators, sometimes working into languages the PM is not familiar with. Then, some sort of quality assurance control must be in place for all situations. It might also require explaining to clients that not all language combinations require equal time and economic investment, thus clarifying unrealistic expectations regarding the translation process. In some cases, PMs are the ones that can advise on using indirect translation depending on the availability of suitable translators. As Olohan and Davitti (2017) claim, trust is a key factor in this relationship.

In projects where pivot translation plays a role, the quality of translation may be improved by assigning translations to those who are not only proficient in the pivot language but also have knowledge of the source language. Given that translation will happen from the pivot language (most likely English), translators do not need to be proficient in the source language but use that knowledge to improve the output. Such improvement would not be hard to implement if agencies kept a database of translators' additional language knowledge. In their research on quality assurance in subtitling, Robert and Remael (2016, 591) mentioned how "quality assurance at the level of human resources was taken seriously by all the stakeholders in the period covered". That is, there was an effort in their sample to hire the best qualified translators. Source language knowledge could be an added level of qualification.

Fields where multilingualism, and sometimes also pivot translation, is the norm might already work with adequate technology to manage complex workflows. In general translation assignments, this may not have been implemented, complicating the management process but also giving PMs a certain degree of flexibility.

Technology and project management tools

Basic resources such as a generic project management tool, a workflow app or a spreadsheet could be considered adequate for planning and managing a small project. Given the growing complexity of translation projects, and in line with the technological advances in translation today, the market offers several tools that are specific to translation and cover every step of a big project. Some even allow for pivot translation control (see Gridly software configurations in Figure 8.2).

PM tools are increasingly connected to traditional CAT tools. Actually, one of the time-consuming tasks for PMs relates to managing CAT tools (e.g., translation memories, termbases or machine translation engines, including their server versions). Server tools are prepared to deal with multilingual projects but do not

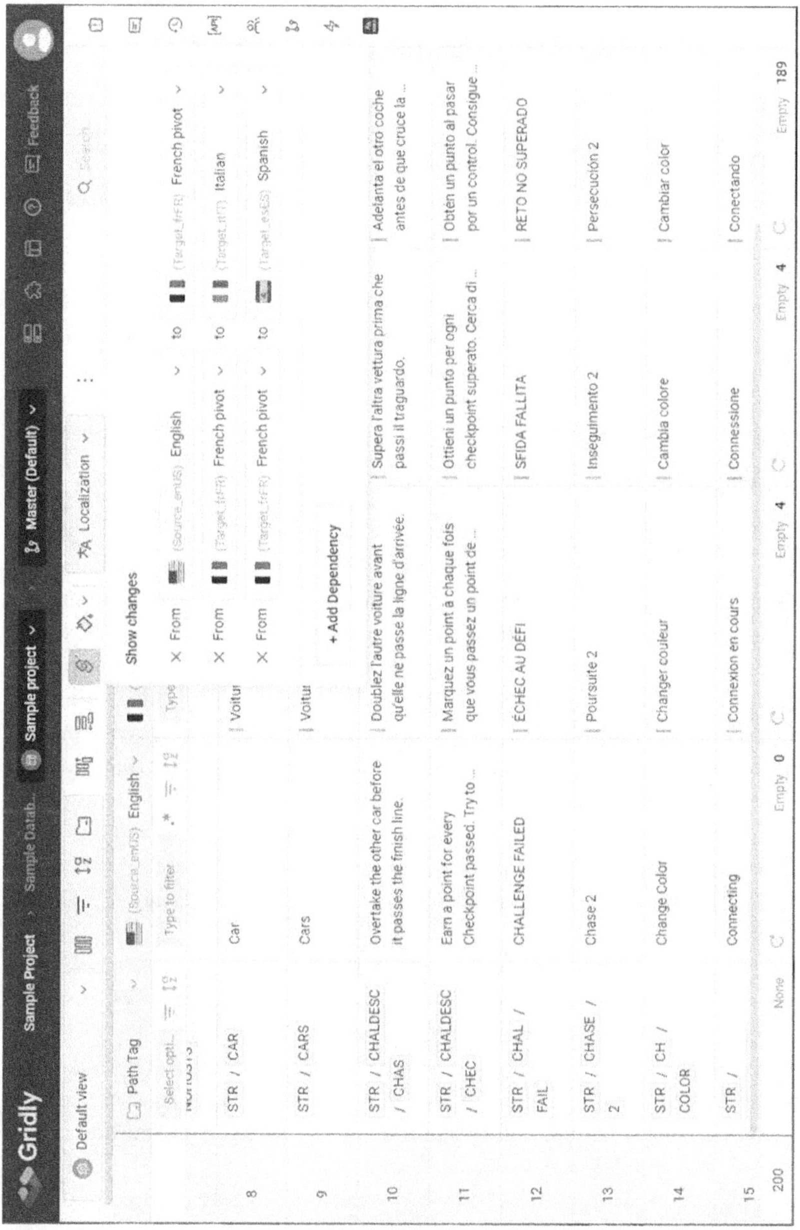

FIGURE 8.2 Screenshot of spreadsheet-based content manager Gridly (sample multi-step localization project)

always clearly cater to indirect translations. Using them for this purpose tends to require some ad hoc adaptation.

Among the benefits of current technologies, automatic word counts and role specifications can help the process of budgeting, quoting, pricing and invoicing. Texts can be divided, updated and merged, outsourced to several languages and their terminology combined in a single database. Quality assurance can be automated by enforcing certain workflows, translation memory plugins and automatic checks (that can identify untranslated segments, detect inconsistencies, sort out technical gaffes and more, as explained in the localization section).

However, there are downsides to the implementation of technologies. On the one hand, technical glitches can be bothersome, especially with highly formatted files, and the need to deal with upgrades and new versions might have a negative impact on time. On the other hand, translators might be concerned about the constraints imposed by these technologies as well as new calculation methods that might reduce offered rates (e.g., by discounting fuzzy or exact matches or by assuming a lower rate for post-editing). The PM must be aware of these possible frictions and intervene before they occur to ensure a smooth completion of the project.

Communication

A traditional view of a PM might give the idea that communication in a translation project is unidirectional (in the line of "issuing instructions"); however, communication must take place among all participants, with the PM working as a hub (see Figure 8.3). According to ISO 17100/2015, a PM's responsibilities include "monitoring constant conformity to the client-TSP agreement, project specifications, and, where necessary, communicating with all parties involved in the project, including the client" (ISO 2015, 9). That is, the PM is not only the voice of the client, but also the voice of the workers. They must communicate clearly to dispel uncertainties and clarify expectations, which "serv[e] the purpose of protecting the trusting relationship over time" (Olohan and Davitti 2017, 413).

In general terms, communication in the pre-translation stage must include confirmation with the client regarding source texts and translation resources, as well as the commercial terms to be included in the contract. In this regard, PMs can play a very important role in advocating for fairer working conditions by educating clients on the realities of translation or, if clients opted for a language service provider (LSP) in order to avoid dealing with translation-related details, the advantages of adequate rates and delivery dates.

Communication with translators should clearly state the working conditions (rates and delivery times), provide all necessary materials (if possible, in a single location/communication) and information on the translation flow. The PM must consider whether direct communication between revisor, translator and pivot translator should be encouraged and whether communication channels should be open.

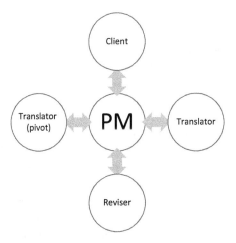

FIGURE 8.3 Hub-style communication flow

If the extent of the project means that this would create an unnecessary burden, then indications on how to provide feedback or ask questions is also encouraged (Q&A sheets, comments, email, etc.).

In this respect, more challenges are likely to occur when coordinating a large pool of workers with different tasks and needs; therefore, some contingency measures are always recommended. Negotiating reasonable delivery dates with some time planned for possible delays can help if something happens. However, a balance must be made to not push deadlines too early just to be safe.

Communication is also important after the translation has been submitted, both to clear any financial issues that have not been sorted out and, whenever possible, to provide feedback on the work. As Olohan and Davitti (2017, 391) claim, "the project manager's ability both to confer and to instill trust is highlighted as key to the successful operation of the company".

Finally, post-production communication and project review also include client satisfaction management.

Project management in interpreting

Conference interpreting

As discussed in the chapter on indirect translation in interpreting, according to the professional standards agreed upon by the International Association of Conference Interpreters (AIIC), "teams of interpreters must be put together in such a way as to avoid the systematic use of relay" (AIIC [2004] 2017). Nevertheless, "when there is no alternative to the use of relay for a given language, the team shall comprise at least two interpreters able to provide a relay from that language" (AIIC [2004] 2017). The nature of relay as an imperfect yet inescapable phenomenon is a cornerstone of indirectness in simultaneous interpreting.

In interpreting, and especially in situations where several language mediations might take place at the same time, the chief interpreter (PM) is the person in charge of planning and rearranging tasks. All in all, the PM must assign people to tasks, make sure the documentation is uploaded and in order, confirm the correct functioning of the technology, make sure allocated interpreters are in the right place when they need to pivot, and mediate if conflicts arise.

The PM should first make sure relevant documentation is available for all interpreters. Ideally, he or she should also recommend that the chairperson reminds speakers to pause when they move on to the next slide (AIIC [2004] 2017). This deliberate breathing space allows relay-takers to catch up.

So, the first task for the PM is to discuss and determine working arrangements. Assuming that interpreters were selected based on their language combinations, the chief interpreter must consider any special expertise that exists within the team (field speciality, regional accents, passive languages, etc.). An important aspect to ponder is whether the relayer would work best into their L1 or L2 depending on the interpreter's abilities. Then, arrangements must consider the needs of all the booths and the overall language coverage: it is key to have a clear understanding of who does what and when. Wrong time allocations can easily cause trouble.

Initial planning must consider working conditions: working shifts and resting times must be respected. However, slavish adherence to the initially agreed schedule can be counterproductive at times. An inflexible division of the work based on the number of presentations might not best serve the interests of the interpreters or the interpreted. For example, it is rarely advisable to change interpreters in the middle of a speech unless it is very long. The PM must have a plan for contingencies and make quick decisions when unexpected changes to sessions or schedules occur.

The chief interpreter is responsible for managing arrangements between different booths. Therefore, they need to be kept informed and updated about relevant changes in the booths. This will avoid a sudden absence of a given pivot, a given language combination, or an unnecessary systematic relay in situations where all the working languages are sufficiently covered in each booth. (AIIC [2004] 2017).

As in the remaining fields, personal acquaintance with the interpreters might help avoid personality clashes and identify teams that work especially well together, thus making less trouble for the PM.

Consecutive interpreting

Regarding consecutive interpreting, project managers or language service providers must make the client aware that relay interpreting can double the time of a regular appointment: the number of steps increases and the interpreting usually takes extra time (see Chapter 2). Therefore, PMs must allocate enough time for the meeting and warn the translation buyer about it. For court relay assignments, it would be advisable to confirm that this setting will not be a problem and discuss how to follow court procedures appropriately (Allen et al. 2018, 373). If possible, interpreters should be encouraged to meet beforehand in order to decide how they will handle introductions, address communication problems, and manage turn-taking. Debriefing with the translation buyer and the interpreters is also highly recommended in order to look at ways of improving in this setting.

Ideally, interpreters should have access to any documents they need to sight translate, although, often, this is not possible due to data protection responsibilities or a simple lack of communication with the client.

Project management in scientific-technical translation

If we assume that scientific-technical projects might not necessarily be of the size of localization projects, PMs may be able to use simple management tools. If that is the case, there are some key factors that PMs must bear in mind.

First, if the project allows, the PM might consider which text would be a better source for translation: the source text or the pivot text. Inclusion of both can also be considered. In any case, always remember that changes in the source text need to be reflected in the pivot and target text. Therefore, appropriate source file preparation might save trouble later.

Keeping the files organized will make the translation process easier for you and the subsequent translator. It may help prevent needless organizational efforts and errors across all languages. Include all relevant files in an ordered folder structure. Be sure that all are indeed relevant for the subsequent translator: extraneous or unused files will slow down their translation process considerably.

When receiving files that will be reused by further translators, make sure adequate background information is provided, including a glossary of technical terms and/or abbreviations that have been used previously. Earlier correspondence or other documents relating to the subject matter can also be helpful, as subsequent translators do not necessarily have the same amount of information about the subject matter as the first translator had.

Q&A worksheets can help improve the final outcome: if the source text is ambiguous, encourage translators to share any problems they had trouble solving as well as any ingenious solutions they discovered. If time allows, it is advisable to approach pivot translation as team work and pass on this vision to all the translators. Open communication channels where the text can be discussed. In this context, if translators are willing to follow up, an open dialogue maximizes the chances of a successful result.

Project management in localization

Localization is one of the translation fields that, by definition, is most accustomed to multilingual project management. During localization, products are translated to meet the technical, linguistic and cultural demands of the target markets. Therefore, current localization tools are already designed to help project managers address problems related to extra files, graphical user interfaces (GUI) and simultaneous translation into multiple languages.

Human resources

As happens in other specializations, some knowledge of other languages involved in the process can add an extra layer of quality. In localization, technical skills bring added value.

Moreover, crediting everyone involved in the translation process can be a stepping stone to ensuring that a team that works well together can stay involved in the project. This is sometimes challenging in localization projects that require updates and revisions. In game localization, for example, periodically launched special events must be translated every few weeks. Crediting should also include relayers. That is, this practice should be fully implemented regardless of the quantity of languages or genre of the project.

Testing internationalization

Internationalization, understood as designing and testing software to prevent globalization errors, is introduced at the development stage. Among the features reviewed, good internationalization allows for text extraction in translation-accessible files, and compilation and loading of the translated text (extensive details in Roturier 2015). PMs can provide feedback to clients (or, in Roturier's terminology "**translation buyers**") on how to best prepare files to avoid translation problems.

Translation

The translation kit includes all the files required to produce a translation. Before the translation process starts, all these documents should be reviewed, especially glossaries and accompanying documentation. If the platform used does not integrate a follow-up of the shared files, the PM must make sure that a suitable archiving system is in place to monitor all received and sent files.

If the localized text is to be shipped simultaneously with the source language product, documentation (like Help files) might be in the making. That usually provides little room for quality assurance and testing and should be taken into consideration. In this situation, the PM must draft a clear schedule of deliverables and make sure that these milestones are reached on time. Also, communication channels between production and localizers can speed up the process if problems arise.

Finally, there are different positions regarding the copyright of MT data, with some arguing that online MT falls under the text and data mining exception of the Directive on Copyright in the Digital Single Market entered into force on June 6, 2019 and the fair use exception in the US (see Seinen and van der Meer 2020 for details). Pivot machine translation would then fall into this category.

Quality assurance monitoring

Modern CAT tools integrate quality control mechanisms that take care of user interface problems such as tagging, truncated texts in user interfaces, overlapping elements or inconsistent access keys; technical mismatches such as missing translations, inconsistent use of tab and spaces or inclusion of incorrect characters in the target code; and linguistic consistency, such as terminology use, maintenance of key words and the avoidance of prohibited words.

Ideally, the localized product should be tested by a third party.

Project management in literary translation

Large scale projects in literary translation are not all that common. Well-known exceptions might occur in Bible translation and excerpts for literary journals or book fairs. Even in those situations, the use of CAT tools might not be the norm. As stated before, indirect translation in literary contexts is often considered undesirable but, actually, it can become an opportunity for enhancement. If the delivery schedule allows it, challenges posed by a translation into a given language can be reported back to the PM and used to clarify the pivot text or even improve it.

Since global consistency is one of the requisites of large-scale projects, glossaries with key elements of the story (character names, frequently used terms and register considerations, to name just a few examples) should be provided. Moreover, clear instructions on expected strategies, platforms for shared documents or queries can also be provided to promote communication and collaboration between translators to find one solution for all.

As indicated in the chapter on literary translation, issues with ethical concerns and copyright infringement could easily arise in this context, since authors of mediating texts are rarely acknowledged in the paratexts of indirect translations and relayers are not paid for the use of their intellectual work. The PM should take the necessary steps to discuss the workflow, collect queries and comments and circulate them. Regarding copyright, Standard EN 15038:2006 indicates that "copyright can be covered in the initial contract details" as an option to the obligatory indications on service specifications and commercial terms (European Committee for Standardization 2006, 8). Currently, ISO 17100:2015 mentions "copyright on deliverables" as a commercial term that can be included in the contract but also "restrictions to the use of by-products such as translation memories" (ISO 2015, 13). Championing for the inclusion of copyright provisions in all contracts by default would probably be useful for PMs.

Project management in AVT

In the human resources process, the quality of translation could be improved by assigning translations to those who have knowledge of the source language or culture in addition to proficiency in the template language. Even a basic acquaintance with the key peculiarities of a given culture can be a step forward in quality.

Moreover, a comprehensive collection of source text materials is encouraged. In a survey on quality control in subtitling (Robert and Remael 2016, 593), respondents were asked about the source text material they received: video file only, script only

(= dialogue list), template only, or a combination of these. As noted, over 80% had access to the video file and a written form (Robert and Remael 2016, 594). In the context of online streaming, the inclusion of project management and translation tools (like OOONA) probably facilitates the sharing of resources.

Experienced translators can feel resistance to the use of templates due to their lack of flexibility to specific conditions, fears of mistranslation, and lower rates that might result from higher competitiveness in translations between major languages. The PM can play a role in attracting and retaining translators. PMs can advocate for open templates, whereby subtitlers can change some of the spatial or temporal features e.g., merge or split segments and adjust in and out cues, at least slightly for certain languages and traditions. Revision of the instructions provided to templators on what information to include in their annotations can also help reduce mistrust in the pivot. If such revisions cannot be included in the process due to time limits—we should not forget that the need for quick global distribution is usually behind the use of templates in AVT—they can be noted for future projects.

Regarding rates, templators' fees should be reviewed: they are not only translating but facilitating the translation into multiple languages by adding annotations. Also, in some legal systems, subtitling is considered a creative endeavour, so contracts should address whether copyright compensation of some kind should be paid to templators. It must be noted that, while rights belong to the translator or translation company, they are often transferred to the publisher or translation company who hires the translator (Van der Meer 2013).

Last, and in line with previous recommendations, clients must be made aware that templates only reduce the time invested by the translators in the process (not the pivot translators) if they are asked not to consider technicalities. In doing so, however, a revision layer is lost.

Project management in news translation

Since journalists/translators do not consider their (re)writing tasks as translating, there is no such thing as a multilingual project manager in newspapers, even though, as explained in Chapter 7, editors usually train young journalists in source text assessment and collection.

Conversely, global news agencies put forward different project management models in order to assign translation tasks, send them to clients, control quality and assess commercial impact. Hence, it makes sense to focus on the case of news agencies in this chapter, as one of their declared tasks is to translate from translations and for translation. Reuters' "Guide to Operations" stipulates that "Reuters stories have to travel beyond your own country or market. You will often need a higher level of context and background. A Reuters story should be written so that a single version of the story can be sent, if necessary, to all relevant products or wires" (Reuters 2008, 25). Meanwhile, regional bureaux for Associated Press France (APF) and Inter Press Service (IPS) both localize global news to local wires—"This means that events of global significance are reported at the same time in Spanish, in English and in French, through articles that incorporate regional nuances are thus designed for their specific audiences from the start" (Bielsa 2010, 36)—and also work with further translation in mind—"Translation is thus an integral part of journalistic work at both regional offices, where news reports are processed, which will further be translated into other languages at the local level" (Bielsa 2010, 39).

Since news agencies work both locally and globally, PM-equivalent positions are to be found in news agencies headquarters (editor-in-chief) as well as in local bureaux (desks). These meet virtually or over the phone on a regular basis (Bielsa and Bassnett 2009, 77; Davier 2017).

According to Reuters, desks fulfil many of the PM tasks listed in Drugam's (2013) three phases: pre-translation, translation and post-translation. First, some desks have the function of "tasting", i.e., prioritizing urgent breaking news, on the one hand, and, on the other, planning more in-depth coverage stories. As far as local offices are concerned, tasting also entails selecting what stories matter to that specific market.

Moving on to the translation phase, Reuters (2008, 58–59) considers that desks also work as sub-editors, believing that extra pairs of eyes are often needed to ensure quality and readability, particularly when dealing with stories aimed at different markets. In the case of APF, desks often become communication hubs. In the newsroom, usually all journalists/translators will work in an open space, exchanging ideas, but they will all gravitate around *deskers* (Davier 2017, 121). Finally, they also play the role of gatekeepers: "The desk guides the copy in accordance with the type of client, filters certain texts and ensures that the 'rules of agency writing' are respected" (Davier 2017, 113, our translation).

At the post-translation phase, the Reuters' desk files the news dispatches for clients, decides which news dispatch goes to which client and sees if they have landed correctly (Reuters 2008, 59). In addition, corrections are also seen as a post-translation task (Reuters 2008, 60). Bielsa saw how, in both APF and IPS, journalists/translators read daily local media and their working space is filled with TV sets showing ongoing news programmes so that the impact of the produced news dispatches may be evaluated (Bielsa 2010, 38).

Last but not least, the quality control desk reads all news dispatches and is responsible for style and accuracy.

Recently, IPS proposed an alternative management model. In line with IPS aims to enhance global inclusion in multilingual news, it has developed a different model of translation, which consists of hiring translation professionals in addition to journalists and creating a new PM figure in news translation—the translation coordinator (Bielsa and Bassnett 2009, 77). This alternative model, giving more visibility to translation and enhancing specialization in news translating, might be replicated in other news translation organizations and, in the long run, help fight copyright infringement (see Chapter 7).

> **Further discussion**
>
> - *Managing crisis translation projects.* Does project management change in crisis translation? How? Why not? Some food for thought might be found in several publications issued in 2020–21 that focus on the translation response to the Covid-19 pandemic. Check our portal for links to these publications.
> - *Project management in non-professional settings.* Try to find out how translation projects work in fansubbing, on Wikipedia and in other non-professional environments. What can we learn from the way they are managed? Should we encourage the use of previous translations as support translations? You may want to read Wao (2014, 6) for some views on the topic.

Activities

Activity 1 Be aware of and comply with the current market demands and conditions for translating for and from a translation in different fields

Activity 1.1 Rates by field

In Chapter 5 we asked you to look at different rates based on language combinations. Now, please look up different rates based on field/text genre. How different are the rates for general translation, literary translation, technical translation, subtitling and dubbing? Are the rates listed by individual translators on their webpages (or on translation platforms like proz.com) equal to the rates quoted in job offers (again, for the same linguistic combinations)? What can we learn about market conditions based on your findings? What are the options when the rates offered and rates requested differ immensely (if they do)?

Activity 1.2 Rates for relay

In some situations, the reuse of translations might incur higher rates. If your translation is going to be the source text for other translations, should you request higher rates?

a. Yes, as my work is also copyrighted and the company will make use of it.
b. No, because I would not do anything differently.
c. No, but I would charge separately for further information requests and file for copyright if it is a literary endeavour (including subtitles).
d. No, because I would lose the job if I did.

Activity 2 Take account of and adapt the organizational and physical ergonomics of specific working environments

PART A. Ideal situation

How do you envisage an ideal indirect translation workflow (people and tools)? What would be the responsibilities of each party?

PART B. Translation workflows

The following are some collaborative projects that include translation/localization. Find how their workflow is set. Do they indicate different roles for different participants? Can anyone adopt any role? Is there an explicit revision process? Is there information on how CAT tools, glossaries or machine translation are used? Try to find out as much information as possible for each and consider what their strongest and *weakest* points are. Do they align with the ideas you presented in Part A?

- Bible Translation Platform, https://bibletranslationtools.org/.
- Benjamins' *Handbook of Translation*, https://benjamins.com/online/hts/main.
- Rakuten Viki, https://contribute.viki.com/.
- TED Translate, www.ted.com/participate/translate.
- Wikipedia Translation, https://en.wikipedia.org/wiki/Wikipedia:Translation.
- Square Enix Video Games, https://finalfantasy.fandom.com/wiki/Localization_of_Square_Enix_video_games.

PART C. Tools

In 2021, the DGT launched a contest to design the best translation tool (see www.philol.uni-leipzig.de/fileadmin/Fakult%C3%A4t_Philo/IALT/Dokumente/DGT_EMT_Challenge_2021_rules.pdf for details of the 2021 contest). Mimicking this idea, what features would your ideal CAT tool include for indirect translation to be effective in a multilingual project? How would you provide instructions to users that would like to use the platform? What key ideas would you stress?

Activity 3 Organize, budget and manage translation projects that make use of previous translations or produce texts to be used for further translations

Consider how you should react in the following situations. What variables would you consider before acting one way or another?

SITUATION 1

A client wants a certain clip to be subtitled in 25 languages. They offer a competitive rate for translation into English and lower rates for translation from English into other languages. All languages must be submitted at the same time. Several translators working out of English decline the offer. The client recommends MT and post-editing.

SITUATION 2

You are managing a large project into multiple languages. You receive the same terminology query from eight out of the ten translators working on the project. You ask the client and they request that the term be kept in English throughout. The other two translators claim that is not the norm in their languages and the term should be translated.

SITUATION 3

A client requires a multilingual translation of a Thai short story. No further specifications are provided. Once the ten versions are received, you notice that three of them have translated the main characters' names. The translated names are the same.

SITUATION 4

A client wants to release a Japanese game simultaneously in several European markets (simship). Studies show how there are clear national preferences regarding subtitling or dubbing (and especially AI lip-syncing). The client asks for your advice on the release.

SITUATION 5

A client wants to translate a help video into the three most likely spoken Indian languages. They are working with a low budget and short deadlines. Advise on how to localize the video considering the financial constraints and urgency of the execution.

Activity 4 Critically approach the use of mediating languages in online translation tools

Read Anastasopoulos et al. (2020) on the translation initiative for Covid-19 (available here https://tico-19.github.io/data/paper/ticopaper.pdf). How do you evaluate the process for compiling TMs and terminology in a multilingual project? If you would like to reflect on the final results, they are available here: https://tico-19.github.io/memories.html.

Resources: Readings to inform "Further Discussion". Links to project management tools online.
Activities: Extra activities and adaptations.

References

AIIC (International Association of Conference Interpreters). [2004] 2017. "Practical Guide for Professional Conference Interpreters." https://aiic.org/document/547/AIICWebzine_Apr2004_2_Practical_guide_for_professional_conference_interpreters_EN.pdf [Accessed December 12, 2019].

Allen, Katherine, Victor Sosa, Angelica Isidro, and Marjory A. Bancroft. 2018. *The Indigenous Interpreter. A Training Manual for Indigenous Language Interpreting.* Salinas, CA: Natividad Medical Foundation.

Anastasopoulos, Antonios, Alessandro Cattelan, Zi-Yi Dou, Marcello Federico, Christian Federman, Dmitry Genze, Francisco Guzmán et al. 2020. "Tico-19: The Translation Initiative for Covid-19." arXiv preprint arXiv:2007.01788.

Bielsa, Esperança. 2010. "Translating News: A Comparison of Practices in News Agencies." In *Translating Information*, edited by Roberto Valdeón, 31–49. Oviedo: Ediuno.

Bielsa, Esperança, and Susan Bassnett. 2009. *Translation in Global News.* New York: Routledge.

Chan, Sin-wai. 2015. "Computer-aided Translation." In *Routledge Encyclopedia of Translation Technology* edited by Sin-wai Chan, 32–67. London: Routledge.

Davier, Lucile. 2017. *Les enjeux de la traduction dans les agences de presse.* Lille: Presses universitaires du Septentrion.

Drugan, Joanna. 2013. *Quality in Professional Translation: Assessment and Improvement.* London: Bloomsbury.

Dunne, Keiran J., and Elena S. Dunne. 2011. Translation and Localization Project Management: The Art of the Possible, Amsterdam and Philadelphia: John Benjamins.

Esselink, Bert. 2000. A Practical Guide to Localization, revised edition, Amsterdam and Philadelphia: John Benjamins.

European Committee for Standardization. 2006. *European Standard EN 15 038. Translation Services – Service Requirements.* Brussels: European Committee for Standardization.

ISO 17100: 2015. 2015. *Translation Services: Requirements for Translation Services.* Geneva: ISO. www.iso.org/obp/ui/#iso:std:iso:17100:ed-1:v1:en [Accessed November 25, 2021].

Olohan, Maeve, and Elena Davitti. 2017. "Dynamics of Trusting in Translation Project Management: Leaps of Faith and Balancing Acts." *Journal of Contemporary Ethnography* 46(4): 391–416. doi.org/10.1177/0891241615603449.

Reuters. 2008. *Handbook of Journalism.* www.trust.org/contentAsset/raw-data/652966ab-c90b-4252-b4a5-db8ed1d438ce/file [Accessed November 25, 2021].

Robert, Isabelle, and Aline Remael. 2016. "Quality Control in the Subtitling Industry: An Exploratory Survey Study." *Meta: Journal des Traducteurs/Meta: Translators' Journal* 61(3): 578–605.

Roturier, Johann. 2015. *Localizing Apps: A Practical Guide for Translators and Translation Students.* London: Routledge.

Seinen, Wouter, and Jaap van der Meer. 2020. *Who Owns My Language Data? Realities, Rules and Recommendations. A White Paper.* Amsterdam: TAUS Signature Editions. www.bakermckenzie.com/en-/media/files/insight/publications/2020/02/17022020-whitepaper--whoownsmylanguagedata--wouter-seinen.pdf.

Van der Meer, Jan. 2013. *Clarifying Copyright on Translation Data - TAUS - The Language Data Network*. [online] Taus.net. Available at: www.taus.net/insights/reports/clarifying-copyright-on-translation-data [Accessed October 21, 2021].

van Rooyen, Marlie. 2019. *Tracing the Translation of Community Radio News in South Africa: An Actor Network Approach*. PhD Thesis. KU Leuven.

Wao, Baorong. 2014. "Interview with Julia Lovell: Translating Lu Xun's Complete Fiction." *Translation Review* 89(1), 1–14. doi:10.1080/07374836.2014.931268.

9
CONCLUSIONS

Introduction

This final chapter ties together some of the most salient points that have emerged from the previous chapters in relation to the central theme of this textbook. This chapter also mentions areas that were not covered in this book but which need, or may come to need, specific training in translating for/from a translation. To complete the picture, this chapter includes some activities to help you get a bird's eye view of indirect translation as an area of professional practice and research.

> **Warm-up activity**
>
> Figure 9.1 shows the logo of the IndirecTrans Network (www.indirectrans.com/news.html). What do you make of this logo? Which features of indirect translation does it bring to mind? Do you think the logo is up to date?

Bringing it all together

The writing of this book was a truly enriching experience. Having worked on indirect translation for some time, we circumscribed case studies which suggested that indirect translation is present in many fields of the translation profession but remains virtually absent from university curricula. However, we had never addressed the key questions: where is indirectness in real-life professional milieux? And are there guidelines on how to efficiently translate from a translation or with a further translation in mind?

DOI: 10.4324/9781003035220-9

FIGURE 9.1 The logo of IndirecTrans Network

These two questions led us to read many pages on translation and interpreting but also on other related areas, such as plain language, academic writing, computational linguistics, creative writing, journalism, ethics, patent filing, technical writing and ergonomics, to name but a few. At the same time, we organized and participated in different scholarly and professional meetings (academic conferences, train-the-trainer workshops, translator meet-ups), pitching the idea that hands-on practice in indirect translation should be included in translation courses. We were also actively looking for feedback on this still marginal topic.

Our readings and feedback from colleagues both led to the same conclusion: as a field of professional practice, indirect translation is everywhere. Books portraying translation in diverse professional settings included many descriptions of real-life professionals translating for and from a translation. At the same time, colleagues encouraged us to think about ways of teaching how to translate indirectly. Their rationale was that indirect translation is a fact of life, and indirect translation can be a useful tool for many trainers, especially those who teach how to translate in classrooms filled with students from multiple and diverse language backgrounds.

So, indirect translation is everywhere but remains rather invisible, although to different degrees. In interpreting, for example, relay is comparatively well institutionalized and discussed, whereas in news translation, journalists/translators do not acknowledge their work as translation, let alone indirect translation. This lack of institutional acknowledgement made finding the right examples and tips more challenging. An additional challenge related to the negative connotations surrounding indirect translation was the following. Since the practice is often associated with cheating and deficient outcomes, many sources that mention indirect translation were limited to depreciative comments and a few short recommendations ("avoid it", "but if you must", etc.).

Against this background, we believe that this book has at least three merits. First, it demonstrates that indirect translation is a practice of both peripheral languages (often in the position of translating for) and central languages (often the pivot languages translated from). This book shows that indirect translation is not a marginal practice, relevant only to peripheral languages. Therefore, it should not be treated as such in academia.

Second, this book brings together disparate sources which, collectively, will help you develop knowledge about indirect translation. More importantly, this book suggests ways on how to better translate for and from a translation, thus prompting you to think about potential pitfalls and possible solutions.

Third, this book provides time and space for reflective learning, where you can put the above-mentioned knowledge into practice. We truly hope that this book will help foster critical thinking on indirect translation and serve as inspiration for developing further research and teaching activities. We believe that incorporating indirect translation into the curriculum will put training institutions in a better position to keep pace with the fast-evolving professional practice and teach real-life skills to future translators. Training in indirect translation may also have a positive impact on the global translation market, as it may contribute to reducing inequalities. This is because high-quality indirect translation has a key role in achieving the Agenda for Sustainable Development, where everyone has the same access to opportunities, regardless of the language they speak. By teaching how to translate indirectly, trainers will contribute to this aspiration for global sustainability. They will help empower peripheral languages and, ultimately, render access to information more equal and democratic.

Each chapter of this book locates indirect translation in different translation fields and professional milieux. To break the ice, we adopted an exploratory approach in the Introduction (sometimes called the "5 W's and one H" approach) to problematize the concept of indirect translation and debunk some misconceptions regarding indirect translating. We felt the need to add one supplementary W-question, namely: "What are the consequences of indirect translation?". This entailed looking at the negative consequences that indirect translation is often said to cause. More importantly, this additional question made us reflect upon the positive outcomes of indirect translation. Finally, we briefly looked at the history of indirect translation and tried to foresee its future. Indirect translation is age old but alive and kicking, and it is here to stay.

Chapter 2 dealt with one translation field where indirectness is more visible and more commonly discussed, so much so that it was possible to extract specific guidelines for relay interpreting from documents issued by professional associations, research work and coursebooks. We discussed the challenges of relay interpreting for both relayers (e.g., pronunciation of foreign words) and relay-takers (e.g., time lag), stressing that much can be improved by good teamwork. Communication between the different agents (speaker, interpreters, etc.) is key. Indirect translation is multiple, hence inherently collaborative.

Chapter 3 discussed indirect translation in relation to scientific and technical knowledge. We looked at scientific texts and technical texts for both specialists and lay users. We argued that instructional texts are often written to be translated, as the majority of products are meant to be launched on the global market. This is why we focused on translator-friendly writing. In this chapter, we also outlined how indirect translation helps establish a dialogue with previous works in one text and with other researchers through conferences and published articles. Indirect translation is all about translator-friendliness and dialogue. We also proposed that indirect translation can play an important role in quality assurance, if one has access to all the language versions involved.

Chapter 4 explored indirect translation in the field of localization. We stressed that digital content is often designed and launched with further translation in mind. Building on this rationale, in this chapter we establish a parallel between internationalization and translating for further translation, whereby both processes try to facilitate a better reception in multiple target cultures/locales. To explore this parallel, we often go beyond the narrow definition of indirect translation in this chapter (a translation involving more than two languages) and open it up to situations where there may be only two languages but several mediating agents, texts and processes. In localization projects, key aspects affecting the final product need to be tackled before translation begins. This creates an opportunity for indirect translators: if consulted at the early stages of the localization process, professionals with skills in relay translation may help anticipate challenges downstream. Moreover, the use of pivot languages has the benefit of being more cost efficient.

Chapter 5 discussed indirect translation in literature. Despite its longstanding history, indirect literary translation is still laden with negative connotations and frowned upon in many codes of ethics. For this reason, this chapter focuses on copyright and ethical issues related to indirect translation. We argue that, since international law considers translation to be a creative work, covert indirect translations should be forbidden. What is more, relayers should be paid for their creative work, and efforts should be made to eradicate plagiarism of mediating texts. Indirect translation should also be seen as ethical: direct translators should not downgrade indirect translators.

Chapter 6 tackled the widespread practice of pivot audiovisual translation, while focussing on the use of pivot templates in interlingual subtitling. In the spirit of cooperation mentioned in earlier chapters, template makers should make good use of annotations so as to assist further subtitlers who may not understand the language spoken in the video. Regarding rates, and in line with the take aways from the chapter on the indirect translation of literary texts, the fees of template makers should be reviewed. Indirect translation is a way of exporting creative works, and relayers should be paid according to the specific task of translating for translation.

Chapter 7 focuses on news translation, where determining how many source texts there are for a particular translation is often impossible. Likewise, it may be impossible to verify how many translations one piece of news has yielded, as the translations are spread across spoken and written news articles and social media. Due to this reality, indirect translation, as it is broadly understood, may actually be the norm in news translation rather than the exception. To provide you with a better understanding of the complex indirect translation processes taking place in this domain, two subsets of indirect translation were discussed: back translation and eclectic/compilative translation. Indirect translation is pervasive and multi-sourced and may be linear or circular.

Finally, the chapter on project management, Chapter 8, provides an overview of the challenges that need to be tackled in translation projects that include indirect translation. This chapter aims to explore basic ideas that were not developed in the previous chapters. Indirect translation has an important impact on workflow. This is why communication between mediating text producers and final translators should be strongly encouraged all throughout a translation project.

Initially, we considered the inclusion of other translation fields where indirect is likely to occur, such as legal translation, advertising and the translation of sacred texts. We also considered providing more details on sign language interpreting and medical translation in some of the existing chapters. However, in some cases, the related know-how was already covered in other chapters. In other cases, the specific domain was beyond our expertise and there was no systematic, reliable research to draw on. We hope that future revisions of this book will include some of the topics that could not be covered here. Other topics will hopefully be explored by other researchers. At the same time, many new challenges are still to come due to ongoing societal and technological developments. Our hope is that ample research-based tips on how to efficiently translate via a third language will be developed to address these future challenges. We see this book as a first step in this direction.

We tried to include perspectives from outside Europe, to the best of our knowledge and expertise. For this, we provided some examples involving non-European languages, and many challenges and solutions are non-language dependent. That said, our knowledge and expertise are inevitably limited. As a result, and despite our best efforts, the book still largely presents a Europe-centred perspective, with many examples involving our strongest languages: Polish, Portuguese and Spanish.

If you have managed to read this far, you will probably agree that indirect translation as a process is often different from direct translation. Essentially, all the principles that make a good translation still apply, but there are some additional issues that need to be addressed, often from an alternative perspective. Giving or taking relay tends to require a different attitude towards the translation task. Therefore, instead of trying to classify indirect translation as good or bad, it makes more sense to consider that the pivot forges a chain of communication. The pivot link plays a key part in this communication. If the link is strong, it will lead to a more successful communication. However, a weak link will cause communication problems throughout.

All in all, we believe that, in an increasingly globalized world, knowing how to translate from a translation, and with a further translation in mind, is an important part of a translator's skillset in different domains. We trust this book has helped you hone those skills.

Activities

Activity 1 Past facts and myths about indirect translation

Here are some statements you may hear about translating for and from a translation. Based on discussions in this book, your observations, readings, knowledge of the field and experience in it, decide how far you agree or disagree with these statements (strongly agree, agree, disagree, strongly disagree). Explain your rationale.

If you want, you can use the table provided on the portal. Your decision should be based on a fact you can show to others rather than on your personal opinion.

a. Translating from the original always brings better results.
b. Literary texts should never be translated for the purpose of further translation.
c. When a translation cannot be made from the original, the translator should secure the permission of the translator responsible for the translation that is being used.
d. When a translation cannot be made from the original, the translator should translate from a version in a language cognate to the target language.
e. When translating from an already translated text, the translator can take more liberties with their source text than when translating from the original.
f. If the idea is to retain as many culture-specific items of the original as possible, the translator should avoid translating from English language translations, as they typically involve various instances of domestication.
g. Indirect translations should be evaluated vis-à-vis their mediating texts and not the source texts.
h. Indirect translation entails competences different from direct translation.
i. Indirect translation is easier than direct translation.
j. Pivot versions should be done by native speakers of the original language (not by native speakers of the pivot language)
k. When translating from a translation, it is impossible to avoid content deviations that have been introduced in the first translation.
l. When translating from a translation, it is impossible to avoid stylistic deviations that have been introduced in the first translation.

Activity 2 Is indirect translation a niche nowadays?

Activity 2.1

Try to think of an example of an entirely direct translation either in interpreting, scientific-technical translation, localization, literary translation, audiovisual translation or news translation. Can you describe a translation act that does not involve mediation by a third language, text, mode, culture or agent (be it human or machine)?

Reflect on what your answer tells us about:

- The usefulness and sustainability of direct translation as a theoretical notion.
- The usefulness and sustainability of indirect translation as a theoretical notion.

Activity 2.2

In his 2008 article, Cay Dollerup wrote:

> It is not worthwhile making relay the object of major scholarly studies. At best such critical studies can argue that special types of error that turn up

frequently in specific language combinations in "relay" chains are typical of these chains. But it is unlikely that studies of "relay" are relevant except in the broadest terms (…) to Translation Studies in general.

Dollerup 2008, 13

Do you agree with Dollerup's defeatist statement?

Look for mentions of relay and indirect translation in the Translation Studies Bibliography (Gambier and van Doorslaer 2010) and BITRA (Franco 2001). You can also check Google Scholar. How has research on indirect translation evolved since the publication of Dollerup's article?

Activity 3 The foreseeable future of indirect translation

Think about how fast the professional ecosystem of translation is changing and will change in the near future. Factors that are currently shaping the future of the translation profession include technological developments (e.g., artificial intelligence), workflow automation, collaboration, the 2030 Agenda for Sustainable Development, increased migratory movements, big data, developing policies for multilingualism, hybrid meetings and online teaching, to name only a selected few. Considering these factors, how do you imagine indirect translation in the future? How might it change compared to what it is like today? What other factors do you think will likely influence the future of indirect translation?

Resources: Questionnaire to give your opinion on the book.
Activities: Table for Activity 1. Extra activities.

References

Dollerup, Cay. 2008. "Relay in Translation." *Bucharest Working Papers in Linguistics* 2 (10). http://bwpl.unibuc.ro/wp-content/uploads/2017/02/BWPL-_2008_2_Dollerup.pdf [Accessed November 2021].

Franco, Javier Aixelá, ed. 2001. *Bibliography of Translation and Interpreting*. Alicante: Universidad de Alicante. [Accessed November 2021]. http://aplicacionesua.cpd.ua.es/tra_int/usu/buscar.asp? idioma=en.

Gambier, Yves, and Luc van Doorslaer, eds. 2010. *Handbook of Translation Studies*. Amsterdam: Benjamins. [Accessed November 2021]. www.benjamins.com/online/hts/.

GLOSSARY

audio description Narrative inserted into audiovisual products to describe essential details; the aim is to allow blind people to understand and enjoy audiovisual products.

audio subtitling Audio translation of subtitles that are then read by a voice talent for the benefit of blind individuals; the aim is to compensate for the foreign dialogue in the audio. Audio subtitles are often combined with audio description.

author Creator of the source text.

back translation Translating a translated document back to the source language (from A to B then back to A).

bridge language Synonym for pivot language.

bylined article Opinion piece published under the author's name.

central language Languages in the third level of the language hierarchy developed by Heilbron (1999). They are usually official languages with linguistic resources. They are more likely to work as relay languages for speakers of peripheral languages.

circular indirect translation In news translation, a synonym of "back translation" (Valdeón 2022).

clear writing Orderly writing style that relies on everyday language in order to achieve clarity.

compilative translation A translation not from one but several source texts.

consecutive interpreting Interpreting that takes place after the source-language utterance, which the interpreter records in notes.

controlled language Subset of natural language with restricted grammar and vocabulary that aims to reduce ambiguity.

cultural references Terms for ideas or situations that are specific to a given culture.

dialogue interpreting Spontaneous communication mediated by an interpreter in a face-to-face situation. Often used in health, legal and crisis settings.

dialogue list File that contains a verbatim transcription of all dialogue exchanges heard in the audio of a motion picture. Frequently it also contains annotations with extra information that explains any instances of challenging idiomatic expressions. It is also called screenplay, script, dialogue transcript or combined continuity (Díaz-Cintas 2001).

directionality Choice of the source and target languages within a translator or interpreter's language combination.

double-relay Third-hand, third-generation translation. That is, a translation from language A to B to C and finally to D.

dubbing Insertion of a synchronized translation of the original dialogue into audiovisual material.

dummy booth Pivot interpreting booth whose output does not reach the general public but is produced solely for the sake of enabling another language interpretation.

eclectic translation Synonym of "compilative translation".

equivalence The assumption that a source text and its translation can have the same value.

ethnicize To make something more representative of the diverse ethnic groups that make up a society.

fandubbing Dubbing done by the fandom of a product, often organized in collaborative translation settings.

fansubbing Subtitling done by the fandom of a product, often organized in collaborative translation settings.

genesis file See "template".

gisting Employ machine translation for personal use in order to get the gist or comprehend the general idea of the meaning of a text that has been written in another language.

hypercentral language In a global hierarchy of languages, the language or languages that connect the speakers of supercentral languages. Currently, English plays this part.

interlingual translation Translation between two (different) languages.

intermodal translation Translation that occurs between different modalities.

internationalization Process after which content is ready to handle multiple languages and cultural conventions without the need for re-design.

intertextual references Ideas or situations in a text that allude to other texts or create their meaning based on references to other texts.

intertitles A piece of filmed and printed text (short sentences on a dark background) that appears on the screen between scenes. Common in silent movies, they are the older relatives of present-day subtitles.

intralingual translation Translation within one (and the same) language.

intramodal translation Translation within one (and the same) modality.

212 Glossary

language service provider Company that sells translation and localization services.

live subtitling See "speech-to-text interpreting".

locale Combination of language and country or region that defines a specific target for translation, e.g., Portugal and Brazil are different locales.

localization Making a product linguistically and culturally appropriate to the target locale (country/region and language) where it will be used and sold.

low-resource languages Languages that have few human and digital resources, mostly because they are less translated, less spoken and/or less studied as a foreign language.

master file See "template".

master (sub)titles See "template".

media service distributors Companies in charge of the provision of programmes to the general public via telecommunications networks (e.g., Netflix).

mise-en-scene Arrangement of actors and scenery on a stage for a production.

multimodal texts Texts that combine more than one modality (e.g., audio, visual).

peripheral language Languages at the lowest level of a global language hierarchy developed by Heilbron (1999), which are rarely learned by non-native speakers. They are often vulnerable or endangered languages, although not necessarily small in the number of native speakers. Languages into which you translate more often and from which you translate less frequently.

pivot language Intermediary language for translation.

post-editing Correcting and improving raw machine translation output in line with specific recommendations.

post-gold model Process of localization where local versions are released consecutively.

pre-editing Processing texts before machine translation. Typically involves correcting mistakes in the source text (e.g., grammar, punctuation and spelling), removing ambiguities and simplifying structures.

project manager Person responsible for the process of a translation project, who manages its specific aspects.

pseudotranslation Written text presented as a translation, despite the lack of a source text.

quality assurance Full set of procedures applied not just after but also before and during the translation production process by all members of a translation organization to ensure that quality objectives important to clients are met (Mossop 2020, 131). Also known as quality management.

quality control A set of procedures that deals with the identification and resolution of problems, often taking the shape of text revision undertaken by non-experts in translation, such as reviewers (Mossop 2020, 117).

relayer The agent who bridges the source text and target text by producing a mediating text, which will then be further translated. Also known as mediating text producer, template maker or first translator.

relay-taker The agent who translates from the mediating text produced by the relayer. Also known as indirect translator or second translator.

remote interpreting Communication situation in which the interpreter and the speakers are not in a shared physical location.

respeaking Process of repeating what is heard into a voice recognition software, which, in turn, generates the caption text.

retour Process of working into a language that is not your native language.

retranslation Translating a source text which has been rendered into the same target language at least once before (A-B-B).

review In specialized translation, the reading of a text by subject-matter experts in order to evaluate the content.

revision Checking a translation for linguistic problems and amending them.

SDH Subtitling for D/deaf and hard-of-hearing people.

shifting A systematic moving from one language to another.

sign languages Visual-spatial languages that can create meaning using space, location, referents and other visually descriptive elements. They are used by deaf individuals as their first or preferred language of communication.

simship model Process of localization where all local versions are released simultaneously. Short for "simultaneous shipping".

simultaneous interpreting Interpreting that takes place at the same time as the source-language utterance is being made.

speech-to-text interpreting Process whereby the source speech is first interpreted simultaneously into another language by a speech-to-text interpreter who is, at the very same time, rendering the oral output into a written text (e.g., using a speech recognition software). Sometimes called "live subtitling".

spotted subtitles Timed subtitles with defined in and out times.

subtitling Presenting a written text, typically at the bottom of a screen, to translate verbal information being transmitted in the audiovisual content.

supercentral languages Second level of languages in a global hierarchy that serve as connectors between central and peripheral languages. Heilbron (1999) identifies the following: Arabic, Chinese, French, German, Hindi, Japanese, Malay, Portuguese, Russian, Spanish, Swahili and Turkish.

support translation Use of fragments of previous translations as a part of the documentation stage in a translation process.

surtitling (theatre) Translation of foreign language dialogue or songs in a play, usually projected above the stage.

template A subtitle file consisting of the spotted subtitles of a film done in the source language, usually English, sometimes with annotations, which is used for further translation. Also known in the industry as template file, master file, master (sub)titles, or genesis file.

template maker Subtitler who produces the English template for further translations. A type of relayer.

transediting Combination of translation and editing that highlights the textual intervention of translators in the field of news translation (Stetting 1989).

transfile See "template".
translatable elements In localization projects, elements that may require translation.
translation buyer Client.
university courses A series of classes that follow a plan (the syllabus) to study one subject or topic. They function as a unit at the institutional level.
university programme A series of courses designed to acquire knowledge and skills in a given area, the completion of which leads to a diploma or degree.
vernacular languages A linguistic variety spoken in daily life by the inhabitants of a certain region or country, usually chosen over a literary, cultured or foreign language.
video on demand (VOD) Media distribution system that allows users to access videos without requiring specific playing devices.
voice-over Insertion of a voice, which is not part of the narrative, in audiovisual material.

References

Díaz-Cintas, Jorge. 2001. "Striving for Quality in Subtitling: The Role of a Good Dialogue List." In *(Multi) Media Translation*, edited by Yves Gambier and Henri Gottlieb, 199–211. Amsterdam and New York: John Benjamins.

Heilbron, Johan. 1999. "Towards a Sociology of Translation: Book Translation as a Cultural World-System." *Acoustics, Speech, and Signal Processing Newsletter, IEEE* 2(4): 429–444. DOI: 10.1177/13684319922224590.

Mossop, Brian. 2020. *Revising and Editing for Translators*. London: Routledge.

Stetting, Karen. 1989. "Transediting – A New Term for Coping with the Grey Area Between Editing and Translating." In *Proceedings from the Fourth Nordic Conference for English Studies* edited by Graham Caie, Kirsten Haastrup, Arnt Lykke Jakobsen et al. 371–382. Copenhagen: University of Copenhagen.

Valdeón, Roberto. 2022. "On the Role of Indirect Translation in the History of News Production." *Target 34 (2)*.

INDEX

Note: Page numbers in **bold** refers tables and Page numbers in *italics* refers figures.

4th century 3
12th century 4
16th century 3, 23
17th century 10, 110, 160
18th century 110
19th century 110, 134, 161
20th century 3, 4, 5, 13, 69, 80, 172
21st century 5, 12, 69, 162, 166, 177

aboriginal languages *see* vernacular languages
abstracting *see* compressing
accessibility 14, 43, 135; *see also* audio description
access rights 10
acronyms 32, 33, 60
adaptation 88, 169, 181
addition 130, 175, 176
Agence France-Presse (AFP) 161, 163, 164, 169, 172–5
agency 6, 177
Al Jazeera 169
Amanda Gorman 177, 178
American Associated Press (AP) 161, 163, 164, 169, 172–5
Anne Frank's Diary 168, 180
annotations 59, 102, 136, *137*, 196, 206
argumentative text 66, 70, 175, 182
audio description 86, 135, 210
audio mismatch 145
audio subtitling 135, 210

audiovisual translation 5, 12, 195–6, 206; project management 195
authorial control 10, 210
automation 84, 190, 195, 209

back translation 2, 148, 166–8, 210
BBC 163, 166, 178
bible translation 3, 9, 195, 199
blindfolded translation 89, 101
bridge language *see* pivot language
briefing 34, 39–40, 192
bugs 88, 92
bylined article 164, 210

CAT tools 84, 85, 89, 199
censorship 4, 9, 134, 161, 177
central language 4, 17, 30, 110, 204, 210
change of speaker 36
chief interpreter *see* project management
circular indirect translation 173–4, 210; *see also* back translation
clear writing 76, 210; *see also* plain language
CNN 163, 166
codes of ethics 115–17
codes of practice 15, 115, 131; *see also* codes of ethics
cognate languages 38, 208
cognition load 31
collaborative translations *see* crowdsourcing
combined continuity *see* dialogue list
commercial translation 4, 12

communication 186, 190, 191, 195, 207
compensation 40, 142
compilative translation 3, 112, 145, 165–6, 168, 210
compressing 34–5, 142
computational linguistics 12
concatenation 97
concatenation effect 111
condensing *see* compressing
consecutive interpreting 7, 23, 28, 40–2, 210, 211; project management 40, 192–3
content writing *see* technical writing
controlled language 84, 107, 210
copyright 114, 116–20, **164**, 194, 197, 206; breach 13, 121, 195; in China 119; compensation 120–1, 196; in Europe 119; international 6; in the UK 118–19; in the US 118–19
corantos 160
court interpreting 41, 42, 192
covert indirect translation 65, 206
creativity 90, 124
crisis translation 9–11, 24, 70, 102, 198
crowdsourcing 102, 135, 163, 198, 211
cultural mediator 69
cultural specificity 67, 84, 111, 142, 151, 208
cultureme 74, 170; *see also* culture-specific items
culture-specific items 30, 113, 143, 148, 149, 170, 210; kinship terms 140, 149; non-verbal 63, 142, 143; names 39, 84, 98, 141, 150; numbers 99

deletion *see* omission of passages
desker *see* news translation project management
dialogue interpreting *see* consecutive interpreting
dialogue list 5, 136, 152, 196
dialogue transcript *see* dialogue list
directionality 30, 39, 81, 151, 154, 211
displaced indexicality xvi, 43, 150
documentary translation *see* gloss
domestication 33, 43, 70, 117, 127, 130, 143, 148, 172
double-relay 22
dubbing 28, 34, 86, 135, 145, 211
dummy booth 211

eclectic translation *see* compilative translation
El País 165
emotional wellbeing 40
English hegemony 64–5, 112–13
equivalence 14, 55, 59, 176
ergonomics 199, 204
ethics 11, 114–17, 120, 166, 176–7
ethnicizing 113, 211

fake news 167, 177, 180
fandubbing 135, 211
fansubbing 135, 198, 211
file management 193–4
formality levels 141, 142, 149
free translation 208

genesis file *see* template
gisting 74, 151, 169, 211
global language English 161; French 3, 161
gloss 66
glossary 55, 59, 60, 85, 194, 196
grammatical features 149; case 140; gender 62, 83, 84, 140, 142, 149, 156; tense 141

headlines 175, 176
homograph 142
human resources 186, 188, 194
hybrid audience 30
hypercentral language 117, 211

ideological manipulation 113, 168, 176–7
indigenous languages *see* vernacular languages
indirect translation: in literature 204, 206; myths 196, 207–8
information resources 194, 196
informative text 113, 175
institutional translation 2, 24, 54
instructional texts 37, 57–8, 62, 73, 205
intellectual property *see* copyright
interlingual: subtitling 206; interlingual translation 2, 68, 165, 174, 211
intermediary texts 10, 65, 81, 83, 123, 162, 179
intermodal translation 2, 43, 211
international English 58–9, 64
internationalization 211; in localization 5, 80–1, 83–5, 92–3, 102, 194, 206; in news translation 161; process 5, 206; in technical translation 57; testing 194
interpretative text 175
interpreter positioning 28, 41
interpreting technology 5, 26, 33, 37, 155
intertextual references 44, 113, 142, 149, 153, 211
intertitles 134, 211
intralingual: corpora 114; indirect translation 43, 66, 166, **171**; translation 2, 68, 165, 174, 211
intramodal translation 2, 211

Janice Deul 177, 178

L2 translation *see* directionality or retour
language register 85, 101, 174, 195
language service provider 91, 93, 144, 188, 190, 192, 212
languages of limited diffusion *see* peripheral languages
language tiering 82, 88, 93
legal translation 4, 25, 54
lingua franca 9, 12, 70; English as lingua franca 12, 70, 161
linguistic homogenization 11–12
literal translation 134, 143, 169, 176
literary translation 3–4, 7–8, 12, 72, 109–31; project management 195
live subtitling *see* speech-to-text interpreting
locale 68, 78, 81–5, 212
localization 5, 12, 78–107, 170, 187, 193–5, 206; kit 85, 194; workflow 80, 85, 102
local news agencies 180
locked templates 144–5, 153–4
low-resource languages *see* peripheral languages
LSP *see* language service provider

machine translation: agency 7–9; MT data 194; MT output 90, 151; MT use 32, 59, 163, 169; neural machine translation 12; *see also* gisting
magic realism 13
market analysis 95, 102, 103–4, 110
master file *see* template
media dispatches 162, 164, 169, 197
mediating text 72; *see also* intermediary texts
medical translation 25
minor languages *see* peripheral languages
mise-en-scene 135, 212
mistranslations 31, 143, 196
multilingualism 24, 64, 67, 144, 152, 188, 209
multimodality and culture 34, 53, 63–4, 97, 143, 149; multimodal indirect translation 16; multimodal perception 27–9, 46; multimodal texts 53, 63, 135
multiple source texts 3, 162, 165
museum translation 67

naming conventions *see* culture-specific items (names)
narrative 86, 89, 111, 135, 169
negative mediation 166

networking 38, 152
news: agencies 161–4; circulation 160–1; translation 5, 8, 67, 159–82, 186, 204, 206; translation project management 196–7
non professional translation *see* fandubbing and fansubbing
novelization 3

omission 31, 35, 111, 142–3, 177, 195; omission of passages 161, 175
open templates 146–7, 153, 196
O Público 163

parallel corpus 6, 114, 152
partial localization 87, 88
passive voice 62, 74
patent translation 53–6
peripheral language 4, 6, 11–12, 31, 101, 154, 212; and MT 12, 17, 90
personal pronouns 62, 140, 149
pidgins 160
pivot booths 5, 22, 25, 30, 192
pivot language 212; Arabic 4; ASL 25; Chinese 24, 82; Dutch 160; Farsi 69; French 25, 110, 123, 161, 173; German 25, 110, 174; Japanese 14, 24; Latin 3, 4, 52; Maya 23; Middle Low German 4; Portuguese 14, 69; Russian 23, 134; Spanish 25, 165; Swedish 14; Tigrinya 25
pivot translation 2, 6, 80, 134, 143, 154, 212; pivot machine translation 2, 6–10, 70, 194; workflow 8, 70, 102, 116, 136
placeholders *see* tags
plagiarism 13, 123, **164**, 206; *see also* copyright breach
plain language 36, 58, 65, 73, 204
policy makers 8, 43
post-editing 71, 89–90, 107, 200, 212
post-gold model 80, 91, 212
post-production *see* post-translation
post-translation 8, 187, 191, 197
power differences 4, 13, 14, 110–12, 205
pre-editing 57, 70, 84, 106, 212
prestige 9–10, 13, 110, 163
professional associations 8, 115, 152
professional availability 9–11, 17–18, 188
project management 85, 208, 212; PM tasks 190; PM tools 89, 104, 188, 191–2
pseudolocalization 85
pseudotranslation 167–8, 212

Q&A 191, 193, 195
quality assurance 8, 53–4, 72, 92, 186, 188, 190, 194, 206, 212

quality control 212; agents 197; in direct translation 53–4; in indirect translation 65, 72; in literary translation 116; in localization 84, 86, 92, 106; in technical writing 57
quality management 186–7, 212
quotes 67, 162, 171, 180

rates: by field 198; by language 200; pivot translation rates 196, 198, 200; translation rates 9, 17, 138, 144, 153, 190, 206
reading: readability 58, 147, 182, 197; reading conventions 99; reading speed 95, 147, 153, 154
reformulation 32, 175, 176
regionalizing *see* localization
regional varieties 33, 153, 170, 174, 192
relayer 7–8, 25, 30–1, 177, 212
relay interpreting 2, 5, 11, 15, 23–4, 204
relay-taker 8, 25, 30, 37–40
remote interpreting 26, 29, 37, 47, 213
research methodology 13
respeaking *see* speech-to-text interpreting
retour 30, 32–3, 37, 39, 213
retranslation 2, 115, 118, 213
Reuteurs 163, 164, 169, 172–5, 181
review 51, 85, 187, 213
revision 8, 45, 53, 91, 100, 138, 196, 199, 213
rewriting 5, 89, **164**, 170, 172
risk management 10, 34, 83, 90, 111

scientific technical translation: project management 193, 205; *see also* scientific translation and technical translation
scientific translation 4, 9, 51–76, 193, 205
screenplay *see* dialogue list
script *see* dialogue list
SDH 135, 145, 146, 155, 213
semantic shift 162, 166, 169, 176
semi-localized webs *see* partial localization
semiotic resources 27
shifting 124, 213
sight translation 42, 46, 193
sign language 25–6, 41, 42, 43, 213
simship 81, 91, 194, 213
simultaneous interpreting 5, 23, 31–40, 213; project management 191–2
social media 53, 44, 93, 124, 163, 178, 181
source language: Arabic 169; Chinese 111; French 171; German 173; Greek 4; Japanese 80, 82, 88, 116; Korean 68, 123, 135, 141, 143, 152; Latin 65; Polish 123

source language knowledge 15, 40, 55, 112, 153
space limits 95–6
spatial immediacy 27, 30, 34, 143
specialized software 84, 134, 188, 196
speech style 35–6, 39
speech-to-text interpreting 3, 7, 43, 135, 213
spelling 174
spotted subtitles 213; *see also* locked templates
stereoscopic reading 113
strategic mediation 42
style guide 85, 89, 101, 163, 170, 180
subtitling 213
summarizing 169
supercentral language 17, 213
support files 195–6
support translation 3, 5, 7, 68, 125, 152, 198, 213
surtitling 135, 213
sustainability 205, 209
syntactical order 97

tags 59, 90, 94, 95, 99, 100, 194
target audience 2, 8, 30, 32, 175
teamwork 13, 85, 195
technical translation 193
technical writing 57, 67, 70, 204
template 5, 7–9, 15, 79, 136–51, 213; maker 142, 144, 148, 150–213
temporal immediacy 9, 27, 33, 40; lack of 29, 91
terminology 84, 100; database 71, 85, 89, 169; technology 84
testing 85, 194–5
text rearrangement 175, 176, 181
time 34, 169; lag 6–7, 27, 29, 33, 205; management 9, 138, 186, 190, 191, 195
transediting 172, 213
transfile *see* template
translatable elements 86, 90, 91, 102, 214
translatable strings *see* translatable elements
translate for 3–5, 7, 146–51, 156, 169–71
translate from 3, 8, 10, 151–4, 169, 172
translation buyer 8, 116, 192–3, 194, 214; chain 6, 13, 162, 166; competences 15, 80, 111, 208; costs 9, 138, 186, 187, 188, 206; memories 188; process 6, 32, 187–8, 193–4, 206; quality 10, 26, 31, 110, 187
translator intervention 41–2, 56, 100, 122; *see also* communication
translator training 14, 115, 204; *see also* university curriculum

trust 37–8, 190–2
turn taking 30

university curriculum 15, 64, 203, 205, 214

vernacular languages 3, 5, 25, 214

video on demand (VOD) 15, 136, 139, 156, 214
voice-over 135, 145, 214

Wikipedia translation 67–8, 73–4, 198
working conditions 119, 190, 192, 196

Printed in the USA
CPSIA information can be obtained
at www.ICGtesting.com
LVHW011143150324
774517LV00041B/1721